North Puget Sound
& The Strait of Juan de Fuca

Third Edition

MARGE & TED
MUELLER

THE MOUNTAINEERS BOOKS

THE MOUNTAINEERS BOOKS
is the nonprofit publishing arm of The Mountaineers Club, an organization founded in 1906 and dedicated to the exploration, preservation, and enjoyment of outdoor and wilderness areas.

1001 SW Klickitat Way, Suite 201, Seattle, WA 98134

First edition 1988. Second edition 1995. Third edition 2006.

Published simultaneously in Great Britain by Cordee, 3a DeMontfort Street, Leicester, England, LE1 7HD

Manufactured in the United States of America

Editor: Brenda Pittsley
Cover design: Mayumi Thompson
Book design and layout: Marge Mueller, Gray Mouse Graphics
Mapmakers: Marge and Ted Mueller, Gray Mouse Graphics
Photographers: All photos by Marge and Ted Mueller, except as noted
Cover photograph: *Anchorage off Young County Park, Guemes Island*

A Cataloging-in-Publication record for this book is on file at the Library of Congress.

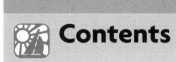

Contents

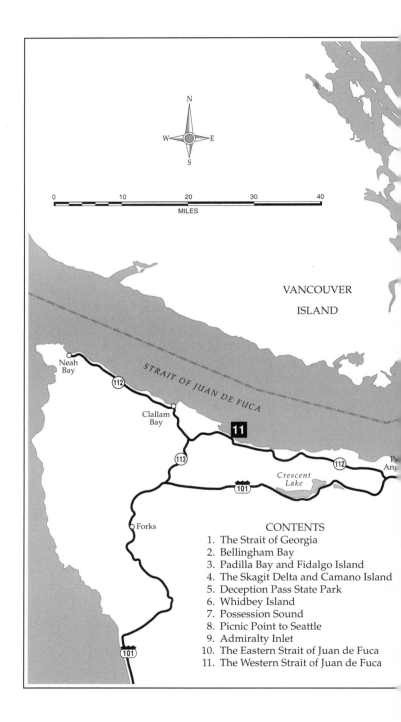

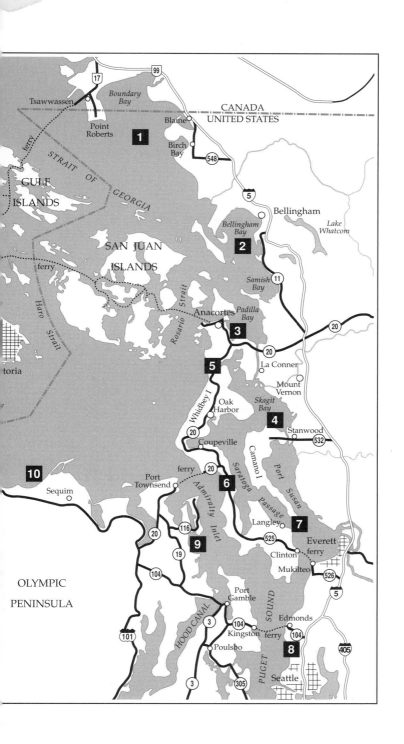

Quick Reference to Facilities and Recreation

Some kinds of marine recreation, such as boating and beachcombing, are found throughout North Puget Sound and the Strait of Juan de Fuca. Others, however, are more specific to particular areas. The following table provides a quick reference to important facilities and activities. Some facilities listed might be at commercial resorts or marinas; some might close off-season. For detailed information read the descriptions of specific areas in the text.

Marine Services include marine supplies and repair; in some places they might be of a very limited nature.

Moorage refers to marinas that have guest moorage. It also includes public docks and buoys at marine parks.

Launch Facilities includes shore access only for hand-carried boats. Hoists and slings are always at commercial marinas. Ramps might be at either commercial or public facilities.

Groceries/Shopping might be of a very limited nature.

Camping is listed under recreation to avoid duplicating it as a facility. However, it also means that campsites, as a facility, are available.

Point of Interest includes such things as educational displays, museums, and self-guided nature walks.

(•) = Nearby; [•] = Freshwater
Fuel: D = On Dock; S = Service Station
Launch Facilities: R = Ramp; H = Hoist; C = Hand Carry
Restroom or Toilet: S = Shower Also
Camping: M = Cascadia Marine Trail Campsite Also
Hiking/Beach Walking: B = Beach Walk

			Facilities						Location				Recreation					
Fuel	Marine Pumpout	Marine Services	Moorage	Launch Facilities	Restroom or Toilet	Lodging	Groceries/Shopping	Restaurants		Fishing	Shellfish	Paddling	Scuba Diving	Camping	Picnicking	Hiking/Beach Walking	Wildlife Watching	Point of Interest
									1. THE STRAIT OF GEORGIA									
									Point Roberts Beach Accesses	•	•					B		
D	•	•	•	H	•/S		•		Point Roberts Marina Resort									
				R	•/S				Lighthouse Marine County Park	•	•			•	•	•/B		

Facilities									Location	Recreation								
Fuel	Marine Pumpout	Marine Services	Moorage	Launch Facilities	Restroom or Toilet	Lodging	Groceries/Shopping	Restaurants		Fishing	Shellfish	Paddling	Scuba Diving	Camping	Picnicking	Hiking/Beach Walking	Wildlife Watching	Point of Interest
S						•	•	•	Blaine									•
D	•	•	•	R	•/S		(•)	(•)	Blaine Harbor	•		•						
					•		(•)	(•)	Blaine Marine Park							•	•	•
D	•		•	H	•/S	•	•	•	Semiahmoo Marina			•						
									Semiahmoo County Park, DNR Beach 372			•	•			B		•
					•		(•)	(•)	Cottonwood Beach and Birch Bay Public Accesses			•	•			B		
				R	•/S				Birch Bay State Park	•	•	•	•	•	•	•/B		•
									2. BELLINGHAM BAY									
D				R/H				•	Gooseberry Point and Portage Island	•		•						
			•						Lummi Island Recreation Site			•		•/M			•	
			•	•					Inati Bay			•		•	•		•	
									Lummi Island DNR Beaches		•	•				B		
S					•	•	•	•	Bellingham									•
									Squalicum Beach							B		
D	•	•	•	R	•/S	•	•	•	Squalicum Harbor			•				•		
					•				Boulevard Park	•		•			•	•		
			•	R			(•)	(•)	Harris Avenue Launch Ramp			•						
					•		•	•	Bellingham Cruise Terminal									•
					•				Marine Park						•	B		
					•				Chuckanut Bay Marsh and Tidelands			•					B	•
					•				Teddy Bear Cove							•/B		
				R	•/S				Larrabee State Park	•		•	•	•	•	•/B		
									Strawberry (Loon) Island Recreation Site			•	•	•/M				
			•	•					Cypress Head Recreation Area	•		•		•/M			•	
			•						Eagle Harbor			•					•	

Marine Pumpout	Marine Services	Moorage	Launch Facilities	Restroom or Toilet	Lodging	Groceries/Shopping	Restaurants	Location	Fishing	Shellfish	Paddling	Scuba Diving	Camping	Picnicking	Hiking/Beach Walking	Wildlife Watching	Point of Interest
		•		•				Pelican Beach and Eagle Cliff	•		•	•	•/M	•	•/B	•	
								Cone Islands State Park			•	•					•
								Guemes Island Public Accesses							B	•	
			•					Young County Park and Clark Point			•				•	B	
			•					Samish Island Picnic Site			•	•			•	B	•
								3. PADILLA BAY AND FIDALGO ISLAND									
								Huckleberry Island State Park			•	•					
			•					Saddlebag Island Marine State Park	•	•	•	•	•/M	•	•		
			C	•/S				Bay View State Park	•		•		•	•	B		
			•					Padilla Bay National Estuarine Sanctuary			•				•/B	•	•
			R	•				Swinomish Channel Boat Launch			•			•			
				•	•	•	•	Anacortes							•	•	•
•	•	•	H	•/S	(•)	(•)	(•)	Cap Sante			•			•			(•)
			R	•/S				Washington Park			•	•	•	•	•		•
•	•	•	H	•/S		•	•	Skyline Marina			•						
								Burrows Island State Park			•	M					
	•		R	•	•	•	•	La Conner	•		•						•
	•	•	H	•/S	(•)	(•)	(•)	La Conner Marina			•						
			R	•				Pioneer City Park			•			•			
								4. THE SKAGIT DELTA AND CAMANO ISLAND									
			R	•				Skagit State Wildlife Recreation Area	•	•	•				•	•	
			R					Leque Island and South Pass Access	•		•				•	•	
			R	•				Kayak Point Regional Park	•	•	•	•	•	•			
			C					Livingston Bay			•						
								Iverson Spit Waterfront Preserve		•					B	•	
			R	•				Cavelero Beach County Park			•			•			

Fuel	Marine Pumpout	Marine Services	Moorage	Launch Facilities	Restroom or Toilet	Lodging	Groceries/Shopping	Restaurants	Location	Fishing	Shellfish	Paddling	Scuba Diving	Camping	Picnicking	Hiking/Beach Walking	Wildlife Watching	Point of Interest
									English Boom Historical County Park							B	•	
				R	•				Utsalady Point and Maple Grove						•			
									Onamac Point	•		•						
			•		•/S	•			Cama Beach State Park			•				•/B		•
				R	•/S				Camano Island State Park			•		•/M	•	•		
									5. DECEPTION PASS STATE PARK									
					•				Deception Pass Area							•		•
D		•	•	R/H	•/S	•	•		Cornet Bay and Hoypus Point Area	•	•	•	•		•	•		
			•		•				Skagit Bay	•	•	•	•	•/M	•	B		
			•	R	•/S				Bowman Bay and Rosario Beach	•		•	•	•/M	•	•		
				R	•/S				Cranberry Lake Vicinity	•		•			•	•	•/B	
				R					Pass Lake	•		•						•
									6. WHIDBEY ISLAND									
					•				Joseph Whidbey State Park					M	•	B	•	
				R					Point Partridge Launch Ramp			•						
					•				Libbey Beach County Park			•			•	B		
					•/S				Fort Ebey State Park	•				•/M	•	•/B		
									Dugualla Bay State Park and DNR Beaches							•/B	•	
				R					Strawberry Point Boat Launch			•						
S						•	•	•	Oak Harbor			•				B		
D	•	•	•	R/H	•/S				Oak Harbor Marina			•			•			
				R	•/S	(•)	(•)	(•)	Oak Harbor City Parks	•		•		•/M		B		
				R					Monroe Landing County Park							B		•
D			•	R	•/S		•	•	Coupeville	•		•			•	B		
					•				Ebey's Landing State Park	•		•				•/B	•	
				R	•/S				Fort Casey State Park	•	•		•	•	•	•/B		

Marine Pumpout	Marine Services	Moorage	Launch Facilities	Restroom or Toilet	Lodging	Groceries/Shopping	Restaurants	Location	Fishing	Shellfish	Paddling	Scuba Diving	Camping	Picnicking	Hiking/Beach Walking	Wildlife Watching	Point of Interest
								Keystone Spit State Park	•			•		•	B	•	•
				•/S				South Whidbey State Park	•	•			•	•	•/B	•	
			R					Mutiny Bay Launch Ramp			•						
				•				Double Bluff Beach Access and DNR Tidelands	•	•				•	B	•	•
			R	•				Dave Mackie County Park	•	•				•			
			R	•		(•)	(•)	Holmes Harbor and Freeland	•	•				•	•		
•		•	R	•/S	•	•	•	Langley	•	•	•			•	B		•
				•		•	•	Columbia Beach	•								
			C					Possession Point DNR Beaches		•							
			R	•				Possession Beach County Park	•	•				•	•	•	
				•				Possession Point State Park	•	•	•	•	M				
			C					Whidbey Island Road Ends		•					B		
								7. POSSESSION SOUND AND PORT GARDNER									
		•	R	•				Tulalip Bay Marina	•	•				•	•		•
								The Snohomish River Estuary	•	•					•	•	
			R					Ebey Slough Launch Ramp			•						
			R	•				Langus Riverfront Park and Trail	•	•				•	•	•	
				•				Spencer Island							•	•	•
			R	•				Rotary Park Boat Launch and Lowell Riverfront Trail	•	•				•	•	•	
								North and South Marine View Parks							•	•	
•		•	R	•				10th Street Marine Park	•	•				•			
				•				Jetty Island Park						•	B	•	
•	•	•	H	•/S	•	•	•	Port of Everett Marina			•						
				•				Howarth City Park	•						•	•	
			R	•	•	•	•	Mukilteo	•	•	•			•	•		•

Fuel	Marine Pumpout	Marine Services	Moorage	Launch Facilities	Restroom or Toilet	Lodging	Groceries/Shopping	Restaurants	Location	Fishing	Shellfish	Paddling	Scuba Diving	Camping	Picnicking	Hiking/Beach Walking	Wildlife Watching	Point of Interest
									8. PICNIC POINT TO SEATTLE									
					•				Picnic Point County Park			•			•	B		
					•				Meadowdale Beach County Park			•		M	•	•/B	•	
S				•/S	•	•	•	•	Edmonds	•		•	•		•	B		
D	•	•	•	H	•/S	(•)	(•)	(•)	Port of Edmonds Marina	•								
					•/S	(•)	(•)	(•)	Bracketts Landing				•		•	B		
					•	(•)	(•)	(•)	Public Fishing Pier and Olympic Beach	•					•	B		
				C	•	(•)	(•)	(•)	Marina Beach Park	•		•	•		•			
					•				Richmond Beach Saltwater Park						•	•/B	•	
									Boeing Creek Fishing Reef	•		•						
					•				Carkeek Park						•	•/B	•	•
									9. ADMIRALTY INLET									
D/S	•		•	R	•/S	(•)	(•)	(•)	Kingston	•		•			•	B		
					•				Arness County Park			•			•			
				R	•				Eglon Beach Park			•			•	B		
				C					Hansville and Point No Point	•	•	•			•	•/B	•	•
				C					Foulweather Bluff			•				•/B	•	
							•	•	Port Gamble						•			•
				R	•/S				Salsbury Point County Park			•	•	M	•	B		
			•		•/S	•			Kitsap Memorial State Park		•		•	•	•	•		
				R	•				William R. Hicks County Park	•	•				•		•	
									Squamish Harbor DNR Beaches		•	•						
				(R)	•				Shine Tidelands State Park and Wolfe Property	•	•	•				B	•	
									Point Hannon (Whiskey Spit) State Park Property		•	•		M		B	•	
D	•		•		•/S	•	•	•	Port Ludlow	•		•			•			

	Marine Pumpout	Marine Services	Moorage	Launch Facilities	Restroom or Toilet	Lodging	Groceries/Shopping	Restaurants	Location	Fishing	Shellfish	Paddling	Scuba Diving	Camping	Picnicking	Hiking/Beach Walking	Wildlife Watching	Point of Interest
				R					Mats Mats Bay	•		•			•			
				R	•				Oak Bay County Park	•	•	•	•	•/M	•	B		
					•				Hadlock Lions Park	•	•				•	•/B		
					•				South Indian Island County Park	•	•	•	•		•	•/B		
					•				Kinney Point State Park Property and DNR Beach 404A					•	M			
					•				East Beach County Park	•	•	•			•			
	•		•	R	•				Mystery Bay State Park	•	•	•			•			
			•	R	•/S	•	•		Fort Flagler State Park	•	•	•	•	•	•	•/B		•
	•		•	R	•/S	•	(•)	•	Lower Hadlock and Hadlock Inn Marina			•						
			•		•/S				Old Fort Townsend State Park	•	•			•	•	•	•	•
			•		•/S	•	•	•	Port Townsend	•		•			•	•		•
•	•	•	•	R/H	•/S	•	(•)	•	Port Townsend Marinas			•			•	B		•
					•				Port Townsend Parks		•	•				•	B	
			•	R	•/S	•	•	•	Fort Worden State Park and Conference Center	•		•	•	•	•	•/B		•
					•				Point Wilson Light Station							B		•

10. THE EASTERN STRAIT OF JUAN DE FUCA

	Marine Pumpout	Marine Services	Moorage	Launch Facilities	Restroom or Toilet	Lodging	Groceries/Shopping	Restaurants	Location	Fishing	Shellfish	Paddling	Scuba Diving	Camping	Picnicking	Hiking/Beach Walking	Wildlife Watching	Point of Interest
									Protection Island									•
				R	•				Discovery Bay and the Miller Peninsula						•		B	•
									Panorama Vista Access								B	•
•		•	•	R	•/S		•	•	Pitship Point and John Wayne Marina	•	•	•			•		B	
		•		R	•/S	•			Sequim Bay State Park	•	•	•	•	•	•	•/B		•
				R	•				Marlyn Nelson County Park			•				•	B	
				R	•				Dungeness Bay Boat Launches	•	•				•			
					•/S				Dungeness Recreation Area					•	•	•	•	

Fuel	Marine Pumpout	Marine Services	Moorage	Launch Facilities	Restroom or Toilet	Lodging	Groceries/Shopping	Restaurants	Location	Fishing	Shellfish	Paddling	Scuba Diving	Camping	Picnicking	Hiking/Beach Walking	Wildlife Watching	Point of Interest
					•				Dungeness National Wildlife Refuge	•	•					•/B	•	•
S					•	•	•	•	Port Angeles	•		•			•	•		
D	•	•	•	R	•/S		•	•	Port Angeles Boat Haven			•						
				•	•	(•)	(•)	(•)	City Pier	•						•		•
				R	•				Ediz Hook							•	•	•

11. THE WESTERN STRAIT OF JUAN DE FUCA

Fuel	Marine Pumpout	Marine Services	Moorage	Launch Facilities	Restroom or Toilet	Lodging	Groceries/Shopping	Restaurants	Location	Fishing	Shellfish	Paddling	Scuba Diving	Camping	Picnicking	Hiking/Beach Walking	Wildlife Watching	Point of Interest
				R	•				Freshwater Bay County Park	•	•	•	•		•			
									Striped Peak Scenic Area							•		
					•/S				Salt Creek Recreation Area County Park and Tongue Point Marine Life Sanctuary	•		•	•	•	•	•/B	•	•
				R	•	•			Whiskey Creek to Twin Rivers	•		•		•	•	•/B		
									Twin Rivers		•					B		
S			•	R	•		•		Silver King Resort	•	•	•			•	•		
				R	•				Pillar Point County Park	•	•	•			•	B		
S					•	•	•	•	Clallam Bay	•					•	B		
S			•	R	•/S	•	•	•	Sekiu Resorts	•		•	•	•				
			•	R		•	•		Sekiu to Neah Bay						•	B	•	•
S			•	R	•/S	•	•	•	Neah Bay	•		•		•	•			•
					•				Cape Flattery							•	•	•

Preface

A "New and Improved!" banner might well be plastered across this book's cover, like a laundry soap slogan. We are always looking for ways to revitalize our books to make them better, easier to use, and more interesting. We hope we have succeeded. In addition to updating all the information, this edition includes:

- Newly formatted lists of attractions to entice you to visit the sites
- Complete "getting there" directions, both by car and boat, and those directions have been moved to the beginning of the site descriptions
- Additional maps and cross-referencing to maps
- Sidebars with interesting facts and trivia about the North Sound
- Navigation notes highlighted with a ❄

A few new sites have appeared since we last surveyed North Puget Sound, and some of the old ones are gone. More important, many existing sites have been improved by repairs, updates, and expansions—giving you good reasons to revisit spots you might have been to before, or try new ones.

And instead of three volumes covering North, Middle, and South Puget Sound, we have merged them into two, North and South, to make them more compact and to make it easier for readers to find information about particular sites.

About the Afoot and Afloat Series

Many guidebooks are written with a specific activity in mind, telling people such as bicyclists, paddlers, or clam diggers where to go to enjoy their favorite recreation. Although the books of our Afoot and Afloat series do cover some activities and areas strictly limited to boaters, we know that boaters frequently leave their vessels to walk beaches, dig clams, or hike trails in nearby forests, and that some boaters even bring bicycles with them to widen their explorations.

At the same time, many people who do not own boats love roaming beaches, hiking bluff tops, and peddling quiet roads, enjoying the bite of salt air, the cries of seabirds, and the rush of waves. The one common thread in this book is shorelines, and all the activities associated with them, no matter how one arrives there.

Descriptions of facilities are kept brief because we believe that such things as marinas and campgrounds are not ends in themselves, but merely places that enable one to enjoy the shorelines and water.

Attractions are described in order to entice visitors to out-of-the-way spots they might otherwise pass by. Because exploration of any region is more enjoyable if spiced with some of its history and ecology, we have included tidbits on history and natural life of some of the areas.

The areas in this book were surveyed over a period of several years and rechecked just prior to publication of this new edition. Changes to facilities do occur, however. The authors and The Mountaineers Books would appreciate your letting us know of any changes to facilities so future editions can be updated. Please address comments to: The Mountaineers Books, 1001 SW Klickitat Way, Suite 201, Seattle, Washington 98134 or send e-mail to *margeted@comcast.net*.

Marge and Ted Mueller

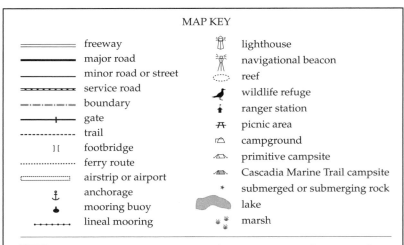

MAP KEY

freeway		lighthouse	
major road		navigational beacon	
minor road or street		reef	
service road		wildlife refuge	
boundary		ranger station	
gate		picnic area	
trail		campground	
footbridge		primitive campsite	
ferry route		Cascadia Marine Trail campsite	
airstrip or airport		submerged or submerging rock	
anchorage		lake	
mooring buoy		marsh	
lineal mooring			

NOTE:
This book's sketch maps are not intended for navigation. Not all hazards, such as rocks or reefs, are shown.

The mileage scale indicates general distances. However, because nearly all the maps are drawn in perspective, as if seen from an airplane, front to back distances are somewhat greater than indicated, due to foreshortening.

Icons for mooring buoys and campsites are placed to show their general location, but the number of icons is not indicative of that item's total number. Refer to the text information blocks for more exact numbers.

🌄 Introduction

NORTH PUGET SOUND IS, IN MANY WAYS, the most interesting and varied of all of Washington's inland waters. It ranges from the harsh, wave-worn, rocky shoreline of the Strait of Juan de Fuca to the seeping saltwater marshes of the Skagit delta. Its attractions include beautiful historic towns, unique nature preserves, fascinating old Army forts, parks for every possible taste, and the best stretches of boating waters to be found anywhere on the West Coast.

These waters, along with the far southern reaches of the sound, were visited by British sea captain George Vancouver in 1792. He explored the area in two ships, the 90-foot sloop of war *Discovery* and the 60-foot brig. *Chatham*. The expedition drew amazingly accurate charts of the area, and named many locations—most notably Puget Sound, named for his lieutenant, Peter Puget.

Another historic name is Lieutenant Charles Wilkes. In 1841 he commanded six vessels of the United States Exploring Expedition. His mission was to explore and chart the region and to establish claims to the area for the government. Many Puget Sound names come from this expedition.

Where Is "Puget Sound"?

The broad seaway on which the major population centers of western Washington front, and on which thousands of boats travel daily, ought to have a nice all-inclusive name. Unfortunately, it doesn't. In precise geographic language "Puget Sound" applies only to the channels south of a line drawn from Port Townsend on the Olympic Peninsula to Admiralty Head on Whidbey Island. That leaves a whole chunk of Washington's inland waters without a name. True, some of these, such as the Strait of Juan de Fuca, Saratoga Passage, and Rosario and Haro Straits have individual names, but the area still lacks an official, overall name that weather reports, government agencies, the populace in general, and beleaguered writers (especially) can use.

Officialdom aside, however, many local people, as well as most state agencies, commonly consider Puget Sound to be all of Washington's inland waters that run north from Olympia to the Canadian border and west to the Pacific Ocean. Thus, we titled this book *North Puget Sound* and its companion volume is *South Puget Sound*. There is no tidy division between north and south, so we set a very arbitrary dividing line for the purpose of these books. We consider North Puget Sound to be the area lying above a line drawn from

Shilshole Bay to Kingston, continuing west and swinging below the Hood Canal Bridge to include the area north of Bangor, then including all of the south shore of the Strait of Juan de Fuca. That pretty group of islands sitting near the center of all this is covered in our third companion volume, *Afoot and Afloat: The San Juan Islands*.

Getting Around in North Puget Sound

To Puget Sound pioneers, the network of waterways was a tremendous asset. The land was covered with forests so thick that even walking was difficult and road building was a herculean task; however, any of the homesteads and infant milltowns along the shore could be reached by boat with a minimum of effort.

In time, as communities were established, the rowboats and sailing ships of early settlers were joined by steamboats—reliable workhorses that churned through the waters of the sound transporting people, mail, and goods with little concern for the vagaries of weather. The quantity of little steamers grew to such a number, swarming hither and yon across wide channels and up narrow rivers and sloughs, that one observer referred to them as the Mosquito Fleet.

Although the automobile and the network of mainland roads it inspired brought an end to seventy years of activity by the steamers of the Mosquito Fleet, the sound still serves as a primary avenue of transportation for residents. A fleet of state-operated superferries, assisted by a few county-run

Before 1935, when the Deception Pass Bridge was completed, a small ferry ran between the two points in the distance, linking Fidalgo and Whidbey Islands.

Using This Book

- This guide is arranged geographically, moving roughly from north to south and east to west. Chapters have an overview map and numerous detail maps. The maps are referenced at the beginning of each site description.
- Sidebars are our digressions of thought into something we found interesting. We hope you, too, will find them interesting.
- Attractions and facilities listed at the beginning of each site description are generally arranged with the most important attractions for that site first and lesser ones following.
- Access directions are given via car 🚗 and boat 🚤, as applicable. Most sites can be reached from a variety of different points, so the access directions and distances are from the most likely spot.
- We have not noted places where fees are charged, because nearly all facilities charge a fee, even state parks. Assume you will need to pay for their use.
- To call attention to navigational imformation, important text is marked at the beginning with a ❋.

and privately operated vessels, now carries goods and passengers to cross-sound destinations. Commercial ships fill the major channels, transporting goods to and from foreign markets. And every year hundreds of thousands of pleasure boaters use the sound to take them to fabled vacation destinations such as those described in this book.

For boaters in large craft, most of the areas in the North Sound are within a day or two's cruising distance from any other point on the sound via protected waterways. The 15-mile-wide Strait of Juan de Fuca, with its winds and waves sweeping in from the Pacific Ocean, can be a serious challenge at times, and its outer reaches present some difficulty in navigating and finding secure anchorages during bad weather.

Trailered or cartop boats, kayaks, and canoes are easily transported to any of a multitude of public or commercial launching facilities for quick access to recreation destinations. For those who want to enjoy the shorelines by foot or bicycle, most points on the North Sound are but a half-day away from the major metropolitan areas via highway and ferry. Interstate 5 is the main north–south route along the east side of the sound; in this book, most driving directions on the east side of the sound are keyed to exits from this thoroughfare.

The Olympic Peninsula—the westernmost point described in this book—can be reached by driving south around the end of the sound and then north on US 101. A shorter but multistep process involves taking ferries from Seattle, Mukilteo, or Edmonds, then driving across the Hood Canal Bridge, and looping around the peninsula on US 101. The Olympic Peninsula can also be reached via the Keystone ferry from Whidbey Island.

Public Shorelines—Separating the Public from the Private

Parks—State, County, and City • "Public" beaches imply ownership by some public agency—city, county, state, or federal—and therefore they are open for public use. State park beaches are generally associated with campgrounds, picnic areas, and other developed recreational features such as fishing piers. County and city parks are nearly always day-use, offering picnic facilities and play space.

On public tidelands, do not stray onto adjacent private land and uplands. Even if lands are unposted, do not assume they are public or that no one cares if you trespass. With the press of people moving to the area, beach-front commands premium prices, and owners are increasingly hostile to trespassers.

DNR Beaches and Other Public Accesses • The Washington State Department of Natural Resources (DNR) owns substantial stretches of public beach. The majority of these beaches are accessible only by boat, and their usability varies. Most of these shorelands are public only up to mean high water line—this is the region just below the layer of driftwood or below the end of grass, trees, or other terrestrial vegetation.

The U.S. Fish and Wildlife Service controls most wildlife refuges. The

The shorelands at Lummi Island's Inati Bay are leased by the Bellingham Yacht Club for public boating use.

state Department of Fish and Wildlife (DFW) which owns some boat launch ramps, and the U.S. Bureau of Land Management (BLM), which maintains Coast Guard–operated lighthouses, are responsible for some of the smaller segments of public shorelands.

City and County Road Ends • In some locations where a platted public road deadends at a beach, the road legally extends across the tidelands and is open to public access, offering an easy place to launch hand-carried boats. Do not assume that all road ends offer beach access, however. Those described in this book were checked by the authors and were legally open at the time of publication.

The Nature Conservancy • The Nature Conservancy, a private conservation organization supported by memberships and donations, has purchased some environmentally important property on the inland waters. In general, lands owned by this group are considered biological preserves and are open to the public for limited use—nature walks are fine, but camping and picnicking are not allowed. However, in some cases the area might be so sensitive that public visits are not permitted.

Cascadia Marine Trail • The Washington Water Trails Association, an organization of paddlers, has created the Cascadia Marine Trail (CMT), which links 150 miles of inland waterways from the southern reaches of Puget Sound to the Canadian border. This marine trail system has set up a chain of campsites that are a reasonable day's paddle apart. Washington State Parks, the DNR, and several city and county park departments have designated primitive shoreside CMT campsites on their properties. An annual permit is required for their use, and in state parks a nominal fee is charged.

Boat Launching and Mooring Facilities

Since this book focuses on boat-oriented recreation, getting boat to water is extremely important; thus boat-launch sites are key to the enjoyment of the area. Both public and commercial launch facilities are noted. A fee is nearly always charged for the use of commercial facilities, and many public ramps have an honor box for depositing fees.

The quality and safety of launch facilities range from the sublime—with excellent surface, drop-off, and protection—to the ridiculously hazardous, where boaters risk getting stuck in mud at low tide or having boats reduced to splinters by ever-present winds or waves. Explore the surface of a ramp before launching, and exercise care using any launch facility until you are familiar with it. At times of wind or surges, extra care must be used to avoid damaging the boat or injuring boaters.

Launch facilities tend to change occasionally. Some are neglected and become unusable. Commercial ones close down for the season or even go out of business. On the plus side, new ones are sometimes built or old ones improved.

Commercial or port authority–run marinas normally set aside space for guest moorage, available for a daily fee. Some accept reservations. Marina facilities run the gamut from meager wooden docks clinging to ancient piers to posh resorts complete with full dockside utility hookups for boats, hot tubs for salt-encrusted crews, and attractions for stir-crazy kids.

Marine state parks are accessible only by boat; they all have mooring buoys and a few have floats, as do a few land-based parks. During busy times, rafting (two or more boats tied together side by side) is encouraged on floats where possible.

Lineal mooring systems, installed in a number of heavily used areas, allow more moorage in a small area and are easier on the environment. They greatly reduce the damage done to the seabed by dragging buoy anchor blocks and boat anchor chains. These 200-foot-long cables, strung between a pair of pylons, have mooring eyes along the cable to which boats can tie.

Park buoy anchor blocks are set reasonably solidly, generally in 2 fathoms of water or more, with sufficient swing room to avoid collisions with neighbors; however, they are not designed in either strength or placement to accommodate a rafted fleet of boats. Follow these guidelines for using buoys:

- Boats less than 24 feet long, four boats
- Boats from 25 to 36 feet long, three boats
- Boats from 37 to 45 feet long, two boats
- Boats more than 45 feet long must tie up singly on buoys

Significantly fewer boats should be rafted during severe weather.

Recreation on Washington's Inland Waters

One of the most remarkable aspects of Puget Sound is the variety of activities the water and shores engender. They offer something for all ages, from tots experiencing the first squish of sand through toes, to senior citizens enjoying retirement with leisurely beach strolls or boat cruises. Here you'll find boating to satisfy every taste from yachting to kayaking and canoeing, as well as bicycling, camping, picnicking, birdwatching, beach walking, hiking, scuba diving, and more. Nature preserves, historical sites, and scenic vistas make this a destination to please nearly every visitor.

Boating and Paddling—And Doing It Safely • Puget Sound residents do like their boating. You have only to take a quick look at the forest of masts in the many marinas, or glance at the parking lots full of boat trailers at the larger launch sites, to quickly establish that fact. Billowing sails and throbbing motors don't tell the whole story, however; peek into any secluded bay and you will probably find kayakers in search of shoreline sights that the crews of larger boats might never find.

Boating, as referred to here, runs the complete spectrum of conveyances that float, from kayaks and canoes to pleasure cruisers and sailboats. Regardless of the size or shape of your transportation, certain fundamentals and cautions apply to all who use these waterways. In many places throughout the text, comments refer to "paddlecraft" or "small boats," a vague category that includes dinghies, rubber rafts, canoes, and kayaks, or any watercraft that is muscle powered or has minimal power. Safety cautions can also apply to boaters in larger boats who have had little experience handling adverse conditions, whatever the size of the craft.

A boater's best ally in navigating safely is "sea savvy"—a generous helping of common sense augmented by boating safety courses and instruction in safely operating one's vessel. Before committing your safety, as well as that of a boatload of family or friends, to your competence, take one of the excellent courses that are available through either the U.S. Power Squadron or the U.S. Coast Guard Auxiliary. Information can be obtained through the U.S. Coast Guard. Note that state law requires each occupant of a boat to have a wearable floatation device available in case of emergency.

Be especially aware that Puget Sound waters are frequently used by scuba divers. Use caution in the vicinity of known dive areas and be on the watch for the red flag with a white diagonal stripe that marks areas where scuba divers are active. When approaching beaches, cut boat speed to a minimum and watch for swimmers in the water.

Renting a boat for a day of fishing or exploration, or chartering one for an extended cruise, is common. This book notes places where such boats are available. No matter what size the craft, to attempt boating without someone on board who is experienced is folly. Most charter operators check out clients before turning a boat over to them; if prospective boaters are obviously unqualified to operate a vessel safely, the charter operator might give them a quick course, or might insist that an experienced skipper go along (for a fee). All required safety gear is included with the rental.

The text makes particular mention of places that are appropriate for paddling—that is, muscle-powered boating in kayaks, canoes, dinghies, or inflatables. While this is the ideal way to reach many of the beaches along the sound, extreme care must be used, with an eye to tide rips and currents, the weather, and even larger boats. Crossing channels can be quite hazardous for the inexperienced. Classes are available in larger cities; guided trips are an ideal introduction to the sport.

NAVIGATION. This book attempts to address major boating concerns, but it is not possible to cover all navigational hazards that might affect all types of boaters. In some places, water depths and particular current problems are noted; however, nothing can take the place of a good navigational chart, an accurate compass, and the knowledge of how to use both. The best chart for close-in navigating is the one with the largest scale—that is, showing the greatest detail.

ROCKS AND SHOALS. Most serious navigational hazards in this area, such as rocks and shoals, are marked with lights, buoys, or similar navigational devices. Long streamers of bull kelp floating on the surface are another warning of a rock or reef—approach any bed of kelp cautiously. However, with a potential tidal variation of 16 to 20 feet at extreme tides, normally submerged and safe rocks and reefs can come dangerously close to the surface at extreme minus tides, and underwater shoals and bars can become a four-hour, or more, resting place for the sailor who doesn't keep a wary eye on the chart, tide table, and depth sounder.

TIDAL CURRENT. Tidal current is not the same as the tide, although one does give rise to the other. Tides measure the vertical distance that water rises and falls above the sea floor due to the gravitational attraction of the sun and moon, as well as more obscure influences. Tidal currents represent the horizontal flow of water resulting from the rise and fall of the tide.

For boaters in small craft with a maximum speed of 6 knots or less, tidal currents are something to be reckoned with—cautiously and deliberately. Obviously, a kayaker would rather be going in the direction of the current rather than struggling to make way headed into it. With long water passages, a typical tidal current of 2 knots abeam can make as much as a 15-degree difference in the course to be steered, even for power boats—a difference that can be critical in conditions of fog and low visibility.

Tidal currents in Puget Sound vary from 1 to 10 knots. In addition, the various interconnecting waterways found in Puget Sound give rise to some rather illogical directions of tidal currents. The small-craft portfolio of charts indicate position, direction, and average speed of the current at maximum flood or ebb tide at specific, measured points. Tidal current tables (not tide tables), which are printed annually, are keyed to station points on the charts. The approximate time of maximum velocity of the current can be computed by referencing the tidal current tables to a chart's station point. Although many other factors enter into the actual surface velocity, and even the direction of the current, general knowledge of the predicted velocity is invaluable for safe navigation.

TIDE RIPS. Navigational charts typically bear notations of "tide rips" off points of land between channels. Tide rips are caused by either the impact of tidal currents meeting from differing directions or the upwelling of currents as they meet underwater cliffs. In either case, the surface appearance is the same: the water appears to dance across an area in small to moderate choppy waves and swirls like a whirlpool. A boat crossing a tide-rip area might have difficulty maintaining course when erratic currents spin the vessel first one way and then another. Persons in small boats such as kayaks might find rips to be an experience best avoided. The positive aspect of tide rips is that the upwelling current also brings to the surface food-chain elements that attract game fish and, therefore, they are ideal fishing spots. They are also a likely place to spot seals and birds attracted by the good eating.

VESSEL TRAFFIC. Some sections of Puget Sound are heavily used by commercial vessels, naval vessels, ferries, fishing boats, and recreational boats, making it seem downright crowded at times. Rules of the road specify who stays clear from whom under what conditions; however, don't risk life, limb, and the hull of your boat assuming another captain knows those rules and will follow them. A sailboat skipper shouting "Starboard tack!" at a large power vessel closing at high speed might end up getting his satisfaction in court—after he has been fished from the sound.

To bring order to large-vessel traffic, the Coast Guard has installed a Vessel Traffic Service (VTS) on Puget Sound. Northbound and southbound traffic lanes have been designated down the center of the sound and are marked on all area charts. The ½-n.m.-wide traffic lanes lie on either side of a ¼-nautical-mile-wide separation zone, which has midchannel buoys marking every point at which the lanes alter direction. Radar stations are located at key points on the sound to track vessel traffic; all radar signals feed into the Coast Guard VTS Center on Pier 36 on the Seattle waterfront.

Large vessels are required to participate in the system. Communication with the VTS Center is over VHF channel 14. Boaters concerned with the location of large-vessel traffic, especially in fog, can monitor this frequency for information. Smaller commercial and recreational vessels generally don't participate in the VTS; however, they will probably appear on the center's radar, depending on their size and radar reflectance. These smaller boats can contact the center in emergencies, and the center will provide assistance, if possible.

Another potential traffic problem, especially at night during commercial salmon fishing season, is dozens of fishing boats with nets deployed. Proper lights on fishing boats and nets should identify areas to avoid, but a sharp lookout is required to spot these lights and avoid snagging nets.

WEATHER. Summer favors Puget Sound and Hood Canal with mild temperatures, moderate weather, and light winds. However, sudden summer storms come up occasionally. In other seasons, the waters in this area can at times be downright nasty and dangerous. Prevailing storm winds come from the southwest; the shift of wind to that direction, plus a falling barometer, bodes of worsening weather.

In sections of North Puget Sound, steep terrain that forces winds along the direction of a waterway can produce an effect called "channeling," or "gap winds," which causes the speed of the wind to increase by as much as double. In the Strait of Juan de Fuca, winds near the west entrance have reached up to 65 knots as a result of channeling.

The middle section of Puget Sound has a particular weather anomaly known as a "convergence zone." Low-level winds from the west off the ocean split as they encounter the Olympic Mountains. A portion loops south around the mountain range then goes back north, down sound. Another portion loops north through the Strait of Juan de Fuca and then heads south, up sound. When these two fronts of winds meet head-on (generally in the area between Seattle and Everett), a violent local weather front is sometimes created, with localized high winds, rain, and at times thunder and lightning.

FOG. In the inland waters, the price paid for warm sunny summer days is often morning fog created by the temperature differential between the sun-warmed landmasses and the perpetually chilly waters. Fog generally lifts by midday, but early departure plans should also include a well-plotted compass course to destinations that might disappear in the sea-level morning mist. Although this fog generally lifts by midday, a planned early departure might have to be delayed. In the Strait of Juan de Fuca, early morning fog can, on occasion, be accompanied by winds of 25 to 30 knots—an unpleasant combination.

CHOPPY WATER. A phenomenon peculiar to long, open, relatively shallow channels such as Rosario Strait or the Strait of Georgia are substantial seas with a very short, steep wave form, in contrast to the broader swells built in the deep channel of the Strait of Juan de Fuca or the open ocean. This generally occurs when wind-built waves are met by strong tidal currents from the opposite direction. The choppy seas chew away at forward boat speed and provide persons prone to seasickness an excellent opportunity to head for the lee rail. The conditions can be very dangerous for small boats, as they might be swamped or overturned. The best defense against being caught by adverse weather conditions is a regular monitoring of the NOAA weather channel, VHF channel WX1 (FM 162.550 MHz).

In Port Gardner, sailors might be rewarded with a view of Mount Baker.

ANCHORING. When anchoring, whether in a marine state park or in another protected area, be sure your hook is properly set and that the swing of your vessel will not collide with others. In a tight anchorage, it might be useful to also set a stern anchor or row a stern line ashore and tie it to a tree in order to reduce swing.

Check predicted tide levels to make sure you have enough water under you for the duration of your stay and that the proper length of anchor rope has been payed out. Contrary to the rules proclaimed in some boating "bibles," an anchor scope of seven times the water depth generally is not necessary, and is almost impossible to achieve in small coves. In all but the most severe weather, a three-to-one scope is quite adequate with a well-set anchor, and considerably more courteous for others who might want to share a crowded anchorage. It is also more environment friendly, because dragging anchor chains damage the seabed—the shorter the chain, the less the damage.

Walking and Hiking • Very little of the foot-bound exercise described in this book is vigorous enough to be categorized as hiking. For the most part, it involves easy strolls to viewpoints, short nature loops through forested glades, or walks along beaches. With time out for birdwatching, flower smelling, rock skipping, or any of many other diversions, most of the walks described are ample enough to fill an afternoon. For extended walks, many public areas can be linked by walking the beach at low tide or following city streets at high tide.

Do not approach too close to the top edge of bluffs as they might crumble. To compound the risk, the tops of many such bluffs are covered with a grass that is quite slippery, especially for smooth-soled shoes. At no time should hikers attempt to ascend or descend a bluff if there is no trail; when trails are present, use care because they too can become treacherously slippery.

Long walks on DNR beaches can be found in some locations. Many are very dependent on tide levels because a wide, gently sloping beach can disappear within 4 or 5 hours beneath an incoming tide. Note the time of the next tide change and plan your walk to avoid getting trapped in some uncomfortable or unsafe place such as below steep bluffs or impenetrable brush.

Bicycling • Nearly all the areas encompassed in this book are well suited to bicycle exploration. Many shoreline roads are quite popular for both one-day and extended bicycle trips. Because traffic tends to keep to the inland highways and freeways, many roads are lightly traveled, yet are level and smoothly paved. Beware of logging trucks, especially on the Olympic Peninsula. They travel fast, are not maneuverable, and require a long distance to stop.

The most difficult bicycling route in the area described in this book is SR 112 along the Strait of Juan de Fuca between Port Angeles and Neah Bay. Some venturesome bicyclists tackle this route as part of an Olympic Peninsula tour; however, the road has numerous ups and downs, curves, narrow shoulders, and occasional logging trucks and hell-bent motorists. Compensation for this is some of the finest scenery on the face of the earth.

US 101 along Hood Canal is popular for long trips and, with a few exceptions, has shoulders wide enough for safe and comfortable bicycling. SR 106 along the south side of the bend of Hood Canal is another well-used bicycle route; however, the road is narrow and twisty and traffic is generally heavy. Follow all bicycling safety rules.

Picnicking and Camping • Picnic facilities, found in nearly all of the developed state, county, and city parks, are for day use only and cannot be used for overflow camping. These sites usually hold only picnic tables and fire braziers, fireplaces, or fire rings. Water and restrooms are usually nearby. Most also have one or more picnic shelters, some with kitchens.

Disabled facilities have increased as funding has become available to make park facilities barrier free. A number of parks have restrooms, parking spots, and one or more picnic sites, shelters, or campsites that have been modified to eliminate access impediments. For more information, contact the individual park.

Toilet facilities are classified in this book as *restrooms, toilets,* and *composting toilets.* When you are in need of one, it probably doesn't matter to you which is which. *Restrooms,* by our definition, have flush toilets and running water for washing up. If they also have showers, it is noted. What we classify as *toilets* are little houses that sit over a dirt pit or have a holding tank that is pumped out at regular intervals. They do not have running water. *Composting toilets* are popular for remote parks because of their efficiency, safety, and decreased odor. In these, disease-causing organisms are destroyed and wastes are broken down by special bacteria and fungi into a compost similar to garden soil. *Note:* Boaters and campers should not empty portable toilets into composting toilets because the addition of other chemicals and water might hinder bacterial growth.

Some state parks will accept campsite reservations online or via a telephone reservation system. Refer to appendix A for phone numbers and website addresses. Camping at unreserved sites is on a first-come, first-served basis. Fees are collected nightly for all campsites, and campgrounds are closed after 10:00 P.M. In this book, we note the different types of sites found in the parks as follows:

- *Standard campsites* have a car pullout, either a fireplace (a ground-level metal enclosure on a concrete pad) or brazier (metal enclosure on a waist-high metal stand), picnic table, and a level tent pad. Water and toilets are nearby. If utility hookups are available for RVs, they are noted with an E (electricity), W (water), and S (sewer). If a trailer dump station is in the park, it is noted.
- *Walk-in campsites*, favored by bicyclists and hikers, are similar but have no vehicle pullout and are a short distance from the road. Some walk-in, primitive, and group campsites have one or two Adirondack shelters. These are three-sided affairs with a sloping cedar roof and usually four wood-planked bunks.

- *Primitive campsites*, as defined by Washington State Parks, hold only a picnic table and fire ring (designated fire area surrounded by rocks), fireplace (low concrete enclosure topped with a metal grate), or brazier. Toilets are nearby, but water might not be available. This type of campsite is found in all of the marine state parks.
- *Cascadia Marine Trail (CMT) campsites*, reserved for kayakers and other paddle-powered boaters, are near water's edge and are usually primitive. Toilets are available at or near the campsites, but other amenities are limited—often the site is just a spot level enough for a tent. Open fires either are not permitted or are strongly discouraged, and potable water is available only at those sites that are associated with other fully developed camping facilities.
- *Group campsites*, which usually require a reservation, have space for large groups to camp together and usually have a picnic shelter and dedicated restrooms.
- *Environmental Learning Centers* (ELCs) in state parks are designed for school and church groups, family reunions, and other gatherings. Although facilities vary by park, they usually include rustic cabins with bunks, cooking facility, mess hall, and other group-use buildings.

Wildlife Viewing and Birdwatching • If you don't bring binoculars with you on your excursion, you probably will wish you had. You are almost certain to see some local wildlife. You might spot harbor seals or river otters. Sea lions often haul out on bell buoy platforms or beaches.

The San Juan Islands are well known for whale sighting; however, whales might also be seen at many places in the inland waters, even in Seattle's Elliott Bay. If you should see a group of whales while boating, move away, or move parallel to them, at the speed of the slowest ones. Look in all directions before approaching or departing. A minimum distance of 100 yards is required by law. Failure to heed this can result in a severe fine.

You could have a good time just trying to identify all the different gulls you see on the shores. However, birdlife extends far beyond gulls, from skittery little shorebirds to tuneful perching birds and soaring eagles and hawks. Grab a bird guide and go!

Harvesting Seafood—Beach Foraging, Fishing, and Scuba Diving • One of the greatest excitements of the seashore is the prospect of gathering food fresh from the water for a seaside feast or a quick trip home to the dinner table. Washington's inland waters are home to more than fifty varieties of sport fish, many of which make excellent eating. Salmon, the prize of Puget Sound sport fish, are frequently caught in areas where opposing tidal flows meet and form tide rips, concentrating food sources for the salmon.

Many state regulations cover seafood harvesting in Washington. Additional regulations cover specific parks, reefs, marine sanctuaries, and similar areas. You are responsible for knowing the regulations, following them, and having appropriate licenses. A pamphlet published by the state Department of Fish and Wildlife, available in most sporting goods stores, lists bag limits, seasons,

Shellfish gathering is one of the delights of Puget Sound. Follow state regulations regarding season, limits, and other restrictions, and harvest only those creatures you intend to eat, as this woman is doing.

licenses required, and other restrictions. Complete current information can be accessed on the DFW website at *wdfw.wa.gov/fishcorn. htm*. Local regulations for parks and similar areas are prominently posted at that site. Before removing anything from a beach, check reader boards for any postings.

Be especially aware that state regulations require that holes dug on a beach for purposes of gathering clams *always must be refilled*. The incoming tide might take three or four cycles to fill holes; in the meantime small marine animals trapped on top of the pile are exposed to the sun and might die of dehydration, and others trapped under the pile might suffocate.

All state parks and some county and city parks have regulations protecting non-food forms of marine creatures, such as limpets, barnacles, starfish, and sand dollars. Although it is not illegal to take a small nonliving souvenir of a beach trip, such as an empty seashell, small rock, or piece of driftwood, please use restraint in the quantity you take, or, better yet, leave it. Even driftwood, rocks, and shells are an important part of the marine environment, forming growing sites for marine plants, homes for small creatures, and helping to control erosion. Many tidelands in populated areas along the sound were once a bright tapestry of marine life, but are now virtually barren due to longtime abuse by beachcombers, coupled with the effects of pollution.

Beachcombers occasionally find historical treasures washed ashore: debris from shipwrecks, some nearly a hundred years old, and pioneer artifacts that were imbedded in eroding underwater cliffs near areas of early settlement. The removal of historical artifacts is prohibited in some areas. Before taking anything away, be sure to check whether it is legal.

PARALYTIC SHELLFISH POISONING (RED TIDE OR PSP). The state Department of Health periodically issues a "red tide warning" and closes particular beaches on

Puget Sound. The name "red tide" itself contributes to the public's confusion, for it is not always visibly red, it has nothing at all to do with the tide, and not all red algae are harmful.

PSP is a serious and sometimes fatal illness caused by *Gonyaulax catenella*, a toxic, single-celled, amber-colored alga that is always present in the water in small numbers. During spring, summer, and fall, certain environmental conditions might combine to permit a rapid multiplication or accumulation of these microscopic organisms. Most shellfish toxicity occurs when the concentrations of *G. catenella* are too sparse to discolor the water; however, the free-floating plants sometimes become so numerous that the water appears to have a reddish cast—thus the name red tide.

Bivalve shellfish such as clams, oysters, mussels, and scallops, which feed by filtering seawater, might ingest millions of the organisms and concentrate the toxin in their bodies. The poison is retained by most of these shellfish for several weeks after the occurrence of the red tide; butter clams can be poisonous for much longer.

When the concentration of the toxin in mollusks reaches a certain level, it becomes hazardous to humans who eat them. *The toxins cannot be destroyed by cooking and cannot be reliably detected by any means other than laboratory analysis.* Symptoms of PSP, beginning with tingling of the lips and tongue, might occur within a half hour of ingestion. The illness attacks the nervous system, causing loss of control of arms and legs, difficulty in breathing, paralysis, and, in extreme cases, death.

Shellfish on Puget Sound are under regular surveillance by the state Department of Health. Marine toxin/PSP warnings are issued, and some beaches are posted, when high levels of toxin are detected in tested mollusks. Warnings are publicized by the media; for current information as to which beaches are closed to shellfish harvesting, check the marine biotoxin website at *www.doh.wa.gov/gis/mogifs/biotoxin.htm*, or the phone hotline at 1-800-562-5632.

POLLUTION. Both chemical and biological pollution have so thoroughly contaminated beaches in King County that harvesting of bottomfish, crab, or shellfish is not recommended along any of its shores. Similar problems afflict several beaches and bays in metropolitan areas of Kitsap and Snohomish Counties and some limited areas on Hood Canal in Mason and Jefferson Counties. Fish and shellfish from these areas have been found to have high levels of pollutants in their body tissues. A continuous diet of such animals can pose a health hazard. Hazardous beaches are generally posted. If in doubt, inquire.

Chemical pollution occurs near industrial areas, such as Harbor Island and Commencement Bay. Biological contamination occurs in areas where runoff from barnyards or sewage finds its way into the water or where large numbers of seals or sea lions congregate. In the far reaches of some inlets, where water movement is restricted, such pollution can occur.

Swimming ● Some beaches along the sound are shallow and therefore warm enough for saltwater bathing in summer, especially in the southern reaches.

Because of the close confines, wave action is nominal except in foul weather and, with some notable exceptions such as the Tacoma Narrows, the current is weak near beaches and poses little hazard. However, none of the public beaches, including those in the state parks, have lifeguards; swimming is at the participant's risk and should not be done alone or unwatched.

Using the Public Parks: Rules, Regulations, and Courtesy

Rules and regulations in the various areas are set up to preserve the natural environment and to maintain the safety and pleasure of all visitors, as well as park neighbors.

The following comments apply specifically to parks operated by the Washington State Parks and Recreation Commission. In general, these same rules, where relevant, also apply to county parks. When using any area, check for specific rules and regulations that are prominently posted or are found in pamphlets available at the entrance.

Some activities listed here might not be specifically covered by park rules, but they affect the aesthetics and environmental well-being of the area and the enjoyment of others. While visiting, be courteous and considerate of other park users and treat the park itself with care.

Fort Casey, on Whidbey Island, is one of several World War I and II forts that now see duty as state parks. This former lighthouse is now an interpretive center.

FEES. Fees are charged for the use of some state park facilities. Campsite reservations can be made online at the parks website, *www.parks.wa.gov*, or by calling (888) CAMPOUT or (888) 226-7688. Check the website or contact the specific park for information on group areas. The website also lists current fees.

CAMPING. Camp only in designated areas; camping is limited to ten consecutive days at any one park. Do not ditch tents, cut green trees or boughs, hammer nails into trees, or in any other way mutilate nature in the quest for a perfect campsite. Clean up your campsite after using it.

FIRES. Build fires only in designated fireplaces and fire rings. Fire hazard can be extreme during the summer. Before leaving, be sure your campfire is completely extinguished and the embers are cold. Beach fires are prohibited.

Portable charcoal-burning barbecues or hibachis placed on boat floats can badly char them; when using any such stove, be sure the wood is properly shielded from the heat. Some places prohibit the use of such stoves on docks.

Gathering fallen trees, branches, and driftwood for campfires is prohibited in all state parks. Decaying wood provides valuable nutrients to the forest ecology, and driftwood helps prevent beach erosion. Either bring firewood with you or, where it is available, purchase it at a campground registration booth or at a store.

GARBAGE. Trash receptacles are provided at the larger state parks; please use them. Many of the smaller, more remote marine state parks have neither garbage cans nor garbage collection. In areas where garbage cans are not provided, all trash must be removed. Recycling is encouraged.

When on boats, do not "deep-six" debris, whether it is cans, bottles, orange peels, or chicken bones. It usually does not come to permanent rest six fathoms down, as the slang expression implies, but will eventually wash up on some beach as ugly litter.

LIVING THINGS. Feeding, hunting, or harassing wildlife and discharging firearms is prohibited within the state parks and most other parks. Plants may not be dug up or flowers picked.

VEHICLES AND BICYCLES. Motorized vehicles and bicycles are prohibited on service roads and trails. Observe posted speed limits on public roads within parks.

BOATS. In the moorage area of marine state parks, the boat speed limit is 3 mph (no-wake speed). In addition to being extremely annoying to other boaters, hot-rodding or racing, even in small outboard-powered dinghies, can create a wake that might swamp small craft, send hot food flying from a cruiser's galley range, or cause other damage. Boaters are legally responsible for any damage caused by their wakes.

Moorage on buoys, floats, and lineal mooring systems is on a first-come, first-served basis. The practice of individuals attempting to "reserve" space by tying a dinghy to a buoy or float space is not legal in the state parks. Continuous moorage is limited to three consecutive nights.

It is courteous to use the minimum moorage space possible on a float.

Union Dock in Edmonds is a popular dive spot; however, the water offshore can be treacherous.

Beach small boats whenever you can, instead of tying up to a float. Berth small cruisers or runabouts as far inboard as possible, leaving the end of the float for larger boats that require deeper water and more maneuvering space.

PETS. Pets must be on a leash no longer than 8 feet and be under control at all times. They are not permitted on designated swimming beaches. Pet owners must clean up after their animals; violators are subject to fines.

NOISE. Because sounds carry greater distances over water, use care that radios or overly boisterous noise do not penetrate to nearby boats or campsites. Report disturbances to park rangers.

VANDALISM. It probably does little good to talk about intentional vandalism here. The damaging or removal of park property is, of course, illegal, and if you observe it, you should report it to the proper authorities.

Some acts of vandalism, however, are committed out of thoughtlessness or ignorance. Defacing park property or rocks or other natural features by spray painting or scratching graffiti is vandalism and will be prosecuted.

Digging into banks with shovels, picks, or any similar tool is also prohibited. Holes dug in beaches for clamming or for any other purpose must be refilled.

Safety Considerations

Boating and beach travel entail unavoidable risks that every traveler must be aware of and respect. The fact that an area is described in this book is not a representation that it will be safe for you. The areas described herein vary greatly in the amount and kind of preparation needed to enjoy them safely. Some might have changed since this book was written, or conditions might have deteriorated. Weather conditions can change daily or even hourly, and tide levels will also vary considerably. An area that is safe in good weather at low or slack tide might be completely unsafe during inclement weather or at times of high tide or maximum tidal current. You can meet these and other risks safely by exercising your own independent judgment and common sense. Be aware of your own limitations, those of your vessel, and of conditions when and where you are traveling. If conditions are dangerous, or if you are not prepared to deal with them safely, change your plans. Each year, many people enjoy safe trips on Washington's shores and inland waters. With proper preparation and good judgment, you can, too.

Emergency Assistance and Other Concerns

In parks where rangers or managers are not on duty, the proper authority can be reached by marine or citizens band (CB) radio if immediate action is necessary. From cell phones, the quick-dial number *CG immediately connects the caller to the Coast Guard Vessel Traffic Center in Seattle. The center coordinates marine safety and rescue activities in the region. Be prepared to explain the nature of the emergency and your exact location.

The U.S. Coast Guard has primary responsibility for safety and law enforcement on the water. Marine VHF channel 16 is continuously monitored by the Coast Guard and should be the most reliable means of contact in case of emergencies on the water. The Coast Guard monitors CB channel 9 at some locations and times, but it has no commitment to full-time radio watch on this channel. Several volunteer groups do an excellent job of monitoring the CB emergency frequency and will assist as best they can with relaying emergency requests to the proper authorities

Overall legal authority in all unincorporated areas of the state rests with the county sheriff. The emergency number is 911. Complaints or other business should be referred to the sheriff's office. A list of phone numbers and addresses for parks and legal agencies is included in appendix A. In matters of less urgency, park rangers should be contacted by telephone or in writing.

chapter one

The Strait of Georgia

IN SUMMER, THE STRAIT OF GEORGIA sees a steady flow of Canadian boaters headed south to fabled Washington islands and Yankee boaters headed north to island treasures in British Columbia—proving that even cruisers subscribe to the adage that the grass is greener (or, in this case, the water is bluer) on the other side of the fence. This 10-mile-wide channel spans the boundary between the United States and Canada. Several marine developments near the border on the U.S. side provide facilities and recreation to boaters in transit, as well as permanent moorage for those who

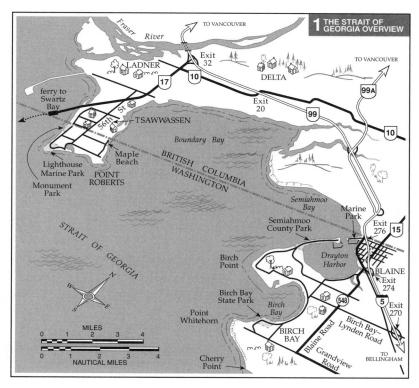

Opposite: *A rock breakwater protects Blaine Harbor Marina.*

like to have their vessels within easy striking distance of vacation waters. Customs checkpoints for boaters entering U.S. waters are at Point Roberts and Blaine marinas.

❋ Incoming boaters will note three sets of range lights in Semiahmoo and Boundary Bays marking the international boundary at the 49th parallel. The white, 60-foot-tall Peace Arch that straddles the boundary onshore is also visible from the water during most weather. The Strait of Georgia is free of obstructions except for Alden Bank, a 3-mile-long shoal marked by buoys that lies northeast of Sucia Island. Tidal currents in the channel rarely exceed 3 knots; however, a hull-jarring chop can occur when the direction of the current opposes that of the wind.

POINT ROBERTS
Map 2

🚗 From BC 99 18 miles (29 km) north of the border at Blaine at Exit 32 (BC 17, Tsawwassen, Point Roberts), head north on BC 17. At a stop light in 4²⁄₃ miles (7¹⁄₂ km), head south through Tsawwassen on 56th Street to reach the border to Point Roberts in 2³⁄₄ miles (4¹⁄₃ km). Crossing the border at either Blaine or Point Roberts is usually a very quick process except on weekends and holidays when heavy traffic might be encountered. Carry photo identification and proof of citizenship (passport or notarized copy of a birth certificate preferred).

🛥 Point Roberts lies 7 n.m. west of Drayton Harbor in Blaine. The nearest marine facilities are at Blaine, Semiahoo, and Bellingham. U.S. Customs clearance is available at the Point Roberts Marina.

A marker at Monument County Park commemorates the settlement of the boundary dispute.

Point Roberts is something of a geographic anomaly: a political island created by a quirk in an early treaty. During the time of pioneer settlement both the United States and Great Britain vied for the territory between Russia-owned Alaska and Oregon. The Yankee cry in the 1840s of "Fifty-four Forty or Fight" meant that the United States wanted to claim sovereignty over all the territory south of a latitude of 54 degrees, 40 minutes, well above the Queen Charlotte Islands. The British insisted on an international boundary at the Columbia River. In 1846 a compromise was reached, with the 49th parallel established as the international boundary from the crest of the Rocky Mountains west to the Strait of Georgia where the boundary dipped south, down the center of the Strait of Georgia, giving

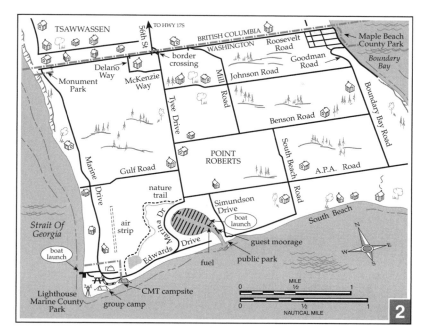

the Gulf Islands and all of Vancouver Island to the British.

The lawmakers back in Washington, D.C., due perhaps to inadequate maps, failed to note two geographical problems: The 5-square-mile tip of the Point Roberts peninsula that hung below the 49th parallel became isolated from the rest of the United States, and the boundary through the San Juan Islands was not clearly defined. The oversight on the San Juan boundary brought the two nations to the brink of war in 1859 during the Pig War standoff. Although a bit awkward, Point Roberts has created no major problems, and the U.S. citizens living there have learned to cope, and perhaps to enjoy their unique status.

Point Roberts Beach Accesses (Whatcom County) Map 2

Historical marker • Paddling • Swimming • Beach walking • Shellfish • Views

Area: *Maple Beach:* 1000 feet of saltwater beach on Boundary Bay

🚐 After crossing the border continue south on Tyee Drive for 1/3 mile. *Maple Beach:* Turn east on Johnson Road, which Ts into Boundary Bay Road/Goodman Road in 1 1/2 miles. Wind downhill on Goodman Road and at a three-way intersection continue east on Elm Street. In two blocks, Elm Street Ts into Bay View Drive, which runs above the beach bulkhead. There is no parking along Bay View Drive, but spots might be found along intersecting streets.

Monument County Park: From Tyee Drive, turn west on McKenzie Way, which turns north in 1/3 mile and becomes Delano Way. In 500 feet, this road Ts into

Roosevelt Road, which can be followed west for ³/₄ mile to the park. Monument County Park can also be reached from the south via Marine Drive.

🛥 *Maple Beach:* The access is immediately south of the border (marked by range marks on piles offshore) on the east side of Point Roberts. *Monument County Park:* The access is south of the border on the west side of the point. For either park the best exploration is by beachable boats, which can be put in at Lighthouse Marine Park, to the south.

Maple Beach County Park ● A concrete bulkhead, stretching southward for

several blocks from the Canadian border, fronts the vacation community at Maple Beach. Staircases that interrupt the bulkhead provide access to the sand and mud beach, which stretches out into Boundary Bay for nearly ¼ mile at minus tides. The water over the shallow, gradually tapering beach warms to pleasant swimming temperatures in summer months. The entire beach from the border south to Elm Street, a length of about five blocks, is publicly accessible property of Whatcom County Parks. Parking is not permitted along the road above the bulkhead.

Monument County Park ● This undeveloped tract of land offers tree-framed

glimpses from English Bluff of the Strait of Georgia, the long causeway at the Tsawwassen ferry landing nearby, and the green stretches of the Gulf Islands in the distance. A stone obelisk next to the parking area marks the boundary between Canada and the United States. It was the first, both historically and geographically, to be placed on the 49th parallel, in 1865.

Attempting to descend the 150-foot-high bluff is only for the foolhardy—it is steep and treacherous. ❊ The park's extensive tideflats, which extend out for more than ½ mile before plunging steeply downward, are best accessed by small shallow-draft boats. From the water, the public beach is easily identifiable by a navigational marker onshore. A great blue heron rookery inland, east of the park, is said to be one of the largest heron rookeries in the United States. The birds often can be seen lunching offshore.

Point Roberts Marina Resort   Map 2

Boating ● Paddling ● Beach walking

Facilities: Guest moorage with power, water, wireless broadband, gas, diesel, propane, restrooms, showers, laundromat, boat pumpout station, boat repair, chandlery, groceries, bait and tackle, pub, restaurant, picnic tables, boat launch hoist, U.S. Customs

🚐 From the Canadian border, drive south on Tyee Drive for 1½ miles and turn east on A.P.A Road. In ¼ mile, turn south on Simundson Drive to arrive at the marina in another ⅓ mile.

🛥 The marina is on the south side of Point Roberts, 7 n.m. west of Drayton Harbor in Blaine.

Convenience, both in facilities and location, is the byword at the Point Roberts Marina. The resort features the latest in moorage amenities, and a wealth of fishing and cruising waters are within a few miles of the entry breakwater. The large comma-shaped yacht basin holds more than 1000 boats. It is reached by water via a 200-yard-long dredged channel, which is in itself guarded by an angled jetty that serves to prevent shoaling of the channel. Being slightly inland gives it maximum protection during even the most severe weather. Guest moorage is along the east side of the entrance channel; the remainder of the basin is reserved for resident vessels.

Lighthouse Marine County Park (Whatcom County) Map 2

Boating • Paddling • Hiking • Camping • Picnicking • Fishing • Beach walking • Shellfish • Whale watching • Nature interpretation

Facilities: 30 campsites, group campsite, showers, CMT campsite, picnic tables, fire grates, boardwalk, picnic shelters/windbreaks, restrooms, view tower, fire rings, informational display, snack bar (weekends in summer), children's play area, launch ramp with boarding float. Day-use fee charged for all but Whatcom County residents. Fees for boat launching or overnight camping vary, depending on the type of boat and whether you are a county resident. *Nearby:* Nature trail.

Area: 22 acres; 4000 feet of shoreline on the Strait of Georgia

🚗 From the border, continue south on Tyee Drive, which in 1²/₃ miles bends westward around the marina basin as Marina Drive. In ¹/₂ mile, this road becomes

The namesake of Lighthouse Marine County Park is rather prosaic; however, the park itself is a delight.

Edwards Drive as it continues to the west for 1²/₃ miles to the park.

🛥 The park is at the southwest tip of Point Roberts. The CMT campsite is above the beach at the east end of the park. The nearest marine facility is at Point Roberts Marina Resort.

Here's a spectacular site for a park: a gravelly cape of land thrusting into the surging waters of the Strait of Georgia, with views sweeping the length of the strait and out to emerald San Juan and Gulf Islands. To the southeast rises Mount Baker, queen of all. The lighthouse, after which the park is named, is a mundane metal framework tower with a rotating beacon.

Because of strong winds that sometimes buffet the point, picnic tables sit in angular wooden covered shelters on a long boardwalk; numerous fire rings near the beach are in the protection of shallow log-rimmed pits. The beach has ample space to spread a blanket for lunching or sunbathing, wind permitting. On one corner of the boardwalk, a 30-foot viewing tower assists in sighting whales that travel in the strait. A shelter displays photos of orca whales (the ones most commonly seen), describes fin characteristics, family pod identification, and behaviors, and tells other fascinating information.

The underwater shelf drops off sharply at the tip of the point, but to the north and east the tideflat flares out more gradually, providing opportunities for clamming and beachcombing. At the northwest edge of the park is a 2-lane launch ramp; an adjacent line of floats, which is in place in summer, is used for boarding boats. Temporary anchorage can be found along the north side of the point in 5 fathoms of water, but wind and current conditions make this impractical for long-term stops.

The day-use area is on the south and west sides of the road, the campground to the east. A few low pines and a slight hill give the campsites some protection from winds off the strait. Owners of large RVs might prefer using one of the two commercial trailer parks located a few blocks inland because the campsites are a bit snug. They are ample for tenters and small RVs, however. None have hookups. A group camp at the southeast end of the park can be reserved. This is also the site of a CMT campsite; paddlecraft can be drawn up on the berm between the group camp and the beach.

The view tower at Lighthouse Marine County Park is used by people hoping to spot whales in the Strait of Georgia.

BLAINE
Map 3

Blaine is best known as a border town, offering a rest stop and fueling station to motorists going to and coming from Canada. Southbound boaters can stop here at the marina to check through Customs, although several other ports near the border provide the same service. Town businesses are geared to persons passing through—heavy on restaurants, lodging, and duty-free shops for northbound motorists.

Blaine lies on Drayton Harbor, a large shallow bay cut off from Semiahmoo Bay on the southwest by a 1½-mile-long sandspit and on the northeast by a man-made landfill jetty that holds the town's marine industries. Only the dredged harbor by the jetty and a small portion of the bay near the entrance are navigable—the rest of it dries at the mere hint of low tide. The tideflats of Drayton Harbor, as well as those north of the marina jetty, are excellent for clam digging and oyster picking.

❄ Shoals in Semiahmoo Bay spread outward for some distance on either side of the narrow entrance to the harbor. Boaters should give Semiahmoo Spit a wide berth and stay in the marked channel when entering.

Blaine Harbor   Map 3

Boating • Paddling • Sightseeing • Fishing • Crabbing

Facilities: Guest moorage with power, water, wireless broadband, boat pumpout station, dump for portable toilets, restrooms, showers, laundry, gas and diesel, repairs, haulout, 2-lane launch ramp with boarding float, public fishing pier.

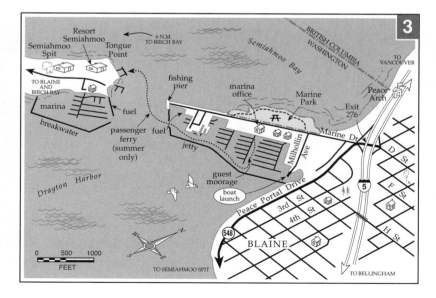

Nearby: Shopping and restaurants

🚗 Take Exit 276 (Blaine City Center) from I-5, just south of the Canadian border. At the intersection of D Street and Peace Portal Drive, head west on Marine Drive to arrive at the marina in ¼ mile.

🚤 The marina is on the north side of Drayton Harbor, with the entrance between concrete breakwaters at its west end. Guest moorage is on H Dock. The launch ramp is at the east end of the marina at the end of Milhollin Avenue.

The 700-slip marina, Blaine Harbor, which is operated by the Port of Bellingham, is a favorite with boaters looking for good mainland moorage within easy range of the San Juan and Gulf Islands. A rock and concrete breakwater along its south and west sides encloses the dredged basin, giving it excellent protection.

A complex of small businesses, mostly marine related, occupies the mile-long landfill pier. Marina offices and accommodations for pleasure boaters are in the middle section, while commercial fishing facilities are at the far western end. Marine Drive terminates at a broad wooden pier where public fishing and crabbing are permitted. Downtown Blaine is about a ¾-mile walk from the visitors' floats.

On Friday through Sunday between Memorial Day and Labor Day, a

Life-size sculptures of orca whales swim and dive in a concrete "sea" at Blaine Marine Park.

seventeen-passenger foot ferry, the Plover, lets you take a ride on a piece of history. Hourly, the boat, a working exhibit of the Drayton Harbor Maritime Society, makes short runs across the mouth of Drayton Harbor to the resort at the end of Semiahmoo Spit. The Plover was built in 1944 and used to ferry workers from Blaine to a fish cannery at Semiahmoo. Catch the ferry at the head of the guest dock; a donation fare is accepted (and appreciated). For more information go to *www.mvplover.org.*

Blaine Marine Park   Map 3

Picnicking • Walking • Nature study

Facilities: Picnic shelters, amphitheater, viewing platform, interpretive signs, restrooms

See Blaine Marina, described previously. The park is on the north side of Marine Drive across from the marina.

The City of Blaine, the Marine Education Foundation, and dozens of local volunteers collaborated to turn what was once a barren strip of landfill into an attractive beachfront park facing on Semiahmoo Bay. A large grass field along the north side of the road that runs past the Blaine marina has been attractively outfitted with picnic shelters, an amphitheater, and a bayside viewing platform fronted by an impressive sculpture of four life-size orca whales. Interpretive signs name the various species of birds that use the bay as a migratory stop, and tell how different species use specific ecological niches found in the bay. The mudflat offshore from the park often dries at low tide; public access is prohibited to preserve its unique ecological features.

Semiahmoo Marina   Maps 3 and 4

Boating • Paddling • Resort

Facilities: Guest moorage in unoccupied slips (contact marina for availability), water, power, wireless broadband, restrooms, showers, laundry, boat pumpout station, dump for portable toilets, chandlery, boat launch hoist, marine repairs, gas, diesel, groceries, gift shop

From I-5, take Exit 274 (Peace Portal Drive, Blaine). Cross west over the freeway and turn northwest on Peace Portal Drive. At a stop light in a short block, head south on Bell Road, which shortly becomes Blaine Road. In 1 mile, turn west on Drayton Harbor Road, and in another mile, go south on Harbor View Road. In 1/2 mile, turn west on Lincoln Road, which becomes Semiahmoo Parkway and reaches the resort and marina in 3 3/4 miles.

Semiahmoo Marina is on the south side of the entrance to Drayton Harbor, behind Tongue Point, the tip of Semiahmoo Spit.

Going from a fish packing plant to a posh marine resort is a big jump, but that's just what occurred on Semiahmoo Spit. Much of the property that was once owned by the salmon cannery, as well as a large portion of the Birch Point peninsula, is a major resort community. It includes a fine yacht basin protected by a floating log breakwater on the eastern side of the spit at Tongue Point. Boating facilities here are new and nice, with concrete floats, utilities, and security gates. The resort has a fine hotel, villas, restaurants, spa and fitness center, and a tournament-class golf course.

Semiahmoo County Park (Whatcom County) and DNR Beach 372   Map 4

Picnicking • Clamming • Crabbing • Beachcombing • Swimming • Birdwatching • Fishing • Paddling

Facilities: Picnic tables, toilet, museum
Area: 322 acres; 6700 feet of shoreline on Semiahmoo Bay and Drayton Harbor
🚗 See Semiahmoo Marina, described previously. The park is a mile southwest of the marina at the head of Semiahmoo Spit.
🛶 The park is accessible only by paddlecraft or beachable boats on either the Drayton Harbor or Semiahmoo Bay side of the spit. It is within walking distance of the boat basin.

This county park, which lies on the south end of Semiahmoo Spit between the residential and marina areas of Semiahmoo Resort, offers a nice combination of the natural and the historical. The natural part is a pair of wonderful beaches—one a windswept, driftwood-laced strand facing west on Semiahmoo Bay, the other a more protected tidal flat that spreads into Drayton Harbor. Both beaches offer the opportunity to capture crabs in the eelgrass beds; clamming is best on the Drayton Harbor side.

The park's historical offering is a group of buildings once used as bunkhouses for the salmon cannery. One of the buildings hosts a museum that displays photos, models, and artifacts recalling the era when the waters were filled with the graceful Bristol Bay sailboats used for gillnetting. A scale

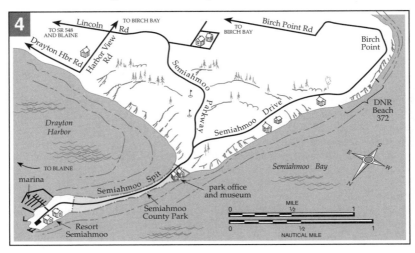

Either the inner shore or outer shore of Semiahmoo Spit are fine for lolling when the sun comes out.

model of the bay shows how it looked in 1917 when it held traps to snare the silvery deluge of salmon. The museum is open Friday through Sunday from Memorial Day to Labor Day, and weekends only for the remainder of September. A few picnic tables are scattered along a grass strip north of the buildings, some with views of the beach.

Boats can be hand-launched at either of the beaches, but in Drayton Harbor only at high tide; ❊ use care there to not become mired when the tide recedes. Semiahmoo Bay also offers paddling possibilities south around Birch Point to Birch Bay, 5 miles away. En route, DNR Beach 372 can be explored. That 2000-foot-long gravelly beach, lying beneath a steep 70-foot bluff ½ mile north of Birch Point, is a likely spot to find some clams. There is no upland access; only the beach below the mean high water level is public. ❊ Strong winds off the Strait of Georgia can be a danger.

BIRCH BAY

Map 5

🚗 From I-5, take Exit 270 (Lynden, Birch Bay), and follow Birch Bay–Lynden Road west for 4 miles to Birch Bay.
🚣 Shallow Birch Bay is primarily of interest to paddlecraft. The nearest launch ramps are at Blaine and Birch Bay State Park.

Birch Bay is best known for the summer resort communities edging its shore. The cabins and condos at the towns of Cottonwood Beach and Birch Bay host families that come to revel in the sun and sand as well as enjoy the nearby golf course, water slide, and other recreational offerings. Even the weather collaborates to make this a summer playland, as this section of Washington's inland waters receives far more sun than in lower Puget Sound.

While entertainment at Birch Bay tends toward the upbeat rather than the sedate, the area has its placid side. Once the summer crowds are gone, it becomes a quiet retreat, both for off-season guests and for flocks of migrating waterfowl that gather in the bay. Black brants, loons, oldsquaws, and harlequin ducks are frequent visitors.

❋The bay itself is an open bight holding less than 2 fathoms of water throughout much of its extent—great for swimming, but offering little to deep-draft boats. A few spots to drop a hook can be found well out in the bay in 4 to 5 fathoms of water. As compensation, a minus tide exposes a 1000-foot-wide tideflat with good opportunities for harvesting seafood. Kayakers or canoeists can enjoy some 7 miles of near-shore paddling within the protected arms of the bay. ❋Strong winds that occasionally sweep in from the west off the Strait of Georgia can pose problems in open water.

Birch Bay Village, a private residential community on the north side of the bay, has a small dredged basin, but it is only for the use of residents.

Cottonwood Beach and Birch Bay Public Accesses   Map 5

Shellfish • Beach walking • Paddling • Birdwatching

Facilities: Toilets

From Cottonwood Beach south to Birch Bay State Park, the beachfront is public, broken only by a few sections of privately owned (well-posted) property. Birch Bay Drive, which parallels the shoreline, has numerous parking areas along its side, each with a toilet.

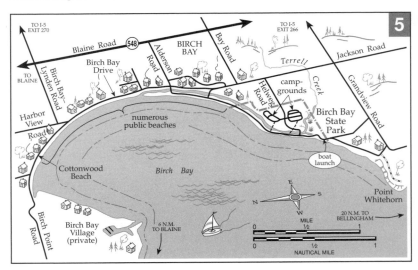

From a narrow band of driftwood, the tideflat recedes gradually into the water, remaining at wading level out for nearly 1/2 mile. The beach is so wide and glorious that not one, but three, sandcastle competitions are held here every summer, with dozens of competitive teams shaping flamboyant architecture or bizarre creatures.

Birch Bay State Park   Map 5

Camping • Picnicking • Boating • Paddling • Fishing • Beachcombing • Shellfish • Crabbing • Scuba diving • Hiking • Birdwatching • Kite flying • Water skiing

Facilities: 147 standard campsites, 20 RV campsites (EW), primitive campsite, 1 primitive group camp, picnic shelters, picnic tables, fire rings, wildlife theater, restrooms, showers, bathhouse, RV pumpout station, nature trail, primitive launch ramp. (Reservation campground, day-use fee area, and south campground closed in winter.)

Area: 193 acres; 8255 feet of saltwater shoreline on Birch Bay, and 14,923 feet of freshwater shoreline on Terrell Creek

🚐 *Campground entrance:* From I-5, take Exit 266 (SR 548, Custer, Grandview Road). In 6 3/4 miles, turn north on Jackson Road, and in another 3/4 mile, turn west on Helweg Road, which arrives at the park in 1/2 mile. *Day-use entrance:* From the intersection of Birch Bay Drive and Alderson Road in Birch Bay, cross Terrell Creek and take Birch Bay Drive south for 3/4 mile to the park entrance.

🛥 See Birch Bay, described previously.

The climax of the Birch Bay shoreline is the state park at its southern end. Here the magnificent beach is complemented by grassy shores with picnic tables and ample space for playing volleyball, tossing Frisbees, flying kites, or for any of the other sports that go so well with sun and sand. The entrances

Paddling in Birch Bay

Beach driftwood at Birch Bay State Park is great to play on.

are gated at sunset to discourage nighttime partying and recreation inspired by moon and sand.

The park's upland section, where the camping area is located, is in a stately old-growth forest of cedar and Douglas-fir. Sites on the north loop are in fairly open forest; a few have views of the bay through the trees. Campsites on the south, in heavier timber with some undergrowth, are more secluded.

From the campground entrances, the road passes picnic tables and picnic shelters in grassy fields shaded by large cedar and hemlock. One of the shelters is equipped with a small stage and benches for interpretive programs during the summer.

Terrell Creek drains into a narrow estuary at the south edge of the park. The marshland here provides habitat for beaver, opossum, muskrat, and a variety of birds. A ½-mile nature trail loops through the forest to the edge of the marsh. Flora at nine marked stations along the trail are identified in a pamphlet available at the park. The trailhead, unmarked on the park road, starts at a kiosk just east of the RV pumpout station. The nearest parking is at the entrance to the campground loops.

Scuba divers entering the water at the park swim west to Point Whitehorn where the bottom drops off more rapidly and the rocky shoreline hosts a diversity of underwater life. A 1-lane gravel launch ramp at the south park boundary is only marginally usable at high tide.

chapter two

 Bellingham Bay

THE SEVERAL ISLANDS CLUSTERED AROUND THE EDGE of Bellingham Bay and Bellingham Channel suffer somewhat from an identity crisis. Although they are frequently referred to as part of the San Juans (which they strongly resemble geologically), they are not part of San Juan County and therefore, by bureaucratic measurement, are not "real" San Juan Islands. Although they lie within a stone's throw of Bellingham and Anacortes, both major population centers, these half-dozen large islands and their entourage of smaller islets have managed to escape industrialization. Real estate developments have made some minor inroads, however, and the threat of development is constantly present.

Boaters seeking to avoid the heavy crowds and hoopla of the San Juans will find this area makes a nice cruising destination, with enough channels and tucked-away coves to hold their interest for a weekend. The city of Bellingham has full marine facilities.

Two of the islands, Lummi and Guemes, can be reached by car as well as by boat, making them accessible for persons with cartop craft or those who want to explore the shores by foot or bicycle. Larrabee State Park, south of Bellingham, is largely inland, but it does have a campground and rocky beachfront with a launch ramp.

The small ferry that leaves from Gooseberry Point connects Lummi Island with the mainland.

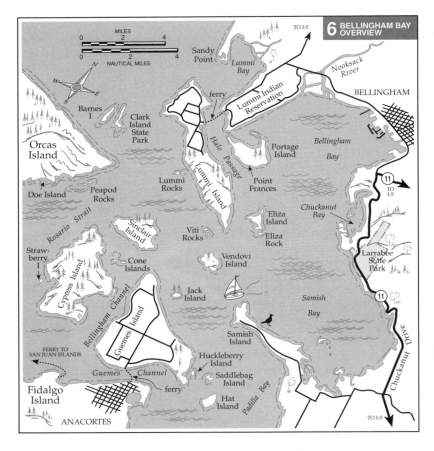

LUMMI ISLAND AND HALE PASSAGE
Map 6

Lummi is the most dramatic of the islands in the Bellingham vicinity—more than 9 miles long and 1 mile narrow, with bluffs at its south end rising precipitously for 1500 feet, while at the north end of the island the terrain abruptly flattens into rolling farmland. Its striking silhouette is visible from many of the northern islands and channels, further adding to the misconception that it is one of the San Juan group.

The island can be reached via a small Whatcom County–operated ferry from Gooseberry Point. On weekdays, the ferry runs half-hourly during times of heavy traffic, hourly when traffic is lighter. Crossing time is about 10 minutes. The only tourist amenity is a store and café a short distance north of the landing. Be forewarned: There is no gas pumped on the island—fill up before you go.

Most of the island's beachfront homes and acreages are on the flat, northern half of the island. The road that follows this northern shoreline offers motorists and bicyclists temptingly scenic views of Lummi Bay and the Strait of Georgia, but there is no public access on the west side. On the south end of the island, roads penetrate for only a short distance before the steep and wild take over.

Hale Passage, a mile-wide channel, runs between Lummi Island and the mainland.

❋ The channel is unobstructed; however, a sandbar that runs north from Lummi Point to Sandy Point, on the west side of Lummi Bay, is covered by only 2 fathoms of water at mean low water. Current in the channel runs up to 2 knots; canoeists and kayakers should time their ventures for a favorable tide.

Gooseberry Point and Portage Island   Maps 6 and 7
Fishing • Paddling • Stommish Festival

Facilities: Ferry landing, launch ramp and sling, gas, outboard mix and propane (onshore), groceries and deli

🚐 Leave I-5 at Exit 260, follow Slater Road west for 4 miles, and turn south on Haxton Way. In another 6 3/4 miles, arrive at the ferry landing at Gooseberry Point on the Lummi Indian Reservation. To reach the Stommish Ground from Gooseberry Point, take Lummi View Drive south for 1 mile.

⛴ Gooseberry Point is on the east side of Hale Passage, 3 1/2 n.m. north of the south entrance to the passage, or 2 n.m. south of the north tip of Lummi Island.

Fisherman's Cove Marina • On the mainland at Gooseberry Point, immediately north of the Lummi Island ferry landing, a marina provides some boating amenities. A pier with short floats on either side facilitates loading and onloading fuel and supplies; there is no overnight moorage, and at minus tide the floats sit on dry land. The marina does haulouts to 34 feet. A launch ramp on the north side of the piers offers access to Hale Passage. Boats launched here have ready access to the popular salmon fishing grounds along the end of Lummi Island and near Eliza and Vendovi Islands.

Portage Island • Gooseberry Point and Portage Island are part of the Lummi Indian Reservation. An early Indian village

Launching at Gooseberry Point on Hale Passage

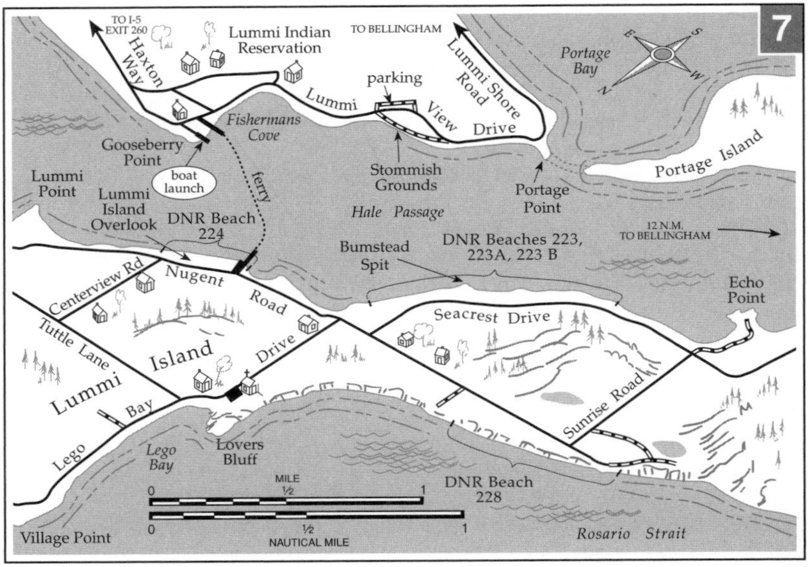

was at Gooseberry Point, and the Natives portaged canoes from Hale Passage to Bellingham Bay across the drying sandbar that joins Portage Island to the mainland. Only members of the Lummi tribe are permitted to remove clams, crabs, or oysters from the tidelands, and crossing Lummi tidelands is not permitted without tribal permission.

For very shallow-draft boats such as kayaks, Portage Island is an interesting circumnavigation in protected waters. Much of Portage Bay is dry at a minus tide, but at extreme high tide even the sandbar is covered. ☸Beware of rocks that ring the south end of the island at Point Frances.

Lummi Stommish Grounds • One weekend in June the Lummi tribe holds war canoe races and other festivities during its annual Stommish ("Old Warrior") and Water Festival. Members of nearly a dozen Northwest tribes take part in the colorful event, which is open to the public. It includes a salmon barbecue, arts and crafts sales, and traditional games. The brightly painted racing boats, ranging up to 52 feet long and holding from two to eleven people, are paddled on a round-trip course. The men's course is 5 to 6 miles long; women and youngsters paddle shorter distances.

Lummi Island Recreation Site (DNR) Map 8

Camping • Paddling • Hiking

Facilities: 1 mooring buoy, 5 campsites, CMT campsite, fire grates, toilets, hiking trail, no water

Area: 42 acres; 2125 feet of shoreline on Hale Passage

⬤ On the southeast side of Lummi Island, 1¼ miles north of Carter Point and due west of the northern tip of Eliza Island. The nearest launch ramps are at Gooseberry Point and Bellingham.

The southeast shore of Lummi Island, facing on Hale Passage, has a number of attractive little coves offering some limited anchorages for moderate-size boats and some delightful exploring for paddlers. The shorelands are densely forested and wild, ensuring a quiet overnight stay interrupted only by the hooting of owls.

Three unnamed coves, adjacent to one another, lying 1¼ miles from the southwest tip of the island are the site of a primitive DNR campground. The largest, most southerly of the little bays is just a few hundred feet across, and has a nice steep gravel beach below a line of driftwood. The second, smaller pocket on the north side of the headland faces east and is fairly open, with a gently tapering gravel and cobble beach. ❈ A baring rock lies in the very center of the cove. The third cove, smallest of the three, is oriented to the northeast and has very little beach—in most places the enclosing rock walls drop abruptly to the shoreline.

The coves, all of which are bounded by steep rocky walls, are linked by wooden steps and a steep trail that climbs to the campsites above, which are part of the CMT. A large onshore sign marking the site is visible from the water. The DNR planned to close the site due to budget cuts, but a kayak group from Bellingham volunteered to maintain it; for now, it remains open.

About ½ mile northeast of the DNR site, the open bight of Reil Harbor

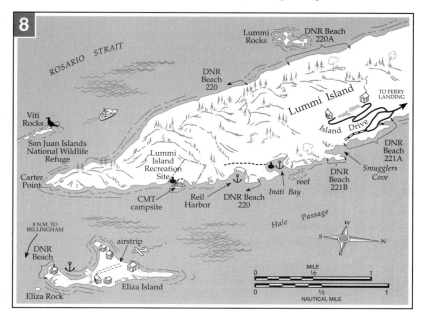

provides space in calm weather for a couple of very scenic anchorages; however, there is no protection from southerly storm winds. The narrow, gravel and rock beach, lined by driftwood, quickly gives way to steep, wild bluffs. DNR Beach 220 is a nearly 4½-mile-long strip of public tidelands below the mean high water level that begins just northeast of Reil Harbor and runs south to the recreation site. The public tidelands then continue around the end of the island and extend northwest nearly to Lummi Rocks. The shorelands are rocky, with a scattering of gravel at the heads of occasional pocket coves.

Inati Bay Map 8

Camping • Picnicking • Boating • Paddling • Hiking • Swimming

Facilities: 2 mooring buoys, toilets, picnic tables, fire grates

On the southeast side of Lummi Island, facing on Hale Passage, 2 n.m. north of Carter Point. The nearest launch ramps are at Bellingham and Larrabee State Park.

The best anchorage on this side of Lummi Island lies ¼ mile around the rock knob to the north of Reil Harbor. Here, at Inati Bay, the north-facing cove offers a pocket of protection for almost any weather, with ample space for a dozen or so boats. The two mooring buoys in the bay are for public use but are privately maintained. The Bellingham Yacht Club has leased land at the head of Inati Bay and has placed toilets, picnic tables, and fireplaces there for the use of boaters.

The bay has a rock shelf offshore about 500 yards, marked on the south by a white can buoy and on the north by a black post. From the south, enter south of the white buoy to avoid rocks and kelp in the entrance; from the north, follow the shoreline closely inboard of the marked rocks.

The last of the bays along the southeast shore, Smugglers Cove, marks the end of the wilderness and the beginning of Lummi Island civilization. A gravel operation occupies part of this bay, but boaters might still find space to anchor. Sunrise Cove, 1¾ n.m. farther north along the shore, has space for some anchorages in the open, north-facing bay. The float and launch ramp onshore are owned by a private beach club, and all beaches in the vicinity are private—stay off.

Lummi Island DNR Beaches Map 7

Paddling • Beach walking • Clamming

On the northeast side of Lummi Island, facing on Hale Passage. The nearest launch ramps are at Gooseberry Point and Bellingham.

Large portions of the tidelands along the northeast side of Lummi Island are DNR beaches. Beach 224 has a staircase access; the others must be reached by boat. Only the tidelands below mean high water are open to the public, except for Beach 220, which fronts the Lummi Island Recreation Site, described previously.

Lummi Island's Inati Bay has anchoring space in the bay and tables onshore for picnicking.

The northernmost of these tidelands runs north from the ferry landing for ½ mile. This beach, the former site of a ferry landing, lies below a high bank and is quite wide at low tide. At its north end, a wooden viewing platform overlooks the beach and the current ferry landing, and a staircase leads down to the beach. There is no parking in the immediate vicinity; park at the ferry landing and walk along South Nugent Road to the staircase. The shore immediately north of the stairs and south of the ferry landing is private—do not trespass. The sand and gravel flat offers good opportunities for clamming at low tide.

BELLINGHAM AND BELLINGHAM BAY
Map 9

Bellingham is the fourth-largest city on Puget Sound. Since earliest times, it has served as a portal for the San Juan Islands. Settlers routinely rowed the 30-plus miles from their island homesteads to Bellingham for supplies, mail, and even a Saturday-night date. With the advent of the steamboats of the Mosquito Fleet, a steady stream of goods and passengers flowed between the islands and their closest mainland point of commerce. Although many visitors now reach the San Juans via the ferry from Anacortes, Bellingham still maintains a strong tie through its marine businesses, with numerous boats chartered or berthed in Bellingham heading regularly for the San Juans.

❋ Bellingham Bay is spacious and deep and has no navigational hazards. The extreme north end of the bay dwindles into mudflats, but south of these flats anchorages can be found in 6 to 15 fathoms.

A full range of goods and services is available in city stores and nearby

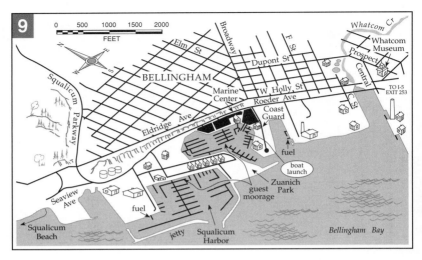

malls. Ornate turn-of-the-century buildings in the Fairhaven business district have been restored and now house restaurants, craft shops, art galleries, and other interesting places to browse. The downtown area is dominated by the Victorian-era brick building at 121 Prospect Street that served as city hall from 1892 to 1936 and now houses the Whatcom Museum of History and Art. The first ordinance enacted in this building by the city council banned cows from walking the streets between 7:30 P.M. and 6:00 A.M.—the mayor's cow was the first to be incarcerated for violating the law.

Squalicum Beach (City of Bellingham)   Map 9

Hiking • Beachcombing

Area: 3160 feet of saltwater tidelands on Bellingham Bay

🚗 From I-5, take Exit 253 and follow Lakeway Drive west to W Holly Street. Follow it northwest to C Street, turn southwest, cross the railroad tracks, and head northwest on Roeder Avenue. Continue past the marina to a road-end parking area in ¹/₂ mile.

On the north side of Bellingham Bay, a ²/₃-mile-long stretch of public beach extends west from the last industrial site. An abandoned coal pier reaching well out into the bay midway along the beach offers testimony to the shoal nature of the bay—at a minus tide it has less than 8 feet of water under its far end. Above the tide level, the shore is sand and driftwood; as the bay drains, it exposes a mucky tideflat offering endless exploration for beach treasures, and possibly a clam or two. The park extends up a wooded, blackberry-laden gully as Little Squalicum Park.

Opposite: *The Port of Bellingham's Squalicum Harbor offers some of the best facilities on Washington's inland waters.*

Squalicum Harbor (Port of Bellingham)   Map 9

Boating • Paddling • Picnicking • Sightseeing • Nature study

Facilities: Guest moorage with power, water, wireless broadband, restrooms, showers, laundry, boat pumpout station, dump for portable toilets, gas and diesel, 2 2-lane paved launch ramps with boarding floats, marine chandlery and repair, hotel, restaurants, deli, Marine Life Center, day-use park, complimentary shuttle to town, U.S. Customs, U.S. Coast Guard

🚗 From I-5 Exit 253, take Lakeway Drive west to W Holly Street. Follow it northwest to C Street, turn southwest, cross the railroad tracks, and head northwest on Roeder Avenue. Reach the marina in another ½ mile.

🚤 The marina's two moorage basins are on the north end of Bellingham Bay. The fuel dock is in the westernmost basin, where there is guest moorage along the inner float next to shore. In the east basin are the launch ramps, U.S. Customs, and more guest moorage on U and P Docks. A float just inside the basin entrance is for day-use only.

The spiffy facilities of Bellingham's Squalicum Harbor provide nearly everything a visiting boater might want. As you enter Bellingham Bay, the two moorage basins are on the northwest side of the town, west of the industrial area. The basin to the west is protected by overlapping rock jetties; entry is in the center or at the northwest end. The commercial fleet is moored here, as well as many permanently berthed pleasure craft. The upper level of the elevated walkway of Squalicum Esplanade affords a panoramic view of the harbor and its bustling activity. Behind the esplanade are Squalicum and Harbor Malls, which house the port offices, a restaurant, and a number of marine-related stores and services.

A 4-lane paved launch ramp lies on the east side of the eastern marina basin. Its protected location makes it excellent for launching in all weather. At the head of this basin is Harbor Center, where visitors can view acres of pleasure boats from planked walkways and elevated decks. A restaurant and other businesses occupy the building. Showers, restrooms, and a laundromat are available for use by visiting boaters. A large open tank at the center of the mall and three smaller aquariums display local marine life such as pipefish, octopus, anemone, and feather worms. A smaller "touch tank" offers marine life for youngsters to squeal and giggle at.

East of this harbor complex, on the jetty protecting the east boat basin, is pleasant little Zuanich Park, a great place to watch the boating activity on all sides and slip goodies to the bevy of squawking gulls that freeload in the area. A large grass knoll is surrounded by park benches overlooking the bay and the boat basin and has a memorial to fishermen lost at sea.

Boulevard Park (City of Bellingham)   Map 10

Picnicking • Beachcombing • Paddling • Swimming • Hiking • Fishing • Crabbing

Facilities: Picnic tables, shelter, fire grates, restrooms, children's play equipment, viewpoint, hiking trail, craft studio, historic and nature displays

Area: 14 acres; 4000 feet of saltwater waterfront on Bellingham Bay

From the north: From I-5 Exit 254 (Iowa Street, Ohio Street), head west for two blocks to State Street. Take State southwest for 1¼ miles to the north end of the upper park. In another 1½ miles, at the intersection of State and 11th Streets, Bayview Drive drops downhill to the lower park beach. *From the south:* From I-5 Exit 251 (Fairhaven Parkway, Chuckanut Drive), go west 1½ miles, then turn north on 12th Street in Fairhaven, which bends into 11th Street and joins State and Bayview Drive in ¾ mile. The south end of the causeway trail from the park reaches a pier at 10th Street and Taylor Avenue in Fairhaven.

The park stretches along the shore on the east side of Bellingham Bay north of the Bellingham Cruise Terminal. A small day-use dock is near the north end of the park. The nearest launch ramp is in Fairhaven.

Every city should be so fortunate as to have a park as gorgeous as this! Bellingham has made the most of a steep bluff and a swath of beach by developing it into a two-level showpiece that seems even more spacious than its 14 acres.

The upper section of the park lies along South State Street, on a bluff 75 feet above Bellingham Bay. A path leads from the overlook past a gazebo, over a bridge, and then down a winding wooden staircase to the lower park area (which can also be reached by car). At the north end of the lower section of park is a short dock, available for day-use boaters and handy for trying your luck at fishing or crabbing. Plenty of picnic tables, trees, and grass offer picnics with a view, siestas with shade, or family games with sunshine.

A path goes north from the park for 1¼ miles, paralleling the railroad tracks all the way to Wharf Street on the south side of downtown Bellingham. Heading south, a trail crosses an old railroad trestle that has been converted into a fishing pier and viewing site. From 1883 until 1925, when

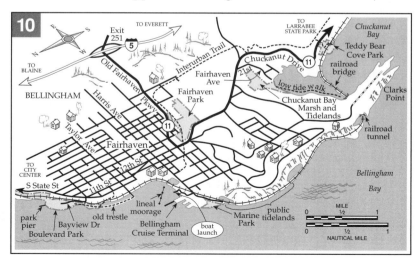

The Boulevard Park Trail follows the route of old railroad tracks.

it was destroyed by fire, this was the site of one of Bellingham's many shoreline sawmills.

South of the trestle, signs describe a short section of beachfront where an effort is being made to remove invasive species and reintroduce native plants such as black hawthorn, ocean spray, juniper, camas, and serviceberry. A paved causeway trail follows the old railroad trestle route south across a cove to reach Fairhaven in ¼ mile.

Harris Avenue Launch Ramp (Port of Bellingham) Map 10

Boating • Paddling

Facilities: 1-lane paved launch ramp with boarding float, offshore lineal moorage system and 2 mooring buoys (fee)

🚗 From I-5 Exit 251 (Fairhaven Parkway, Chuckanut Drive), head west on Old Fairhaven Parkway for 1½ miles. Turn north on 12th Street in Fairhaven. In three blocks turn west on Harris Avenue. Two blocks before the reaching the Bellingham Cruise Terminal, turn north (right) at the Alaska Ferry Terminal sign to reach the ramp in little over a block.

🚤 The ramp is at the southeast corner of Bellingham Bay just east of the Bellingham Cruise Terminal. The lineal moorage system and mooring buoys are about 100 yards offshore.

A boat launch facility is maintained by the Port of Bellingham on the southwest side of town, near the Bellingham Cruise Terminal, and within an easy walk of the Fairhaven business district. The 1-lane paved ramp is not as good as the facility at Squalicum Harbor, but it provides quick access to this side of Bellingham Bay. The lineal moorage system just offshore consists of a pair of cables suspended between buoys with a series of eyes along the length of the cables to serve as tie-up points for boats. Two public mooring buoys are northeast of the lineal moorage. Usage fees for these moorage facilities can be paid at a collection box at the launch ramp. Rentals of canoes, kayaks, dories, sailboards, and small sailboats are available at a nearby business.

Bellingham Cruise Terminal   Map 10

Historical displays • Ferry viewing

Facilities: Ferry terminal, restaurant, viewing areas, gift shop, restrooms

🚐 From I-5 Exit 251 (Fairhaven Parkway, Chuckanut Drive), head west on Old Fairhaven Parkway for 1½ miles. Turn north on 12th Street in Fairhaven. In 3 blocks turn west on Harris Avenue and reach the terminal in 3/4 mile.

In 1989, the Alaska Ferry System pulled up stakes from Seattle's waterfront and moved its southern terminus to Bellingham, lured by the promise of a new terminal. The city made good on its promise with a stunning, $6.4 million facility covering 5.5 acres on the Fairhaven waterfront. Alaska-bound ferries arrive and depart from here every Friday throughout the year; during the last two weeks of May and the first two weeks of June there are additional sailings on Tuesdays. The terminal is also the home base for tour boats to Victoria, B.C., and the San Juan Islands.

The activity on the ships can be watched from the adjacent pier or from the enclosed glass dome of the terminal. Even if a ferry is not in port, the terminal provides fine views of Bellingham Bay. Displays around the edge of the pier give interesting vignettes of early exploration and development of Bellingham and Fairhaven.

Marine Park (Port of Bellingham)   Map 10

Picnicking • Beach walking

Facilities: Picnic tables, shelter, fireplaces, restrooms
Area: 3 acres; 730 feet of shoreline and 2650 feet of adjoining tidelands on Bellingham Bay

🚐 See directions to the Bellingham Cruise Terminal, described previously. Immediately west of the terminal, turn southwest at a signed intersection to reach the park.

Marine Park is another example of Bellingham's dedication to fine parks. The beautifully landscaped site has tables for picnicking and grassy lawns for afternoon meditation (naps). Strategically placed benches look out to Bellingham Bay and passing marine traffic.

The tidelands south from the park to Post Point, a distance of about 2/3 mile, are public. The beach can be walked at low tide, but all uplands are owned by the railroad and trespassing is prohibited (and dangerous).

CHUCKANUT BAY
Maps 10 and 11

A chuckanut is not some kind of local tree, as one might suspect, but an Indian word believed to mean "small cliffy bay next to big bay"—certainly an appropriate description for this site. Paddlers who gain access to Chuckanut Bay by hand-carrying boats to the beach at Chuckanut Bay Marsh and Tidelands, or the launch ramp at Larrabee State Park just around the corner to the south, can explore rocky shorelines and tiny islands that dot the long bay.

Larger boats, too, will find the bay is made to order for gunkholing, with several little side bays offering ample space for anchoring. Local promoters once touted the bay as ample to anchor the entire Pacific fleet—quite a bit of an exaggeration. Aptly named Pleasant Bay, at the extreme south end of Chuckanut Bay, is well protected from southerly winds. ❋A rock ledge, 3 feet below the water surface, just south of Chuckanut Island, has been reported.

At the center of the bay, 5-acre Chuckanut Island is a wildlife preserve of The Nature Conservancy. Day-use is permitted, but no fire building or camping. The island's thick vegetation includes grand fir, madrona, western red cedar, and some Douglas-fir that are more than 250 years old. Two bald eagles nest on the island, and numerous other species of birds frequent its shores and uplands. The intertidal regions serve as a study area for marine biologists. The island was donated to The Nature Conservancy by the family of the late Cyrus Gates and the preserve is named in his honor.

Chuckanut Bay Marsh and Tidelands (City of Bellingham)   Map 10
Beach walking • Paddling • Birdwatching

Area: 69 acres; 1550 feet of saltwater shoreline, and 1800 feet of adjoining tidelands on Chuckanut Bay

🚗 From I-5 Exit 251 (Fairhaven Parkway, Chuckanut Drive), head west on Old Fairhaven Parkway for 1½ miles. Turn south on 12th Street, which shortly becomes N Chuckanut Drive. In 1 mile, at the intersection of N Chuckanut Drive and Old Samish Highway, turn south on 21st Street, which soon bends west as Fairhaven Avenue and arrives at road-end parking in ½ mile.

Although this city park is undeveloped as of 2006, it represents an important potential link in the system of trails interlacing Bellingham. When the tide is in, cartop boats can be launched here, and paddlers can duck beneath the railroad trestle that crosses the bay to gain open water. At low tide, the long mucky tideflat makes launching here impossible.

After following a narrow, brambly path west from the park, at minus tides inveterate hikers can skirt the edge of steep sandstone cliffs for nearly ½ mile to the west. The wave-carved sandstone formations at the base of the cliffs, similar to those found on Sucia and other San Juan islands, seem out of place adjacent to this shallow muddy section of bay. Before the railroad causeway was built, however, this section of Chuckanut Bay was a deep, clear

Large flocks of shorebirds frequent the tidelands at Chuckanut Bay Marsh.

basin where winter storm-driven waves lashed against the base of the cliffs. The construction of the trestle and then the causeway, combined with silt generated by logging and the construction of I-5, altered the bay, changing it to a low-tide mudflat. The beach and adjoining marshlands host hundreds of migrating birds, including flocks of dunlins that bank and sweep through the air with amazing precision.

Teddy Bear Cove (Whatcom County)   Map 11

Hiking • Beachcombing

Facilities: 1-mile trail, toilets (at the trailhead)
Area: 9.5 acres; 1400 feet of saltwater shoreline on Chuckanut Bay

See directions to Chuckanut Bay Marsh and Tidelands, described previously. At the junction of Chuckanut Drive and Old Samish Highway, continue southwest on Chuckanut Drive for 500 feet to a parking area on the southeast side of the road. This is the north end of the Chuckanut Trail System.

The park is on the east side of Chuckanut Bay, about ¼ mile south of the east end of the railroad trestle. The nearest launch ramp is at Larrabee State Park. Hand-carried boats can be put in at Chuckanut Bay Marsh.

Terrific views of Bellingham and Chuckanut Bays and a beautiful white beach composed of shell fragments make this a great spot to spend an afternoon. We could not discover why the cove is named "Teddy Bear." Before it became a county park this was a favorite clothing-optional beach, so perhaps it was originally named "Teddy Bare."

From the shared trailhead for all of the many Chuckanut Mountain trails, take the path to the south across a marsh-covering boardwalk, and switch-back uphill to intersect a paved road and the Interurban Trail. For the next

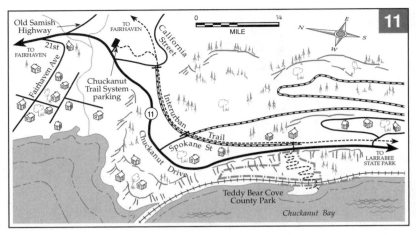

¼ mile the trail leads past residences; opposite the house at 1464 Spokane Street is a sign pointing west to Teddy Bear Cove.

Descend to the west. Cross Chuckanut Drive and drop down a short staircase to a trail that switchbacks down the steep wooded bank to the railroad tracks. (Caution: There are no crossing gates on this live rail line.) West of the tracks, log stairsteps lead down to the beach and up to the top of a small rock bluff at its north end.

The cove is small, maybe 100 feet across, with wave-pocked sandstone rocks at its north end. In the 1920s, a brick factory operated at the north end of the beach, just north of the rock bluff. If you find any relics from the factory, please leave them.

Larrabee State Park   Map 12

Camping • Boating • Paddling • Fishing • Swimming • Crabbing • Tide pools • Waterskiing • Scuba diving • Hiking • Bicycling

Facilities: 51 standard campsites, 26 RV sites (EWS), 8 walk-in sites, 3 primitive sites, group camp, group day-use areas, picnic tables, fireplaces, kitchens, picnic shelters, amphitheater, restrooms, showers, RV pumpout station, 2-lane paved launch ramp, 7²/₃ miles of hiking/biking/equestrian trails, 6 miles of hiking trails

Area: 2790 acres; 8100 feet of shoreline on Samish Bay, 6700 feet of freshwater shoreline on Fragrance and Lost Lakes and other small unnamed lakes

🚗 *From the north:* Take I-5 Exit 251 (Fairhaven Parkway, Chuckanut Drive) and head west on Old Fairhaven Parkway for 1½ miles. Turn south on SR 11 (Chuckanut Drive). Continue south on SR 11 for 7 miles to the park entrance. *From the south:* Take I-5 Exit 231 (SR 11, Chuckanut Drive) and drive north on SR 11 for 15 miles to reach the park. The launch ramp is off Cove Road, ½ mile north of the park entrance.

🚤 The park launch ramp is on Wildcat Cove on Samish Bay, 1¼ n.m. south of Governors Point.

Although most of Larrabee State Park lies inland, embracing the steep, forested slopes of Chuckanut Mountain overlooking Chuckanut Bay, a corner of it touches the shoreline of Samish Bay. This corner contains most of the park's facilities. The camping and picnic area lie in a narrow section between Chuckanut Drive and the railroad tracks. Trails to the beach cross the railroad tracks at Clayton Beach, or reach the shore via a tunnel under the tracks from the main part of the park.

The launch ramp is in an adjacent section of the park, reached by a separate road. At the intersection with Cove Road, ⅓ mile north of the park entrance, a sign points west to the boat launch. The 1-lane ramp is very steep, but well surfaced. Parking nearby is adequate for a dozen vehicles with trailers. Wildcat Cove, into which the ramp empties, is small and rock rimmed—unsuited for large boats. At moderate to low tides, enough gravel beach is revealed to permit beach towels to be spread for sunbathing, or the water to be tested for wading.

Another corner of the park touches the shore a mile to the south at Clayton Beach. The beach can be reached by boat or by a primitive trail that begins at a staircase across Chuckanut Drive from the Clayton Beach parking area, south of the main park entrance. In ½ mile, the trail leads to some steep rock slabs that drop to the railroad tracks (unguarded crossing, caution!). A short path on the west side of the tracks leads to a sandy pocket beach framed by rocky headlands.

Larrabee State Park offers several miles of inland hiking trails on the

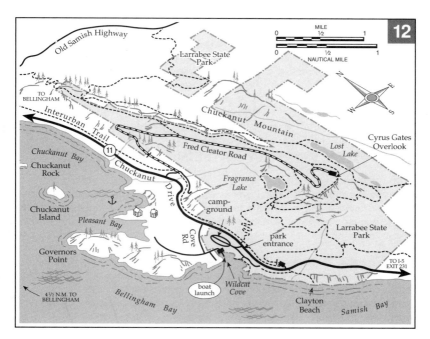

Beautiful madronas overhang the rocky shores of Larrabee State Park.

slopes of Chuckanut Mountain. The trail up the mountainside is steep, gaining over 1500 feet, but the reward of crystal mountain lakes and lookout points with panoramic vistas makes the effort worthwhile. For low-level leg stretching, the Interurban Trail, suitable for both hikers and bicyclists, begins in the park and runs north for 5½ miles to Bellingham with no appreciable elevation gain. The Clayton Beach parking lot is the trailhead for both the route up Chuckanut Mountain and the Interurban Trail.

Steeply tilted layers of sandstone interbedded with lenses of shale are exposed along the park shore. Fossils of large palm leaves believed to be 60 million years old have been found in the shale deposits. The state park holds a distinctive spot in history—it was established on 20 acres of land donated by the Larrabee family and was Washington's first state park.

ELIZA, VENDOVI, AND SINCLAIR ISLANDS
Maps 6 and 13

Three moderate-size islands lying at the front door to Bellingham Bay are privately owned and have little to attract tourists, although their bays and shorelines offer some interesting boat exploration. The nearest launch ramps are at Bellingham and Larrabee State Park.

Eliza Island • This island, which lies closest to Bellingham, is the most settled of the three. Small planes that land at an airstrip bring landowners to their vacation retreats. ❀Shoals and numerous rocks lie off the east and west sides of the triangular-shaped island—visiting boaters should approach with care. A large open bight at the south end, facing the southern tip of

Lummi Island, offers some anchorages, although the holding ground is poor and the bay is exposed to southerly blows.

The only public area on Eliza Island is a DNR beach at the extreme southern tip; however, the shores are so rocky, and the beach so small, that few boaters would care to approach, even in small craft. Eliza Rock, which lies just offshore to the south, and Viti Rocks, ¾ mile southwest of the southern tip of Lummi Island, are both part of the San Juan Islands National Wildlife Refuge. Avoid approaching so close to either area that nesting birds are disturbed.

Vendovi Island • The most primitive of the three islands is Vendovi, lying 2 n.m. southwest of Eliza. Its shorelines are smooth and rocky, except for a small bay on its northwest point. All of the island's shorelines, with the exception of those facing immediately on the bay, comprise DNR Beach 214; the public area lies below the mean high-water level. The beaches are rocky, with some pretty little pocket coves. All the uplands are conspicuously posted with No Trespassing signs—inland, snarling mastiffs presumably lie in wait.

Sinclair Island • Sinclair Island, which at about 1½ square miles is the largest of the three, is the only one to have real roads. It lies at the north end of Bellingham Channel, 1½ miles west of Vendovi Island.

Although most of the island property is private, some limited access to the uplands is possible. A short county dock protected by a pile breakwater is on the southwest end of the island at the community of Urban. Overnight moorage is not permitted on the dock, but anchoring in the open coves to the north and south of the dock is possible. There are no commercial facilities onshore.

❋ Rocks and a large shoal extend out from Sinclair Island on the north and west, reaching almost to Boulder Reef, ¾ n.m. away. This dangerous reef, which bares at half tide, is marked by a lighted bell buoy. Kelp that surrounds the reef, giving further warning of danger, is often towed under by the current.

DNR Beach 213 extends east from the Sinclair Island dock for about a

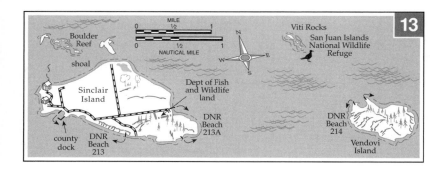

mile. It includes some tiny pocket coves and rocky beaches below a 60-foot bluff—when the uplands dip down and shorelines gentle, the public beach ends. Public beach is only that area below the mean high-water level.

DNR Beach 213A encompasses 2831 feet of shoreline at the southeastern tip of the island. The northern portion of this beach joins to Washington State Department of Fish and Wildlife (DFW) lands, where visitors can extend their beach explorations with an upland nature walk through a small marshland. The DFW lands can also be reached by walking east from the county dock for about 1 1/2 miles. The public land lies south of the road near the east shore.

CYPRESS ISLAND
Map 14

The natural riches of Cypress Island include six small spring-fed lakes, several marshes, three excellent harbors, magnificent fortresslike cliffs, and forested mountains reaching to 1500 feet. More than eighty species of birds and a dozen species of mammals are known to live here, including bald eagles, hawks, deer, foxes, river otters, raccoons, porcupines, muskrats, and weasels. An important peregrine falcon nesting site is in the vicinity of Eagle Cliff. The unusual geological strata of the island support a great variety of flora; however, one notable tree is missing—there are no cypress trees on Cypress Island. Captain George Vancouver named the island erroneously when he identified the local junipers as cypress.

Land ownership on Cypress Island has had a checkered history. The island escaped early settlement due to its steep terrain and scarcity of water. Attempts at mining failed, as did a goat farm, and the land proved too harsh for agriculture. Over the years, private individuals acquired small parcels and

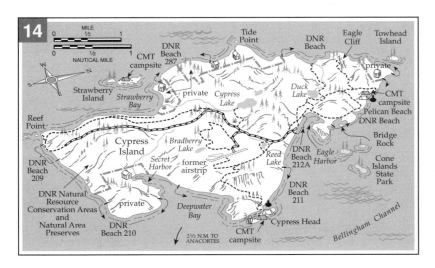

built a few residences, primarily on Strawberry Bay. Some efforts were made to use the island for a nuclear plant, oil port, or fancy resort. These plans were fiercely opposed by local people and environmentalists who realized the effect such development would have on the fragile environment. Fortunately, all plans for development were scrapped. The state has acquired nearly 85 percent of the 5500-acre island and plans to have only limited recreational development.

Ferry travelers have an excellent view of the island as the boat leaves the Anacortes terminal; the island's southern tip lies just 2½ n.m. north, across Bellingham Channel. The northwest shore is a popular salmon fishing ground, and cruising boaters sometimes drop anchor in Strawberry Bay and in small coves along the eastern shore. The pens of a salmon farm in Deepwater Bay make anchoring there difficult.

The northern cove at Cypress Head has good, protected anchorages in 20 to 30 feet of water.

Strawberry (Loon) Island Recreation Site (DNR) Map 14

Boating • Paddling • Scuba diving

Facilities: 3 campsites, CMT campsite, picnic tables, fire grates, toilets, no water
Area: 11 acres; 4000 feet of shoreline on Rosario Strait and Strawberry Bay
🚢 Strawberry Island is off the southwest side of Cypress Island between Rosario Strait and Strawberry Bay. The nearest launch ramps are at Sunset Beach on Fidalgo Island, 4 n.m. southeast.

Strawberry Island, a ¼-mile-long narrow ridge of an island, offers a few picnic and camping sites along with pleasant shoreline scrambles and views of boats parading past in Rosario Strait. Like other small park islands such as Saddlebag and James Islands, it has a familiar "dog bone" configuration, with two high, rounded shoulders of land joined by a low, narrow neck. In this case the northern shoulder is considerably larger and higher than the southern one—more like an exclamation point.

The shores of the main section of the island are so steep that going ashore there is quite difficult. A sandy cove on the west side of the island between the small southern knob and the remainder of the island provides the only landing for small boats. Offshore waters, which are quite deep, have defied

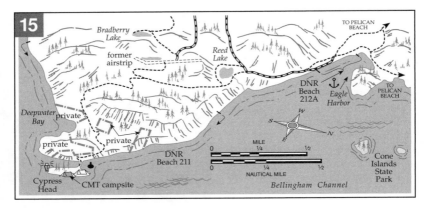

attempts to place buoys. Boaters in large craft should anchor in Strawberry Bay and dinghy across to the recreation site.

Strawberry Bay was visited in 1792 by William Broughton of the Vancouver Expedition. Lieutenant Broughton, who first explored the inner channels of the San Juan Islands, anchored his brig Chatham here, and was delighted to find great numbers of wild strawberries onshore. Some days later, when Vancouver stopped over in the same spot at Broughton's recommendation, the strawberries were out of season, and his crew had to settle for wild onions.

Cypress Head Recreation Area (DNR)   Map 15

Boating • Paddling • Fishing • Hiking

Facilities: 10 campsites, CMT campsite, fire rings, 5 mooring buoys, toilets, no water
Area: 16.5 acres; 4800 feet of shoreline on Bellingham Channel

Cypress Head is on the east side of Cypress Island between Eagle Harbor and Deepwater Bay. Mooring buoys are set on the north side of the head. The nearest launch ramps are at Sunset Beach, 4 n.m. south, and Larrabee State Park, 9 n.m. northeast.

The tiny peninsula of Cypress Head lies on the easternmost bulge of Cypress Island. The wooded headland, which is joined to its parent island by a low grassy sandspit, has been developed by the DNR as a boat-in recreation area, with overnight campsites.

This pretty little spot, not far from Fidalgo Island's Sunset Beach, makes an ideal cruising destination. ✿The long south-facing bay formed by the head is quite shallow and has a rock near the entrance; use care entering. The northern cove, which holds the mooring buoys, is somewhat deeper. Boats too large to be beached must tie to a buoy or drop a hook. Good anchorages can be found in 20 to 30 feet of water.

A rough trail circles the outer edge of Cypress Head on a 10-foot-high bank, passing vistas gorgeously framed by twisted madrona and juniper. Low tide reveals some nice beach scrambles along the Cypress Island shore, but at high tide the beach is almost nonexistent—don't get caught at the wrong spot on an incoming tide!

The Cypress Head Trail leaves the sandspit, climbs 1½ miles to a junction with a spur to an abandoned airstrip, and then continues for ⅔ mile to Reed Lake. A short distance north of the lake, the trail joins the Cypress Mainline Road as it descends to Eagle Harbor.

Weathered, gnarled trees make the shores of Cypress Island exceptionally beautiful.

Eagle Harbor Map 15

Hiking • Paddling • Boating

Facilities: Toilets, information kiosk

Eagle Harbor is on the northeast shore of Cypress Island, 1 mile south of Pelican Beach. The nearest launch ramp is at Anacortes 5½ n.m. away.

Eagle Harbor offers anchorages nicely protected from northerlies. ❄However, deep-draft boats must use care as it is shallow, holding a skimpy 8 feet of water or less at a minus tide, and a shoal lies in the middle. Submerged piles along the southeast side and an old paved launch ramp were used when the island was logged in the 1970s.

Existing jeep roads link with trails, forming a system of some 15 miles of hiking trails running the length of the island, touching many of the lakes, and reaching the shore at Pelican Beach, Eagle Harbor, Smugglers Cove, Cypress Head, and Strawberry Bay. Many make interesting loops.

Pelican Beach and Eagle Cliff (DNR) Map 16

Boating • Paddling • Picnicking • Fishing • Swimming • Scuba diving • Hiking • Beachcombing • Wildlife watching

Facilities: 3 campsites, CMT campsite, fire rings, 3 picnic sites, composting toilet, 6 mooring buoys, hiking trails, no water
Area: 5 acres; 7207 feet of shoreline on Bellingham Channel
Pelican Beach is on the northeast side of Cypress Island, midway between the Cone Islands and Towhead Island. The nearest launch ramps are at Anacortes and Larrabee State Park.

One of the nicest spots on Cypress Island is a forested strip spanning the northern end of the island. On the eastern shore is Pelican Beach, a beautiful little boat-in campground; on the west is the spectacular rocky face of 750-

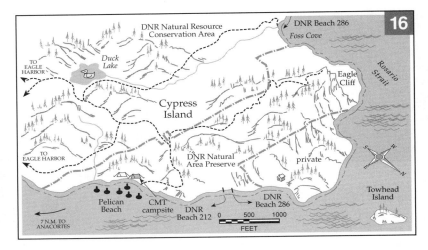

foot-high Eagle Cliff; and between the two is a swath of deep woods holding a few miles of hiking trails for exploration and enchantment.

The gently sloping gravelly shore at Pelican Beach invites wading (chilly) or sunbathing among the driftwood (warm). At its northern boundary, the beach becomes quite rocky. The shore, with its countless little tide pools, can be followed for some distance around the point. However, be aware you can become trapped between an incoming tide and the steep, high bank.

Leaving the campground, the Eagle Cliff Trail heads inland and rises gradually, but steadily, through open second-growth timber. In ¼ mile, a fork is reached. The left leg, signed to Duck Lake, ties into the inland road network for more extensive hiking. The leg to the right heads to Eagle Cliff, 1¼ miles away. The upper portion of the trail to Eagle Cliff follows a sparsely wooded ridge to the final rocky outcropping of the summit. Look down to Smuggler Cove on the west side of Cypress Island and out to toylike boats bobbing in Rosario Strait. The viewpoint is not a place for toddlers or persons afflicted with vertigo. The trail is closed between February 1 and July 15 to protect a peregrine falcon nesting area.

Cone Islands State Park (Undeveloped)   Map 6

Scuba diving • Paddling • Birdwatching

Area: 9.9 acres; 2500 feet of shoreline on Bellingham Channel

The islands lie off the northeast shore of Cypress Island. The nearest boat launch is at Washington Park on Fidalgo Island, 5½ n.m. south.

Cone Islands, a cluster of three tiny forested islands and low-tide rocks are undeveloped state park lands. The northernmost of the islands has especially interesting geology, displaying tilted beds of shale along its east side.

❉Because they are surrounded by kelp beds, and their steep, rocky shores

The sheer face of Eagle Cliff rises above the northwest end of Cypress Island.

drop sharply into the water, most boaters are content to enjoy the islands from the distance as they cruise by, although scuba divers sometimes stop and explore from anchored boats. The island walls are so abrupt that going ashore is nearly impossible.

GUEMES ISLAND
Map 17

Although separated only by 1-mile-wide Bellingham Channel, neighboring Cypress and Guemes Islands are totally different in character. While Cypress Island is steep, rocky, and densely wooded, with deeply notched bays and cliffy shores, Guemes is a rural setting, with wide expanses of flatland and a long, smooth shoreline.

Guemes Island would be just another Anacortes suburb were it not for ½-mile-wide Guemes Channel, which serves to keep urban sprawl and industrial boom at arm's length. The island remains quietly pastoral, providing sanctuary for retirees, artists, farmers, summer vacationers, and Anacortes workers who commute daily from their homes.

The little Skagit County–operated ferry scurries back and forth across the channel like a busy water bug, carrying a few cars on its open deck each trip. The voyage takes about ten minutes; runs are made half-hourly during morning and evening commute hours, and hourly the rest of the day. The ferry leaves from a terminal in downtown Anacortes at 6th and I Streets.

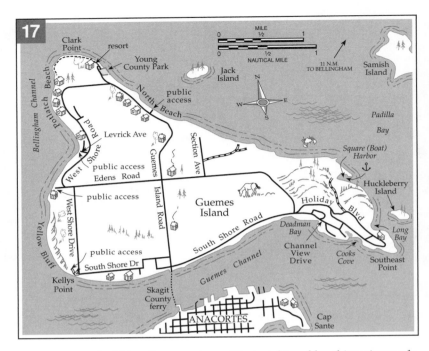

Guemes is ideal bicycling country, with straight and level interior roads that pass by farms and orchards, while perimeter roads wind around the shores, with views out to cool sea and mist-shrouded islands. The only commercial development is a small rustic resort on the northern tip of the island. There are no boat-launch ramps on the island, although hand-carried boats can be put in at several spots.

Guemes Island has a refreshing approach to public use of lands: Here a few beaches are posted as open space. Owners of such lands permit public recreational use so long as such use is compatible with its natural state—observe posted fire regulations, do not litter, and do not deface or destroy either personal property or natural features. The areas at Kellys Point and Clark Point are presently open space. If their status changes, do not trespass—look elsewhere for recreational land.

Guemes Island Public Accesses   Map 17

Beach walking • Shellfish • Birdwatching

North Beach • On the east side of Guemes Island, facing on a huge tideflat, is a settlement of beachfront homes and summer cottages. A 40-foot-wide DFW public beach access is provided here for clam diggers or paddlecraft launching. Traveling north on Guemes Island Road, 1 1/2 miles north of Edens

Square Harbor makes an idyllic boating stop.

Road, watch carefully among the cottages for a gravel lane on the east side of the road, just across from the house at 5336 Guemes Island Road. Nearby parking is limited, and property on both sides of the access is private.

Long Bay and Square Harbor (Boat Harbor) • Nearly all the shoreline of Guemes Island is smooth, with long tideflats. The one exception is at the southeast end where slightly mountainous terrain signals steeper underwater walls. Two small bights are along this shore. The more southerly of these, Long Bay, near Southeast Point, offers boaters some anchoring possibilities, although it is quite open.

An even better anchorage is at sublime little Square Harbor, a mile to the north. The 500-yard-wide rocky inlet has space for two or three boats with good protection from all weather except easterlies. It is a handy, secluded spot when nearby Saddlebag Island is filled to overflowing. The bay is easily located by the 100-foot-high sheer, barren cliff immediately to the north. The beach and all uplands are private.

Kellys Point • On the southwest corner of Guemes Island, at the intersection of South Shore Drive and West Shore Drive, a short road spur to the west ends at a path leading to a beautiful gravel and driftwood beach facing Guemes and Bellingham Channels. The beach can be walked north for more than a mile beneath the imposing 150-foot scarp of Yellow Bluff. Climbing on the bluff or digging caves can be hazardous because the bank is composed of soft glacial till and could collapse. Note the numerous holes that birds (possibly kingfishers) have burrowed in the hillside.

Cliff-nesting birds burrow in the soft bluffs at Kellys Point.

This is said to be a good beach for finding agates—jasper, carnelian, and aventurine can be collected here as well as numerous other stones, some unique to the area. Many residents have extensive collections of agates gleaned from Guemes Island beaches.

The point is named after the notorious outlaw, Lawrence "Smuggler" Kelly, who had a hideout here in the late 1800s. Kelly brought illegal Chinese aliens into the country from Canada, as well as cargoes of opium and wool, which were heavily taxed at the time.

Edens Road • From Kellys Point, on the west side of Guemes Island, West Shore Drive heads due north, and in 1½ miles ends at a T intersection with Edens Road. Turn west and in 200 yards, where the main road turns north and becomes West Shore Road, continue straight ahead for another short distance to the dead end at the beach. The beach access, which has parking for a few cars, is framed by private property.

Lervick Avenue • On the west side of Guemes Island, a short side street heads left ¾ mile north of the Edens Road/West Shore Road intersection. In a short distance a large log blocks the road end at the beach, but the street turns north, continuing to some private homes. The road end by the log offers a narrow beach access between private property on either side. There is parking for a few cars.

Young County Park (Skagit County) and Clark Point   Map 17

Picnicking • Paddling • Clamming • Swimming

Facilities: *Park:* Picnic tables, fire grates, toilet. *Resort:* Cabins, boat launch (fee for nonguests)
Area: 11 acres; 500 feet of shoreline on Padilla Bay

From the ferry landing, drive north on Guemes Island Road for 3¾ miles to its junction with West Shore Road. Continue north on Guemes Island Road for a half-mile to the resort and park.

The park is on the northeast side of Guemes Island, about 1 mile south of Clark Point, the northern tip of the island. The nearest boat launches are in Anacortes.

A small county park at the north end is Guemes Island's only public recreation site. Its tree-shaded grass strip faces on a nice driftwood-edged beach and a gradual, gravel tideflat. Tiny Jack Island, ¾ mile due east, is an enticing small-boat destination. ❀ Even shallow-draft boats should approach the park with care at minus tide to avoid getting mired on the flat. The small resort adjacent to the county park has two rental homes and cabins.

Nearly 2 miles of beautiful clean gravel beach wrap around Clark Point to the north, providing terrific views first into Bellingham Bay, and then north to Sinclair, Vendovi, and Lummi Islands, and finally swinging westward to lovely little Cone Islands and the rumpled mountains of Cypress Island.

To reach the beach, walk north from the resort. As it nears the point, the beach narrows, but it should be passable at all but the highest tides or during heavy wave action. The bank above the beach is steep and heavily wooded, and there is no inland egress, so use care not to get trapped by high water. Open space ends at private property on Potlatch Beach on the west side of the point.

SAMISH BAY AND SAMISH ISLAND
Map 18

Samish Bay, a 2-mile-wide lobe on the southern edge of Bellingham Bay, bares for nearly half its extent during low tides. Most boaters avoid its shallow waters; however, it does offer some fine paddling opportunities.

During migratory season, Samish Bay is as good as Padilla Bay, to the south, for sighting a variety of waterfowl. Great blue herons from the rookery on Samish Island frequent the flats, and visitors are virtually assured of

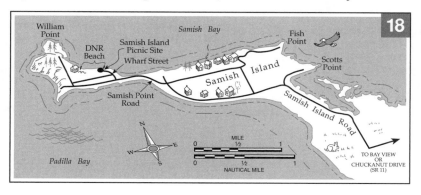

seeing these large, elegant birds. Flocks of black brants, canvasbacks, and Eurasian widgeons winter here.

Samish Island Picnic Site (DNR)   Map 18

Beachcombing • Paddling • Scuba diving • Picnicking • Birdwatching

Facilities: Picnic tables, toilets, no water
Area: 0.5 acre; 1436 feet of shoreline on Samish Bay

🚗 From I-5 Exit 231 (SR 11, Chuckanut Drive), head north on SR 11 for 7½ miles. Turn west on W Bow Hill Road. In ¾ mile, drive through the tiny community of Edison and head south on Farm-to-Market Road. In ¼ mile turn west on Bay View–Edison Road. At an intersection in ¾ mile, continue west on Samish Island Road. Follow this road for 4½ miles onto the island to Wharf Street. Turn north on Wharf and in two blocks reach the picnic site.

🛥 The site is on Samish Bay about ¼ n.m. southeast of the north tip of Samish Island. Only 1500 feet of shoreline are public. The nearest launch facility is Larrabee State Park.

A large great blue heron rookery is on Samish Island.

When the last land-shaping glaciers withdrew from Puget Sound, Samish Island was two islands. Today, it is a peninsula, joined to the mainland by necks of sand. The huge flat delta lands adjoining Samish Island were built up by the Skagit River, which now enters the sound several miles to the south. On the drive through Samish Flats, watch for peregrine falcons, snowy owls, eagles, and gyrfalcons, attracted by rodents and bunnies in the nearby farmland.

The small park is perched at the top of an 80-foot-high bank. A short trail reaches a set of stairs that descends steeply to the shore. The public beach extends west from the stairs for about 1500 feet and east from them about 300 feet. Low tide reveals a cobble shore and the massive tideflats of Samish Bay, but at high water there is no beach. Views are north to Hale Passage and Eliza and Lummi Islands, and across to the rocky cliffs of Chuckanut Drive. The summit of Mount Baker peeks over the horizon.

chapter three

Padilla Bay and Fidalgo Island

🚗 From I-5 Exit 230 a mile north of Mount Vernon, follow SR 20 west. In 8¼ miles, the 75-foot-high arches of a pair of concrete bridges cross the Swinomish Channel onto Fidalgo Island. In 4 miles more, at Sharpes Corner at the end of Fidalgo Bay, the highway splits at a T intersection. The branch to the south continues to Whidbey Island as SR 20, reaching Deception Pass State Park in 6½ miles. The leg to the west and north, SR 20 Spur continues for 2½ miles more to Anacortes.

🛥 Fidalgo Island's two unique waterways, the Swinomish Channel and Deception Pass, serve as boating portals to the San Juan Islands and Canada's Gulf Islands for hordes of pleasure vessels traveling up Saratoga Passage from Puget Sound. The southern entrance to Swinomish Channel is about 50 n.m. from Shilshole Bay in Seattle, and Deception Pass is 6 n.m. farther.

Fɪᴅᴀʟɢᴏ sᴇᴇᴍs ʜᴀʀᴅʟʏ ᴀɴ ɪsʟᴀɴᴅ ᴀᴛ ᴀʟʟ, lying so close that bridges bind it to the mainland and provide easy access to mainland conveniences. Yet it has an island's advantages of mile upon mile of shoreline, with beaches and bays to suit every purpose, and that sense of unique character that only

The 100-yard-wide waterway of Swinomish Channel separates Fidalgo Island from the mainland.

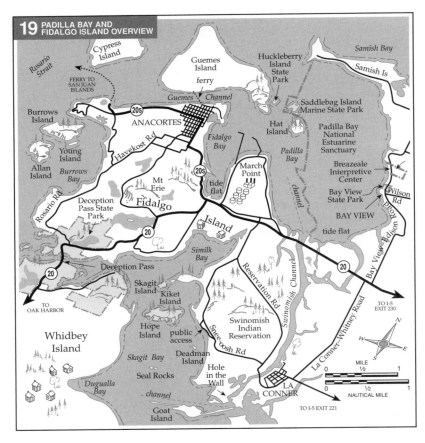

19 PADILLA BAY AND
FIDALGO ISLAND OVERVIEW

true physical separation, and not political boundaries, can create.

The island is divided into three distinct sections, or "lobes." The southeastern lobe, bordered on the east by the Swinomish Channel and on the west by Skagit and Similk Bays, is almost entirely comprised of the Swinomish Indian Reservation.

The long amoebaelike foot of March Point, extending north into the tideflats of Fidalgo and Padilla Bays, occupies most of the middle section of the island. Huge storage tanks and oil refineries with billowing smoke stacks and flaming gas vents seem strange bedfellows to the small farms dotting the surrounding lands.

The western lobe of the island, its largest section, displays the true "San Juan" character, with rugged shorelines, glacier-scrubbed granite domes, and pocket lakes nestled in the folds of forested hills. Here, in its several public parks, visitors can explore beaches and bluffs to their hearts' content and gaze out to the enticing shores of myriad islands, near and distant.

PADILLA BAY
Map 19

Huckleberry Island State Park (Undeveloped)
Kayaking • Scuba diving

Facilities: None
Area: 10 acres; 2900 feet of shoreline on Padilla Bay
The island is in Padilla Bay off the southeast shore of Guemes Island near Long Bay. The nearest launch ramps are in Anacortes.

Centered in the channel between the southeast corner of Guemes Island and Saddlebag Island is small, steep-walled Huckleberry Island, an undeveloped piece of state park property. The only accessible shoreline lies in a break in its precipitous shores on the south side of the island. Here a wide gravel beach extends below a high bluff. ❋ Water off this beach is less than 2 fathoms deep, and dotted with submerging rocks, so it is not a particularly appealing spot for large boats. But it does make a nice spot for a lunch break for passing kayakers.

Saddlebag Island Marine State Park   Map 20
Fishing • Crabbing • Scuba diving • Hiking • Boating • Kayaking

Facilities: 3 campsites, 2 CMT campsites, picnic tables, fireplaces, toilets, no water
Area: 23 acres; 6750 feet of shoreline on Padilla Bay
The island is in Padilla Bay east of the southeast tip of Guemes Island, and north of Hat Island. The nearest launch ramps are in Anacortes.

Conveniently located only 2 n.m. northeast of Anacortes, near the mouth of Padilla Bay, Saddlebag Island Marine State Park is heavily used by boaters who drop by for the day to try their hand at crabbing and fishing, and by

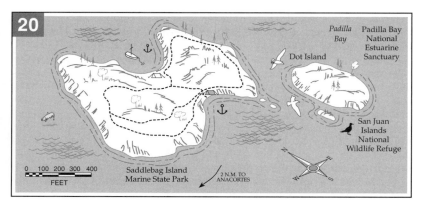

Boaters enjoy a quiet anchorage in the north cove of Saddlebag Island State Park.

those on their way to somewhere else who use its coves as handy anchorages. For visitors who take the time to go ashore, the trails that circle the island's grassy bluffs give boaters a chance to steady their sea legs and enjoy views of bay activity: sailboats with bright spinnakers looking like flowers blowing in the wind, fishing boats drifting offshore, and behemoth tankers heading for the oil refinery at March Point. Dot Island, just a clam toss away from Saddlebag, is a bird nesting area and animal refuge of the San Juan Islands National Wildlife Refuge.

Saddlebag Island is cast in the familiar San Juan pattern of two rocky, scrub-covered headlands joined by a low, narrow neck, creating the outline that inspired this island's name. The two coves formed on either side of the landmass face north and south, with the northern one slightly larger and more deeply indented.

❀ The water east of the island is extremely shallow—approach from the west, especially during a minus tide. There are no mooring buoys at the park, but numerous good anchorages are available; the best are in the northern cove. The southern cove is shallower, with a thick growth of eelgrass, making it difficult for anchors to dig in.

A small camp area is at the head of the northern bay; toilets are along the trail that crosses the middle of the island. The southern bay has space for picnicking on the beach. Two CMT campsites are on the south side, above the narrow driftwood-choked beach.

Saddlebag, Dot, and Hat Islands are perched on the edge of a huge submarine shelf; to the east there is less than a fathom of water, while immediately

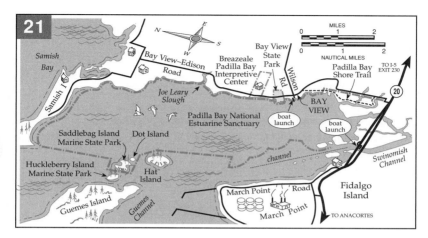

west the shelf plummets to a depth of 30 to 40 fathoms. The rich variety of marine organisms living on the long flat and in niches of the steep walls of the shelf make this a feeding area for seabirds, fish, crabs, and river otters, as well as a mecca for scuba divers.

Bay View State Park   Map 21

Camping • Picnicking • Swimming • Fishing • Paddling • Birdwatching

Facilities: 46 standard campsites, 30 RV sites (EW), 3 primitive campsites, group camp, group day-use area, picnic shelter, picnic tables, fireplaces, restrooms, showers, toilets, RV pumpout station, playfield, volleyball court

Area: 25 acres; 1320 feet of shoreline on Padilla Bay

🚐 Leave I-5 at Exit 230, a mile north of Mount Vernon, and follow SR 20 west 6½ miles. At a stoplight, turn north on Bay View–Edison Road and follow it north for 3 miles to the small town of Bay View, on the edge of Padilla Bay. The park is on Bay View–Edison Road at the north edge of the town.

🛶 Padilla Bay is shoal at all but high tide, so water access to the park is only available to paddlecraft. The park is at the southeast side of the bay. The nearest launch ramps are at Bay View and the Swinomish Channel bridge.

Bay View State Park is split in two by Bay View–Edison Road. The overnight camping area is to the east, in stately old-growth timber. RV sites with power and water hookups are in open grassy areas near the entrance. Some tenting campsites lie around the perimeter of a grass field, but most are on shady forested loops.

A wooden staircase leads from the picnic area, on the east, down an embankment to meet the park road, which ducks through a highway underpass and emerges on the west at a large parking lot and broad, sandy beach. This lower, day-use area of the park has picnic tables, fireplaces, a picnic shelter, and plenty of places to loll in the sun or test the water of the bay.

Kayaks or inflatable boats can be carried the short distance from the parking lot and launched here for exploration of Padilla Bay. For trailered boats, a state DFW launch ramp is in Bay View, a short block north of the Wilson Road intersection. The 1-lane paved ramp is usable only at high tide; it ends in a mucky tideflat at low tide. Parking space for a half dozen cars with trailers is adjacent to the ramp.

Padilla Bay National Estuarine Sanctuary   Map 22

Paddling • Birdwatching • Walking • Jogging • Bicycling • Educational displays

Facilities: *Shore Trail:* Informational displays, picnic tables, benches, toilet. *Interpretive Center:* Nature trail, view tower, restrooms, interpretive displays

Area: *Padilla Bay National Estuarine Sanctuary:* 11,600 acres. *Interpretive Center:* 64 acres

🚗 See the directions to Bay View State Park, described previously. *Shore Trail:* The north end of the trail is at the south edge of Bay View, and the south end of the trail is 2⅓ miles farther south on Bay View–Edison Road. *Interpretive Center:* On Bay View–Edison Road ½ mile north of Bay View and ¼ mile north of Bay View State Park.

🚤 Launch ramps can be found at the town of Bay View and at the south end of Padilla Bay, where SR 20 crosses the Swinomish Channel. Hand-carried boats can also be put in at Bay View State Park

Padilla Bay lies in a protected pocket between Fidalgo and Guemes Islands and the mainland. The north end of the Swinomish Channel, running along the western edge of the bay, is dredged. The ideal way to view the bay is by kayak or other small boat at high tide, when most of the bay is 6 feet deep or less. Avoid this area from September to November and February to May so migrating birds are not disturbed. Boaters are likely to sight seals, herons, and a variety of waterfowl. Below, in the shallow water, is a teeming display of plant and animal life. ❁ At low tide, the bay becomes a mucky flat where even kayaks might become mired. The best place to launch hand-carried boats is from the beach at Bay View State Park. Strong winds can cause problems for small boats.

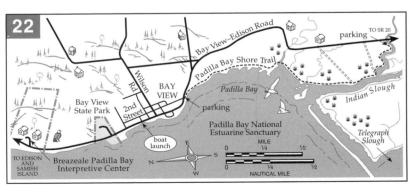

Padilla Bay Shore Trail • During the late 1800s (and long before the days of environmental impact statements), settlers in the Skagit Valley built a network of dikes to hold the saltwater at bay and claim the delta for farmland. A 2¼-mile-long section of these dikes is open as a walking and bicycling path along the edge of Padilla Bay.

The south end of the trail is on one of the branches of Indian Slough, on the Bay View–Edison Road ¾ mile north of its intersection with SR 20. There is parking here for a dozen cars on the shoulder. The north end of the trail is at the southern edge of the town of Bay View; parking is two

Padilla Bay National Estuarine Sanctuary

Until recently most boaters have looked on Padilla Bay as just a place to hurry through—the huge shoal areas marked on marine charts were enough to make any sea captain wary. Now, thanks to the work of some Skagit County residents, the bay has received recognition as the ecological wonder that it is, and more people are pausing to learn about and enjoy the estuary. In 1980, a large section of the bay was established as a national estuarine sanctuary, encompassing 11,600 acres of marsh and tidelands stretching along the east side of the bay from the Swinomish Channel to Samish Island. The vegetation, marine creatures, fish, birds, and mammals living in this area are all part of an important ecological system that has been preserved in its natural state for study and for the benefit of future generations.

The eelgrass beds offshore from Bay View State Park and north to Joe Leary Slough are vital wintering areas for black brants. These small geese with a particular palate dine almost exclusively on eelgrass and sea lettuce such as that found in the brackish water of the bay.

Black brant frequent Padilla Bay.

A rock bulkhead keeps the Padilla Bay Shore Trail high and (more or less) dry above the tidelands.

blocks away on Second Street. Parking for physically disabled persons is by the trailhead; disabled access to the trail requires a gate key, available from the interpretive center.

The wide path atop the dike, surfaced with fine crushed gravel, is ideal for jogging or family bicycling. Interpretive signs tell about the wetland habitat and the effect of the dikes upon it. The Breazeale Padilla Bay Interpretive Center provides a checklist of more than 125 different species of birds that might be spotted here; take binoculars to scan the marshes and bay. Hunting is permitted from the dike, in season.

Breazeale Padilla Bay Interpretive Center • To better appreciate the many forms of life in Padilla Bay, stop at the Breazeale Center, which serves as headquarters of the sanctuary. While walking or driving to the center, watch for birds. Eagles nest near here, and there is a heron rookery on Samish Island. Hawks are commonly seen foraging above hedgerows.

At the interpretive center, models, illustrated displays, dioramas with preserved animals, saltwater aquarium tanks, and a "hands-on" room for young visitors present a fascinating explanation of the marine environment. The center regularly offers programs and other environment-related activities for visitors, schools, and teachers; films are shown at 1:00 P.M. and 4:00 P.M. on Sundays. The center is open Wednesday through Sunday from 10:00 A.M. to 5:00 P.M., closed Monday and Tuesday.

North of the building, a ¾-mile nature trail loops through the wildlife habitat area. Posts along the route are keyed to a descriptive pamphlet available at the center. A second short path leads west from the building to a beach observation deck and a staircase that winds down to the beach. The observation deck is open from April to September; the beach access is open only from July to September; both are closed other times to avoid disturbing nesting and wintering birds. Visitors in small boats can land here to visit the interpretive center when the staircase access is open.

Swinomish Channel Boat Launch (Skagit County)   Map 21
Boating • Paddling • Birdwatching

Facilities: 2-lane paved launch ramp with boarding float and protective booms, toilets, picnic tables

From I-5, take Exit 230 (SR 20, Burlington, Anacortes) a mile north of Mount Vernon. Head west on SR 20 for 8½ miles and exit the highway at the east side of the Swinomish Channel Bridge to reach the launch ramp under the bridge.

The ramp is on the east side of the north end of the Swinomish Channel, underneath the SR 20 bridge.

The easiest boat access to Padilla Bay is from this fine launch ramp maintained by Skagit County Parks and Recreation at the north end of the Swinomish Channel. The 2-lane paved launch ramp has a float for loading boats and booms outboard of the ramp to protect the launch area.

Tangled high grass and cattail-laden marshes that flank the launch ramp site provide forage and protective cover for birds such as red-winged blackbirds. You might want to come here just to birdwatch.

ANACORTES
Map 23
Hiking • Viewpoints • Shopping • Museum • Boating

To reach Anacortes, leave I-5 at Exit 230, a mile north of Mount Vernon. Head west on SR 20. In 12 miles, SR 20 splits; one branch goes left to Deception Pass while the other, SR 20 Spur, angles right to Anacortes. The way is well signed. The total distance from the freeway to Anacortes is 15 miles.

Anacortes is a nautical crossroads that can be reached by boat from the south, north, and west via the Swinomish Channel, Bellingham Bay, or Rosario Strait.

Anacortes serves as the portal to the San Juan Islands, with its ferries transporting more than 1.5 million visitors and residents to the islands annually. Its marinas charter boats and offer marine services to thousands more. A second ferry, operated by Skagit County, provides service to Guemes Island from its terminal in downtown Anacortes at 6th Street and I Avenue.

Many tourists hurry through the city on their way to distant islands, not realizing that Anacortes itself has beaches, bays, viewpoints, and natural treasures to rival those found on the more remote islands. The city's parks range from Cap Sante Park, and its bird's-eye views, to Washington Park, with its rugged weatherworn bluffs.

Anacortes has stores, restaurants, and services to meet every shopping need; most are on Commercial Avenue. The old section of the town, at the north end of Commercial, is a mixture of a few new stores and a number

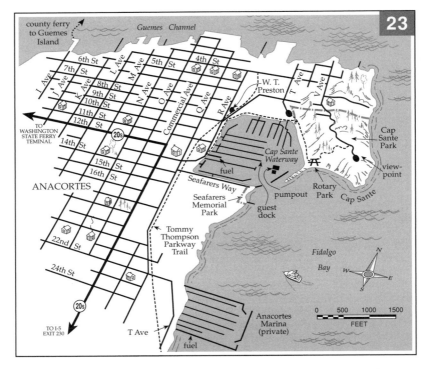

of buildings dating from the 1800s that have been nicely renovated. Some have murals showing old-time Anacortes.

For tourists arriving at Anacortes on their own boat, or those planning to charter one, marinas are at Flounder Bay on the southwest and on the east behind Cap Sante. Anchor Cove Marina and Wyman's Marina, facing on Guemes Channel, have only permanent moorage. Other marinas at Cap Sante and Burrows Bay have guest facilities. A public launch ramp for trailered boats is at Sunset Beach in Washington Park.

Cap Sante Map 23

Boating • Paddling • Picnicking • Hiking • Viewpoints

Facilities: *Anacortes Marina:* Fuel dock, boat pumpout station. *Cap Sante Boat Haven:* Guest moorage with power, water, wireless broadband, gas, diesel, and propane, laundry, restrooms, showers, boat pumpout station, dump for portable toilets, boat launch hoist, U.S. Customs, boat rentals and charters. *Nearby:* Restaurants and shopping. *Rotary and Cap Sante Parks:* Picnic tables, fire braziers, picnic shelter, trail. *Seafarers Memorial Park:* Picnic tables, restrooms, shower, float, meeting room.

Area: *Rotary and Cap Sante Park:* 40 acres; 15,000 feet of shoreline on Padilla Bay. *Seafarers Memorial Park:* 6 acres; 700 feet of shoreline on Fidalgo Bay

🚐 *Rotary Park:* From 4th Street, north of Cap Sante marina, turn south on T Avenue. At 6th Street, a short spur road leads southeast past the Anacortes Yacht Club to the parking lot for the park. *Cap Sante Park:* From the east end of 4th Street turn south on V Avenue, which bends uphill to W Avenue and then climbs southeast to the park entrance. *W. T. Preston:* At the northwest corner of the Cap Sante boat basin, at 7th Street and R Avenue. *Seafarers Memorial Park:* At the south end of Cap Sante marina, turn east from R Street on Seafarers Way and in five blocks arrive at the park.

Cap Sante, an imposing rock knob, rises 200 feet above Anacortes and Fidalgo Bay. The jutting headland shelters a large boat basin, while its heights provide breathtaking views of Fidalgo Island, March Point, and surrounding islands.

Anacortes Marina • This large facility behind a pile breakwater facing on Fidalgo Bay, south of the headland of Cap Sante, has a fuel dock and boat pumpout station, but no guest moorages.

Cap Sante Boat Haven (Port of Anacortes) • Moorages and amenities for visiting boaters are available at Cap Sante Boat Haven. ❅ A dredged channel leading into Cap Sante Waterway is marked with daybeacons and lights. Do not stray out of the channel, because several submerged rocks lie near the headland. The harbormaster's office is on C Dock, on the west shore.

Guest moorage is on the main floats at C Dock, just inside the breakwater and on the north side of the harbor; check in with the harbormaster before tying up here. The harbor office, restrooms, showers, and laundry are in the building at the head of E, F, and G Docks. By foot, to reach the old section of the marina from the newer section, one must mosey around the shore a couple of blocks on a blacktop path. The restaurants and stores of downtown Anacortes are within easy walking distance.

The W. T. Preston *Snag Boat Museum* • An interesting highlight of the Cap Sante waterfront is the *W. T. Preston*, a historic sternwheeler, built in 1929, that for many years worked as a snag boat on Puget Sound rivers and Lake Washington. It was used to tow away tree snags and stray logs that endangered boats. Restored as a museum, it now rests onshore just south of the old Burlington Northern Railroad depot (also restored). The boat is open for viewing daily from 11:00 A.M. to 5:00 P.M. during summer months, and other times when volunteer staff is available. A self-guided tour explains the intricacies of the unique paddlewheeler.

Rotary Park and Cap Sante Park (City Of Anacortes) • Rotary Park is a pleasant hike from the Cap Sante Marina. The top of the headland, with its stunning views, makes a challenging alternate destination. To reach a paved path leading to the park, follow a sidewalk at the east side of the new section of the marina. The path ends at the rock jetty that protects the harbor; here a picnic shelter and picnic tables offer fine views of the harbor. Stairs

Cap Sante Park affords views of the city of Anacortes and Cap Sante Marina.

descend the short distance to the beach, and a rough trail leads steeply up the timbered hillside to Cap Sante Park at the top of the cape. Total distance by foot from the marina to the top of Cap Sante is about ¼ mile, with an elevation gain of nearly 200 feet. The road can be walked for a more gentle, albeit longer, hike.

Whether you reach the top of the cape by way of car, bicycle, or foot, views are outstanding. To the west is the marina complex; to the east, the islands in Padilla Bay nestle below distant Mount Baker. Boats in the bay and Guemes Channel seem like toys plying the blue waters.

The west side of the cape is rolling grassy hillside, giving way to light timber. The south and east slopes are glacier-polished granite broken by patchy grass. Midway down these later hillsides a row of iron posts marks the point where "rather steep" becomes "extremely steep" (and dangerous). End your exploration here.

Seafarers Memorial Park (Port of Anacortes) • Once the site of a paper mill, this waterfront park serves as a memorial to sailors who have died at sea. Its focal point is a bronze statue of a woman with raised lantern, awaiting a seafarer's return. Picnic tables scattered around the lawn offer a nice spot to enjoy views of Cap Sante and Fidalgo Bay.

A 200-foot-long float south of the statue has barely 3 feet of water under the end at low tide, so it is suitable only for launching or landing hand-carried boats. By water, the park float is about 300 yards south of the entrance to Camp Sante Marina.

Washington Park   Map 24

Camping • Picnicking • Boating • Paddling • Hiking • Fishing • Viewpoints • Scuba diving

Facilities: 46 RV sites (EW) 22 campsites, group camp, group day-use area, picnic tables, fireplaces, restrooms, showers, bathhouse, 3 kitchen shelters, children's play area, horseshoe pits, 4 1/2 miles of hiking trails, scenic loop road, 2-lane paved launch ramp with boarding float

Area: 220 acres; 40,500 feet of shoreline on Guemes Channel and Rosario Strait

🚐 From Commercial Avenue in downtown Anacortes, head west on 12th Street, which becomes Oakes Avenue. In 3 miles, at its junction with Ferry Terminal Road and Sunset Avenue, continue west on Sunset Avenue to reach the park in another 3/4 mile.

🛥 The launch ramp is on the north side of the park at Sunset Beach, on Rosario Strait between Shannon Point and Green Point. Boaters staying at Skyline Marina in Flounder Bay (see Burrows Bay, following) can reach the park by walking the road, a distance of about 3/4 mile, to the park entrance.

The crowning glory of the Anacortes city park system, Washington Park has 220 acres of forest and beach and panoramic viewpoints. Immediately to the right of the park entrance are the picnic shelters and tables of the Sunset Beach day-use area on a large grassy field above the beach. To reach the boat launch, continue past the picnic area for 500 feet and take the next right. An excellent 2-lane paved launch ramp drops into the bay. The huge parking lot, accommodating about 100 cars and boat trailers, attests to its popularity. For visitors arriving by boat, Sunset Bay is the only possible landing spot within the park. There is no overnight moorage; for long-term stays boats must be beached or anchored out in the bay.

A few hundred yards beyond the day-use area are the three campground loops, with pleasant sites inland, shaded by second-growth timber but with little

The bulbs of camas, found in abundance at Washington Park, were a food staple of early Native Americans. Today we enjoy seeing their delicate blue blossoms.

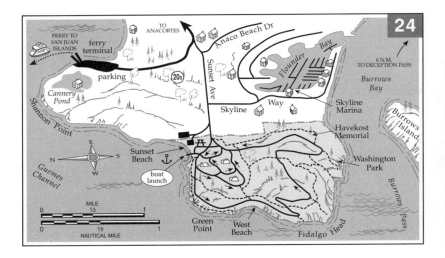

undergrowth for seclusion. The campground is open year-round.

In addition to the steady flow of auto-bound sightseers, many others use the park for hiking, road walking, jogging, or cycling, traveling slow enough to fully soak in its beauty. Pedestrians can choose to walk the loop road from sea-level forest upward to grassy knolls and glacier-scoured rocks 250 feet above the water, or hike the rocky beach from Sunset Bay westward until tide and the steep bluffs of Fidalgo Head force the route inland. The road can be avoided almost entirely by following forest paths near the edge of the bluff from West Beach all the way to the Havekost Memorial. A loop trip is about 1 2/3 miles—longer if enticing side trails are explored.

An inviting wayside stop is West Beach, where waves from Rosario Strait toss driftwood logs onto the narrow bedrock beach. The south side of the park, beyond Fidalgo Head, is a favorite with scuba divers experienced enough to handle the strong current and deep water. Uprising cliffs of Fidalgo Head prevent a complete beach circuit of the park, but southside views can be seen from the road or trail. The bluffs drop off abruptly, so there are no beaches, but the vistas more than compensate. As the road makes its final loop before heading back down to the park entrance, a viewpoint features a small marble monument to T. H. Havekost, a pioneer industrialist who gave the city the original 8 acres of land for this park.

BURROWS BAY

Map 19

The most notable features of Burrows Bay are the two islands that separate it from Rosario Strait. Lifting greenly forested shoulders from the waters of the bay, Burrows and Allan Islands might seem to be everyone's dream of an island hideaway; however, the very rugged nature that gives the islands

The slopes of Washington Park overlook Burrows Bay. Forested Burrows Island is center right.

their beauty, coupled with the lack of water, has served to limit settlement. Spanish explorers, viewing the fortresslike slopes, named them Las Dos Islas Morrows—"Two Islands of the Forts." Mountainous Burrows Island, rising abruptly to a height of 650 feet, is often admired from promontories in Washington Park.

Burrows Bay is on the west side of Rosario Strait, immediately north of Deception Pass. ❀ Boaters attempting to run between Young and Burrows Islands should be wary of a large rock that lies in the middle of the channel. A rocky shelf extends out from the south side of Allan Island; use care approaching this shore. Small bays around the two islands serve as pleasant fair-weather lunch stops; however, all shorelands on Allan Island are private. Washington State Parks owns a large portion of Burrows Island, but, respect posted property.

Skyline Marina   Map 24

Boating • Paddling

Facilities: Guest moorage with power, water, restrooms, showers, wireless broadband, gas and diesel, propane and CNG, groceries, marine supplies, marine repairs, yacht brokers and charters, boat storage, moorage, ice, fishing supplies, boat pumpout station, boat launch slings and Travelift, restaurant

🚙 Follow directions to Washington Park, described previously. At the junction of Ferry Terminal Road and Sunset Avenue, continue west on Sunset Avenue for ½ mile and turn south on Skyline Way to reach the marina complex.

🛥 Skyline Marina is on the north end of Burrows Bay, behind a jetty topped by residences.

This large commercial marina on Fidalgo Island is a favorite stopover for pleasure boaters traveling through Deception Pass. It lies within Flounder Bay, a dredged harbor on the north side of Burrows Bay. The Anacortes city center is 4 miles away; however, the marina can meet most boating needs.

The entrance to the harbor is at the east end of the protective jetty. The channel is marked with lights and daybeacons on pilings. To secure overnight moorage, stop at the fuel dock and check in with the harbormaster. Hand-carried boats can be put in at the jetty for easy exploration of Burrows Bay and its islands.

Burrows Island State Park (Undeveloped)   Map 19

Beachcombing • Kayaking • Boating

Area: 407.6 acres; 12,660 feet of shoreline on Rosario Strait and Burrows Bay

🛥 Burrows Island is at the northwest end of Burrows Bay. The only safe approach for small beachable boats is at a tiny cove on the west tip of the island just north of the lighthouse. The nearest launch ramps are at Washington Park in Anacortes or Skyline Marina.

When the Coast Guard automated all of its light stations, property at Burrows Island Light became surplus, and it was acquired by Washington State Parks. Subsequent acquisitions have led to about 84 percent of the island being owned by State Parks. Ultimately, it might become a marine park or a CMT hostel for kayakers. During calm weather, small boats can be landed near the lighthouse for onshore picnics or exploration. A stairway leads up the bluff from the cove. Overnight camping is permitted; however, there is no potable water. Take all trash away with you.

SWINOMISH CHANNEL
Map 19

Fidalgo makes the grade to island status by virtue of the Swinomish Channel, a 10-mile-long waterway that separates it from the Skagit mainland. The slough, 100 yards wide for most of its length, is dredged throughout to a depth of 12 feet and both entrances are well marked with navigational devices for the use of boaters seeking to avoid the turbulent waters of Deception Pass.

✤ When approaching the Swinomish Channel from either end, even shallow-draft boats should have on hand a navigational chart and follow it closely; only the marked channel is dredged and all the surrounding area is tideflat, where in places even a kayak can run aground. Travel at a no-wake speed—La Conner has a strict law against boats throwing wakes. Stay on the starboard side; there is ample room for two good-sized boats to pass, unless one insists on taking the half right down the middle. On rare occasions, a raft of logs under tow might be encountered. Don't panic—there should be room if you pass cautiously.

❀ The southern entrance, Hole in the Wall, is a dogleg run between the 100-foot-high walls of two rock knobs. A lovely spot, but no fun in a fog. West from Hole in the Wall follow the dredged channel past Goat Island to the buoys marking deep water in Skagit Bay. Range markers at Dugualla Bay help vessels keep aligned with the channel. North from Hole in the Wall, the canal straightens out to gently flow through Skagit flatland edged by levees.

❀ Because the waterway connects two large bodies of saltwater (Skagit Bay on the south and Padilla Bay on the north), water flows inward at both ends of the channel during a flood tide and outward during the ebb. The precise location of the transition is hard to predict; however, general knowledge of the forecasted tides can be useful to boaters in small craft. Tidal current in the channel can exceed 2 knots.

❀ At the north entrance to the Swinomish Channel, the dredged channel runs along the west side of Padilla Bay. It is well marked by buoys and day marks on pilings. Run the channel all the way to its northernmost navigation markers, as any shortcut can end up with your craft mired in mud.

The rock jetty stretching between Goat and McGlinn Islands and running west from Goat Island for 1000 yards was built to divert the flow of the North Fork of the Skagit River and prevent it from filling the Swinomish Channel with silt. Near McGlinn Island a narrow break in the jetty allows migrating salmon to get back to the Skagit River if they mistakenly turn into the channel. The fishway is dry at low tide, but at mid to high tide the narrow slot can be used by kayakers to go between the two channels.

While the run through Swinomish Channel is fun in a large boat, it can be enchanting in a paddle-powered one, with side trips up narrow, meandering sloughs and eye-to-eye encounters with great blue herons, ducks, and other marsh birds. During the winter, whistling swans, snow geese, black brants, gulls, ducks, and terns, common to the Skagit Wildlife Recreation Area a few miles to the south, might also be seen here from the water or from roads and trails along the levees.

Goat Island • The old World War I forts of Casey, Flagler, and Worden are well known to anyone who has done a bit of traveling around Puget Sound, but what about Fort Whitman? It did exist, and right here on Goat Island on the south side of the Swinomish Channel. The fortification was built as part of the system protecting the Northwest's inland waters from enemy attack and was in service from 1911 until 1944.

The island can be accessed only by boat. The best access is at the rock beach on the north side, next to the old dock. From here a trail climbs west to the overgrown battery emplacements on the western end of the island. Four 6-inch disappearing guns at Battery Harrison guarded Deception Pass and Saratoga Passage. The fort also had a mine-control center similar to the one that can be seen in Manchester State Park, but there is no record of mines ever being planted in the passage.

Goat Island is now part of the DFW's Skagit Wildlife Recreation Area. Hawks and eagles nest in the tall firs; use care to not disturb them, especially in spring. Camping is not permitted.

La Conner   Map 25

Boating • Paddling • Fishing • Bicycling • Museums • Historic sightseeing

Facilities: Restaurants, lodging, shops, galleries, restrooms, museum, launch ramp

🚗 From I-5, take Exit 230 (SR 20, Burlington, Anacortes). Follow SR 20 west for 6½ miles to a stoplight. Turn south on La Conner–Whitney Road and follow it for 4 miles to La Conner.

🚤 *From the south:* Follow the dredged channel east from Skagit Bay to the Swinomish Channel. *From the north:* Pick up the dredged channel along the west side of Padilla Bay and follow it south. The nearest launch ramps are at the Swinomish Channel bridge and at Pioneer Park in La Conner. The La Conner Marina, on the north side of town, also has launch facilities.

La Conner, on the Swinomish Channel, is the quintessential little seaside tourist village, with waterfront businesses built on piles edging the canal. Founded in 1867, it was a center of commerce during the time of steamboat traffic on Puget Sound. Many of the town's buildings are listed in the National Register of Historic Places. Today, it is an artists' colony and tourist center with interesting shops, restaurants, historic sites, and museums. The museums charge a small admission fee. Town merchants can provide maps of the numerous tourist attractions.

The rich, flat delta land between I-5 and La Conner is favorite bicycling

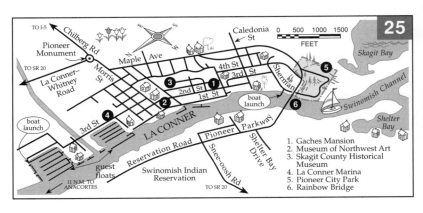

Colorful tulip fields are the hallmark of La Conner.

country, offering views of farms and, in spring, vast fields of brilliant tulips. A public restroom in the middle of town on 1st Street offers welcome relief to touring cyclists.

Several street-end parks on the waterfront provide picnic tables and display sculptures by local artists. On the west shore of the canal, immediately across from La Conner, are boat docks of the Swinomish tribe.

Three of the floats along the La Conner waterfront, below street-end public parks, offer temporary moorage to boaters stopping by to shop or dine. Some might permit overnight moorage, for a fee; however, don't tie up at floats in town without first confirming they are public.

Gaches Mansion • The most elegant landmark in La Conner is the restored, twenty-two–room Gaches Mansion, which is a registered National Historic Place. The home, built in 1891, houses the La Conner Quilt Museum. It is open Wednesday through Saturday from 11:00 A.M. to 4:00 P.M., and Sunday from noon to 4:00 P.M. It is only open weekends in December, and closes the first two weeks in January.

The Museum of Northwest Art • The Museum of Northwest Art, on 1st Street near Morris Street has works by renowned northwest artists such as Kenneth Callahan, Dale Chihuly, Guy Anderson, Mark Tobey, Morris Graves, and Richard Gilkey. The museum is open daily from 10:00 A.M. to 5:00 P.M.

Skagit County Historical Museum • Perched on a small hill above La Conner, the Skagit County Historical Museum has one of the best viewpoints in town, with a breathtaking vista of the pale specter of Mount Baker and green and brown Skagit farmlands. When tulips blossom, the valley is transformed into a tapestry of riotous color.

The museum is at 501 4th Street. To walk to the museum from downtown La Conner, look for a signed stairway on 1st Street, next to a bank. The museum's excellent displays cover a broad range of Skagit Valley life. Youngsters will enjoy interactive displays where they can try on pioneer clothing, operate a telephone switchboard, or guess at the practical function of obscure household and farm utensils. Museum hours are Tuesday through Sunday, 11:00 A.M. to 5:00 P.M.

La Conner Marina (Port of Skagit County)   Map 25

Facilities: Guest moorage with power and water, restrooms, showers, laundry, boat pumpout station, boat launch slings, boat charters, bait, ice, tackle, restaurant, repairs and service, gas and diesel

From Morris Street, the main road into La Conner, turn north on N 3rd Street, and in four blocks reach the south marina basin. Continue north on 3rd Street for the north basin and the marina office.

Many floats in La Conner are open to visiting boaters.

🛶 See directions to La Conner, described previously. The marina is on the north edge of town.

The La Conner Marina, a 500-slip facility operated by the Port of Skagit County, occupies two large dredged yacht basins. Guest moorages are on the two 1200-foot-long outside floats on the south and north basins of the marina. Tying up on the channel side of these floats can be difficult due to strong current in the channel and heavy boat traffic, and these moorages can also be uncomfortable at night due to excessive rocking, but they are fine for a short stay. At the northeast end of the north marina basin, a dual sling hoist launches boats up to 27 feet long.

A number of businesses near the marina provide most boating necessities, and downtown shopping and museums are just a few block's walk away.

Pioneer City Park   Map 25

Picnicking • Viewpoint • Boating • Paddling

Facilities: Picnic shelters, picnic tables, toilets, 1-lane launch ramp with boarding float

🚐 *Launch ramp:* From Morris Street, the main road into La Conner, head southwest on Maple Avenue. In nine blocks, turn northwest on Caledonia Street and in two blocks go southwest on S 3rd Street, which Ts into Sherman Street. Turn northwest on Sherman and find the ramp under the east end of the Rainbow Bridge at the corner of Sherman and Conner Way. *Picnic area:* At Caledonia, continue southwest on Maple, which bends northwest and becomes Pioneer Parkway. In 1/4 mile, the park entrance is on the south side of the road, just before it crosses the bridge.

🛶 See directions to La Conner, described previously. The ramp is on the south end of town at the Rainbow Bridge.

At the south end of La Conner, the orange-painted "Rainbow Bridge" arches dramatically over the Swinomish Channel. From some viewpoints, the design-award-winning bridge picturesquely frames the rustic town stretched along the shore, with the icy crown of Mount Baker rising above. From other vistas, the bridge frames fishing boats moored in the quietly flowing waterway. At the eastern end of the bridge is a combination city park and public boat ramp. The paved ramp is beside the footings of the bridge. A parking area at the launch ramp has room for a dozen cars and trailers.

The more developed section of the park, with tables and shelters for picnicking, sits on the embankment above the ramp. Through trees, boat traffic can be seen in the channel below. Trails lead down to the launch ramp and to the bridge. Walk across the bridge for wide-open views of the Swinomish Channel, La Conner, and majestic Mount Baker, to the north.

chapter four

The Skagit Delta and Camano Island

DELTA FLATLANDS
Map 26

NOT LONG AGO, AS SUCH THINGS ARE MEASURED GEOLOGICALLY, when the last of the land-gouging ice sheets melted, Puget Sound lapped against the rugged Cascade foothills, and mountain streams tumbling down precipitous slopes emptied directly into tidal waters. After the last glaciation, it took 13,000 years for the constant wearing-down of streams and rivers to build up more than 100,000 acres of rich Skagit flatland stretching from the base of the Cascades to its present boundary on Puget Sound. The growth continues at a reported rate of 100 million tons of sediment deposited each year.

A network of sloughs meanders through the Skagit Wildlife Recreation Area.

The two rivers that meander through the Skagit Delta, the Skagit and the Stillaguamish, terminate at an estuary that edges Skagit Bay and Port Susan. ❀ Boaters passing by wisely stay well to the west, in the channel that follows the Whidbey Island shoreline. Although it is not generally thought of

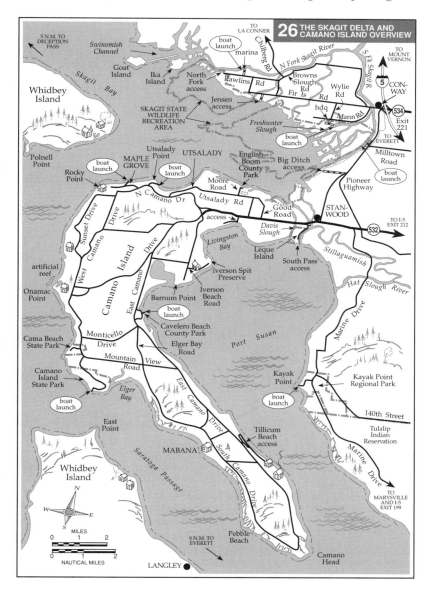

as a cruising-boat destination, it is possible to approach the tidelands from the west in a shallow-draft boat or kayak at mid- to high tide. A cautious approach from the water side can be the best way to observe the enormous flocks of snow geese and other waterfowl that winter in the estuary. Channels lead along the north side of Camano Island into West Pass, and also north into Tom Moore and Boom Sloughs. Consult a navigation chart and proceed with care.

Skagit State Wildlife Recreation Area (Department of Fish and Wildlife)   Map 26

Birdwatching • Paddling • Clamming • Hiking • Fishing

Facilities: Hiking trails, information center, restrooms, toilet, 2 launch ramps
Area: 12,700 acres

🚗 *Launch Ramp on Freshwater Slough:* From I-5, take Exit 221 (SR 534, Lake McMurray) and head west on Old Highway 99. In 500 feet, go west on Fir Island Road, signed to Conway. In 2¼ miles, turn south on Wylie Road, and then in 1⅓ miles, at Moberg Road, take the gravel road to the southeast into the wildlife recreation area. At a fork in ¼ mile, turn east and in 300 yards reach the parking area and launch ramp. *Launch ramp on Tom Moore Slough:* At the junction of Old Highway 99 and Fir Island Road, continue south on Old Highway 99 for 2⅓ miles to Milltown Road. Go west, cross the railroad tracks, and as the gravel road bends north in 50 feet, find the gravel launch ramp. Parking is limited.

The Skagit Delta is a prime birdwatching area to see both waterfowl and land birds.

The Skagit Wildlife Recreation Area (WRA) covers a major portion of the shoreline from Camano Island north to the Swinomish Channel. Here, the state DFW has preserved a natural habitat that supports a wide variety of birds, fish, and small mammals. The tidelands, sloughs, and adjoining fields of the estuary are a major stop on the Pacific Flyway for migratory birds. Hunting and fishing are permitted, in season, but the area is also heavily used by those who hike along the dikes or boat in the channels to simply enjoy the wildlife and scenery.

The most spectacular attraction of the area is the 25,000 to 30,000 snow geese and some 100 whistling swans that winter here. The best time for viewing the flocks is from the end of hunting season in December through April. More than 175 species of birds have been observed here, as well as river otter, rabbit, muskrat, beaver, skunk, and raccoon. Anglers land Dolly Varden, steelhead, and several species of salmon. The tidelands west of Browns Slough offer good clam digging.

The inner edge of the Skagit WRA is bordered by private farmland. Birds can sometimes be seen from the roads, but for best viewing, drive to the area's road-end access points. Personnel at the WRA headquarters can give advice regarding boating in the estuary. ✿The water level and the current in the myriad sloughs and channels at the mouth of the Skagit vary dramatically with the tide. Mid- to high tide is necessary to navigate many of the channels. Improper planning can result in even kayaks becoming stranded in the muck. In the river channels, the current can be quite strong. If it is foggy or if low overcast covers the mountains, it is possible to become disoriented in the reedy marshes; carry a map and compass.

Within the Skagit River delta, there are two launch ramps, both primitive. The one used most frequently is on Freshwater Slough; the other is on Tom Moore Slough at Milltown. Other recreation access points

Raccoon tracks in the sand tell of a nocturnal visitor.

at North Fork, Jensen, Dry Slough, and Big Ditch provide birdwatching and hunting opportunities. Land-bound visitors can also walk trails along the dikes or wander for miles on the tideflats. Rubber boots are a good idea.

At the north section of the WRA, a commercial resort and marina on the North Fork of the Skagit River, just off Rawlins Road, has a launch ramp as well as boat rentals and supplies, RV camping, and a few cabins. Canoes and kayaks can be put in there for a fee.

Leque Island and South Pass Access Map 26

Birdwatching • Paddling • Hiking • Fishing

Facilities: Primitive launch ramp

🚗 To reach Leque Island, leave I-5 at Exit 212 (SR 532, Stanwood, Camano Island) and follow SR 532 west for 5 miles to Stanwood. Continue west on SR 532. Immediately after crossing the bridge over West Pass, a side road to the south, Eide Road, heads back toward the channel, paralleling the bridge abutments. At the channel, a road stub goes straight ahead to the water.

Small Leque Island lies at the mouth of the Stillaguamish River, between the mainland and Camano Island. A road that skirts the southeast shore of the island provides water access to marshes at the south end of the Skagit WRA.

The dirt ramp here is suitable for launching hand-carried boats—trailers might become mired. Parking space for a couple of cars is under the bridge.

Eide Road continues south, paralleling the dike. During hunting season the DFW releases pheasants here and hunters use the area extensively. At other times, wander freely on the south end of Leque Island and onto the tideflats at the end of Port Susan. Eide Road is gated a mile south of the bridge; in the vicinity of the gate, parking is extremely limited. A DFW parking permit is required.

PORT SUSAN
Map 26

Most boaters hurry by on the main highway of Saratoga Passage, rarely lingering to enjoy a detour into the quiet waters of Port Susan. The 11-mile-long inlet leads only to a long, shallow tideflat and limited shoreside marine facilities, but it is a pleasant corner, well worth a visit. The cove offers a few anchorages along the northwest shore in 10 fathoms. ❊ Beware of shoals that rise up abruptly 2 miles from the head of the bay and the extensive mudflat that lies along the northeast shore.

Kayak Point Regional Park (Snohomish County) Map 26
Camping • Picnicking • Boating • Paddling • Fishing • Crabbing • Scuba diving • Swimming • Hiking

Facilities: 33 campsites (2 disabled accessible) with power, 10 yurts, picnic tables, fireplaces, picnic shelters, group picnic shelter, restrooms, showers, launch ramp, fishing pier, hiking trails

Area: 428 acres; 3300 feet of shoreline on Port Susan

🚗 *From the south:* From I-5 at Exit 199 (SR 528E, Marysville, Tulalip), head northwest on Marine Drive for 13 1/4 miles to the park entrance. *From the north:* At 88th Avenue N in Stanwood, turn south from SR 532 on 88th, and in 1/4 mile at a T intersection, head south on Marine Drive to arrive at the park in 8 miles.

🛥 Kayak Point is on the east side of Port Susan, 6 3/4 miles north of Tulalip Bay.

The waters of shallow Port Susan find the perfect complement in the wide beaches of Kayak Point, along its east shore. On hot summer days, the park becomes a northern version of Seattle's Golden Gardens, with mobs of swimmers, sunbathers, picnickers, and sand-encrusted kids. But even in chilly weather, the park has a lot to offer visitors. At one time, the point was occupied by a resort that loaned kayaks to its guests, thus the area's name. The resort is long gone, but the joy of paddling around the placid bay remains.

Cod, perch, flounder, or (with luck) salmon can be caught from the 300-foot-long fishing pier that juts into Port Susan, and crab pots or star traps strategically lowered might result in Dungeness or red rock crab. A 1-lane launch ramp is immediately north of the pier. ❊ Boaters should leave or approach the area with caution, watching for swimmers and scuba divers in the water. The weak current in the bay makes this a popular spot for beginning scuba divers who might find crabs, nudibranchs, moon snails, and orange sea anemones on the smooth bottom. Divers should stay well away from the pier and launch ramp where there are fishing lines and boat propellers.

Hiking trails lace the upland woods between the beach and Marine Drive. On the bluff above the beach, a timbered campground loop offers campsites with power hookups. For those who prefer their camping a bit unique, at the entrance to the campground loop is a yurt village with ten of these canvas-walled cabins surrounding a communal picnic shelter, ideal for a large group outing.

The fishing pier at Kayak Point Regional Park is great for fishing or watching.

CAMANO ISLAND
Map 26

🚐 At Exit 212 (SR 532, Stanwood, Camano Island) from I-5, head west on SR 532 for 5 miles to Stanwood. Continue west from Stanwood on SR 532, and in 1 mile cross Davis Slough onto Camano Island.

Although Whidbey and Camano Islands are joined together politically to form Island County, they are quite different in character. Unlike Whidbey, which is three times larger, Camano Island has neither towns nor major businesses—there are just a few grocery stores and gas stations near centers of population. Camano and Whidbey Islands were more closely allied in early times when boats were the major mode of transportation and Saratoga Passage was seen as a water link, not a barrier between them. Small boats of the Mosquito Fleet shuttled back and forth between the two, carrying goods and passengers. Today, it is not possible to travel directly between the islands other than by private pleasure boat.

Because it lies in the protection of Whidbey Island, Camano has fewer wind-buffeted beaches; ❄however, the western shore does suffer some of the severe weather off Saratoga Passage and the island's shallow bights provide little shelter for boaters.

Livingston Bay • The bay at the northeast end of Port Susan is water-filled only at high tide, and at low tide the water recedes nearly ½ mile offshore leaving behind a mucky mudflat. For kayakers willing to brave this challenge, there is a public access to the bay at a road end on its north shore. To reach it, after crossing Davis Slough onto Camano Island continue west on SR 532 for 1¾ miles. Turn south on Fox Trot Way, which deadends at the beach in ¼ mile. Property and tidelands on either side of the road end are private (and watch tide levels!).

Iverson Spit Waterfront Preserve (Island County) Map 26

Hiking • Birdwatching • Beachcombing • Shellfish

Facilities: None
Area: 330 acres; 3170 feet of saltwater beach on Livingston Bay

🚗 After crossing Davis Slough onto Camano Island, continue west on SR 532 for 5½ miles to the junction of N Camano Drive and E Camano Drive. At a stoplight on E Camano Drive in ¼ mile, turn south on Sunrise Boulevard, and follow it 2½ miles to Iverson Beach Road. Head west on Iverson Beach Road, jog north one block at Moe Road, and in ½ mile T into Iverson Road. Head north on Iverson Road for ½ mile to a road-end parking area at the south end of the preserve.

🚤 The spit is on the southwest corner of Livingston Bay, just north of a string of beachfront residences at Lona Beach. It can only be reached by paddlecraft at high tide.

Below an old dike, a jumble of driftwood more than 100 yards wide fronts a broad sandy beach that tapers gently into Livingston Bay. At minus tides, the water of the bay retreats, exposing sand and mud nearly a quarter of a mile from shore. On the eastern horizon is the western fringe of Cascade peaks, among them White Horse, Three Fingers, and Mount Pilchuck; Rainier looms due south.

The preserve is a birdwatcher's paradise, with more than 125 species recorded in this one spot; eagles, hawks, shorebirds, great blue herons, chickadees, hummingbirds, and thrushes are often seen. This is one of the stopover points for migrating snow geese and trumpeter swans. Walk the beach north for ½ mile to the tip of Iverson Spit, and pick up the faint trail atop the dike and go south to return to the parking area.

Cavelero Beach County Park (Island County) Map 26

Wading • Picnicking • Boating • Paddling

Facilities: Picnic tables, fire brazier, toilet, 1-lane paved launch ramp
Area: 0.6 acre; 300 feet of shoreline on Port Susan

🚗 After crossing Davis Slough onto Camano Island, continue west on SR 532 for 4½ miles to the junction of N Camano Drive and E Camano Drive. Head south on E Camano Drive for 5½ miles, turn southeast on Cavelero Road, and in ¼ mile turn east on a narrow unnamed road signed "County Park."

🚤 The park is on the west side of Port Susan, 1¼ n.m. south of Barnum Point.

The west shore access in this little park gives boaters and beach lovers a chance to sample Port Susan waters. The paved boat launch is at the north end of the park. The narrow access road, the poor condition of the ramp, and the shallow outfall make launching large boats difficult. At low tide, launching of anything except hand-carried boats might be impossible.

Park facilities consist of three picnic tables and a toilet; however, the pretty beach needs no embellishments. Mount Baker and Whitehorse and Three Fingers Mountains line the horizon to the east. The park is a favorite in summer with families who bring toddlers to dabble in the shallow, sun-warmed water.

English Boom Historical County Park (Island County) Map 26

Birdwatching • Beachcombing • Historical site

Facilities: None

Area: 6.7 acres; 900 feet of saltwater shoreline on Skagit Bay

🚐 See directions to Camano Island, described previously. Follow SR 532 west from Davis Slough for 1 mile, and then turn north on Good Road. In 3/4 mile, Good Road bends west and becomes Utsalady Road; in another mile, at the airport, turn north on Moore Road, and reach the park and road-end parking in 3/4 mile.

🚣 The shore of Skagit Bay at this point is extremely shallow, so it can only be approached at high tide by paddlecraft. At minus tides, the shoreline is a mudflat extending 1/4 mile offshore. English Boom Park is 1 1/2 miles east of Brown Point, just east of a beachfront house. The nearest launch ramp is at Utsalady Point.

Between the 1850s and 1880s, Camano Island was logged to supply spar and lumber mills at Utsalady and Stanwood and to meet the demands of a

The former log booming area at English Boom is a prime birdwatching spot.

thriving export of lumber products to worldwide markets. The piles offshore in Skagit Bay were anchor points for log booms. Several of the old booming piles still remain, but their function today is quite different. They now are topped by wooden bird nest boxes for purple martins that migrate from South America to breed in this area. Many other birds might be spotted: osprey surveying the shallow waters for prey, great blue herons wandering at the edge of the mudflat, and eagles and hawks in nearby trees.

Island County plans to install informational panels at the site, but at present there is just a muddy beach, a beachfront salt marsh, a gravel parking area—and birds.

Utsalady Point and Maple Grove   Map 26

Picnicking • Boating • Scenic vista • Historical marker

Facilities: *Vista:* Picnic tables, picnic shelter, toilet. *Utsalady:* 1-lane launch ramp. *Maple Grove:* 1-lane launch ramp, toilet

See directions to Camano Island, described previously. Continue west on SR 532 on Camano Island for 2½ miles to its end at the junction of E Camano Drive and N Camano Drive. Take N Camano Drive west for 3¼ miles, and turn north on Utsalady Point Road. In a few hundred feet, reach a Y; the vista is on Shore Drive, the left leg of the Y, and the launch ramp is to the right and downhill at the end of Utsalady Point Road. To reach Maple Grove, continue southwest on N Camano Drive. In ¼ mile, turn southwest on Maple Grove Road and reach the launch ramp in ½ mile.

Utsalady: The launch ramp is on Skagit Bay, ¼ mile south of Utsalady Point. The numerous offshore buoys are all private, but good anchorages can be found in the muddy bottom in 10 to 20 feet of water. *Maple Grove:* The ramp is on Saratoga Passage, ¾ mile southwest of Utsalady Point. Three piles lashed together about 200 feet offshore mark the ramp.

Utsalady Point marks the northwest tip of Camano Island. Here, a small day-use park provides a grassy, shaded spot on a 100-foot-high bluff overlooking Saratoga Passage. A bas-relief carving on a large wooden panel at the park shows the point in its early days; brass plates relate the history of Utsalady.

The lazy little bay with its swath of beach homes is a far cry from the industrial center it was during the 1870s. At that time, Utsalady had a population of 147, and the shores of the bay boasted a large sawmill and a major shipyard. A number of the steamers of the fabled Mosquito Fleet that plied Puget Sound were built here.

The 1-lane ramp in Utsalady is at a 50-foot-long break in shorefront residences. There is parking nearby for three or four cars with trailers; do not park along the road. All buoys are private.

Just around the point and ¾ mile to the west, in the community of Maple Grove, there is a ramp on a 100-foot-wide stretch of undeveloped beach between a dense collection of shoreside residences. A parking area has room for eight or ten cars and trailers.

The quiet bay at Utsalady is far different from what it was when a sawmill and shipyard were on its shore.

Onamac Point Map 26

Paddling • Fishing

Facilities: Artificial reef

🚤 The point lies 3½ n.m. northwest of Camano Island State Park. The Maple Grove launch ramp is 5 n.m. north.

Midway along the west shore of Camano Island, the meager sandspit of Onamac Point thrusts outward into Saratoga Passage, marked by an onshore navigational light. Immediately north of the point, a pair of buoys indicate an artificial reef placed by the state DFW for the benefit of fish and anglers. Crags and crannies of the broken concrete reef provide habitat for lingcod, rockfish, and other bottom species. Small-boat anglers favor the protected waters of Saratoga Passage; many troll for winter blackmouth and spring chinook salmon in the area between Polnell Point on Whidbey Island and Camano Island's Rocky Point.

Although it sounds quite exotic, Onamac Point is not some ancient Native American word meaning something such as "place where giant fish leap out of the water"—it is merely Camano spelled backwards. The name Camano, by the way, comes from Francisco de Eliza, an early Spanish explorer of the region, who named the island for one of his buddies back in Spain.

Cama Beach State Park   Map 27

Paddling • Boating • Nature study • Historical interpretation • Wooden boat classes • Beach walking

Facilities: (When open) 31 cabins, 4 bungalows, lodge with dining hall, meeting room, restrooms, showers, bathhouse, boathouse, boat rentals, mooring buoys, trail (scheduled to open in 2007)

Area: 438 acres; 450 feet of saltwater shoreline on Saratoga Passage

🚗 From I-5 at Exit 212 (SR 532, Stanwood, Camano Island), head west 5 miles on SR 532 to Stanwood. Continue west for 4½ miles to the end of SR 532 at the junction of E Camano Drive and N Camano Drive. Take E Camano Drive south for 6½ miles; at a Y intersection continue south on Elger Bay Road. In 2 miles, turn west on Mountain View Road, and in 1¾ miles, at the Mountain View Road/W Camano Drive intersection, head north for ¼ mile. The Cama Beach development is on the west side of W Camano Drive.

🚤 The park is on the west shore of Camano Island, ¾ n.m. northwest of Camano Island State Park, where there is a launch ramp.

Cama Beach epitomizes the kind of resort that was popular during the 1930s and '40s. People spent their summer vacations in rustic beach getaways such as this, happy with the tiny cabins and glorious surroundings. However, as it became easier to travel to more glamorous spots, this resort, along with many others like it, declined and eventually closed. A wonderful site is still a wonderful site, however, so the state acquired the property and is restoring some of the old cabins and constructing some new buildings. Plans called for it to open in 2006, but excavations uncovered a Native burial area, and work was temporarily suspended.

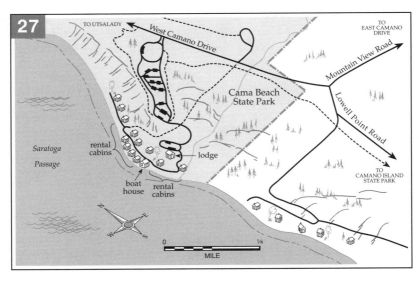

The Center for Wooden Boats leases some of the buildings. It plans to provide programs to complement State Park's interpretive mission. Whether the park is open or not, boats can be beached on the shore and the beach can be walked south for a mile to Camano Island State Park. Offshore mooring buoys are planned.

Camano Island State Park Map 28

Camping • Picnicking • Boating • Hiking • Swimming

Facilities: 87 campsites, 5 CMT campsites, group camp, picnic tables, picnic shelters, fireplaces, restrooms, showers, amphitheater, RV pumpout station, nature trail, hiking trails, launch ramp

Area: 134 acres; 6700 feet of shoreline on Saratoga Passage and Elger Bay

🚙 Follow directions for Cama Beach State Park, described previously. At the Mountain View Road/W Camano Drive intersection, head south on Lowell Point Road to reach the park in another ¾ mile.

🛥 The park launch ramp is on Saratoga Passage midway up the west side of Camano Island, ¼ n.m. north of Lowell Point.

What is perhaps the finest beach on all of Saratoga Passage is, astonishingly, not in an exclusive real estate development but in a magnificent state park where all can enjoy it. The park stretches for more than a mile along the

Sailboarding is just one of many ways to have fun at Camano Island State Park.

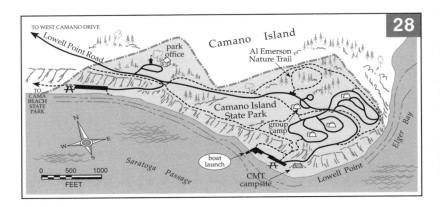

Camano Island shoreline, incorporating both superb upland forests and gently flaring, wave-swept beach.

All regular campsites are upland, in timber away from the bluff; a few sites on the southernmost loop have views of the water. Trails circle the uplands, wander along the edge of the 150-foot-high glacial-till bluff, or drop down to the beach. Rough-hewn benches along the way provide spots to pause and enjoy eagle's-eye views down to boating traffic in Saratoga Passage, out to Whidbey Island, and far beyond to white Olympic peaks. A trail beginning at the picnic area parking lot heads to Cama Beach State Park, a mile to the north.

The road loops steeply downhill to the beach and parking lot at Lowell Point, where CMT campsites, reserved for paddlers, lie south of the day-use area. Picnic tables and fireplaces are stretched along a grassy embankment 30 feet above the beach. At the far north end of the beach, a surfaced, 3-lane launch ramp has a large adjacent parking lot for vehicles with trailers. There is no boarding float, so a bit of wading might be necessary to launch and load boats.

Below a silvery collar of driftwood, the beach slides gently outward—fine swimming or wading for souls brave enough to test the chilly water of Saratoga Passage. A salt lagoon separates the marshy beach and the bluff; by summer the beachside marsh dries enough to host games of Frisbee or one o'cat baseball. In late May, buttercups and wild roses bloom profusely.

chapter five

Deception Pass State Park

Camping • Hiking • Boating • Bicycling • Paddling • Swimming (freshwater and saltwater) • Scuba and free diving • Beachcombing • Birdwatching • Sand dunes • Tidepools • Fishing (freshwater and saltwater) • Sightseeing • Viewpoints

Facilities: 143 RV sites (EW), 167 standard campsites, 5 primitive campsites, 9 CMT campsites, 3 group camps, picnic sites, picnic shelters, restrooms. See individual areas for complete listing of facilities

Area: 3585.25 acres; 77,900 feet of saltwater shoreline on the Strait of Juan de Fuca and Samish Bay, 28,200 feet of freshwater shoreline on Cranberry Lake and Pass Lake

🚗 *From the north:* From I-5 at Exit 230 (SR 20, Burlington, Anacortes), head west on SR 20 for 11¾ miles. Turn south on SR 20, and in 5 miles reach Rosario Road. Pass Lake lies at the junction of the two roads. To reach the Bowman Bay and Rosario Beach sections of the park, turn west on Rosario Road. *For the main park entrance:* Continue past this intersection, cross the Deception Pass Bridge, and in 1 mile reach the entrance on the west and the road to Cornet Bay on the

North Beach provides stunning views up to the Deception Pass Bridge.

east. For the southwest trailhead to the Hoypus Hill area, ¼ mile south of the main park entrance, head east on Ducken Road, and reach the trailhead in 1 mile. *From the south:* Take SR 525 north from the Clinton ferry landing for 22 miles to its intersection with SR 20, and follow SR 20 north through Oak Harbor to the park entrance in another 24 miles.

Bowman Bay is on the south side of Fidalgo Island just west of the west entrance to Deception Pass. Cornet Bay is at the east entrance to Deception Pass just south of Ben Ure Island. Skagit and Hope Islands are on the east side of the north

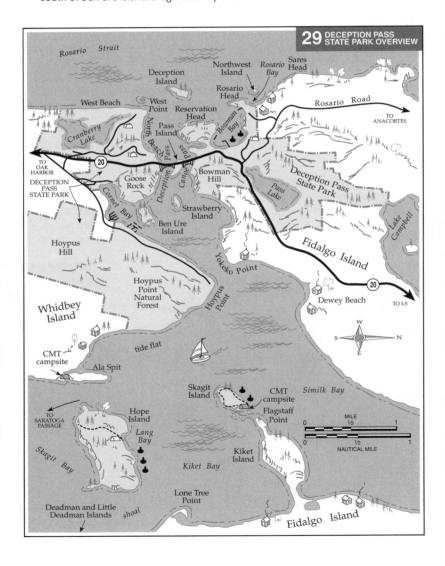

29 DECEPTION PASS STATE PARK OVERVIEW

end of Skagit Bay. Park launch ramps are on Bowman Bay and Cornet Bay. Distance
to the pass from Skyline Marina in Anacortes is 6 n.m., from Oak Harbor 18 n.m.

WITH ITS GENEROUS SAMPLING OF ALL THE TREASURES created when
land meets sea, Deception Pass serves as a perfect introduction to the San
Juan and North Sound Islands. Here are quiet virgin forests; coves, bays, and
wave-tossed beaches; awesome rock escarpments, grassy bluffs festooned
with twisted "bonsai" trees and bright meadow flowers; deer, seals, otters,
eagles, and bizarre marine life; and lakes hosting trout and waterfowl—all
to be enjoyed by motorist, bicyclist, pedestrian, or boater. These attractions
are not unnoticed, however, and the park is swamped by sightseers and rec-
reation-seekers on summer weekends and holidays. More than 1.5 million
people visit the park annually.

Although Deception Pass is separated from the San Juan Islands by bu-
reaucratic boundaries, it has a strong geologic and historic kinship with that
region. The same strata of Late Jurassic igneous rock that underlies Mount
Constitution on Orcas Island forms the enclosing granite walls of Deception
Pass. The Pleistocene glacier that rasped its way across Orcas, San Juan, and
Lopez Islands 15,000 years ago also gouged out the bays and channels of
Deception Pass and scoured the brows of Bowman Hill and Goose Rock.

So captivating are the physical beauties of the park that many visitors
never realize that the area is equally interesting historically. Pioneer life
of the Deception Pass area was colorful, sometimes even lurid—replete
with tales of hardy settlers who tamed the land and of some equally hardy
smugglers, cutthroats, and pirates who sought greater fortune, or perhaps
just greater adventure.

During the late 1800s, a portion of the land within the present park was
designated as a military reservation for the coastal defense of the region. At
the end of World War I, local residents began a movement to have the area,
already a favorite picnicking, camping, and rhododendron-viewing spot, of-
ficially designated as a park. Their hopes were realized in 1921 when 1746
acres were dedicated as Deception Pass State Park. The present acreage
encompasses six entire islands, parts of Whidbey and Fidalgo Islands, two
lakes, and one ocean (as one park brochure describes it).

At the outbreak of World War II, some of the land was temporarily requisi-
tioned by the U.S. government. Three 3-inch guns brought from Fort Casey,
on Whidbey Island, were set up at North Beach and Reservation Head, and
a searchlight was installed at West Point. Some concrete pads from these
emplacements can still be seen.

Deception Pass Area Map 29

Facilities: View walkway, view platform, trails, restrooms

One cannot fail to be impressed by the drama of Deception Pass, whether
viewing it as a land-bound tourist from the heights of the 182-foot-high bridge
or experiencing it as a skipper attempting a first white-knuckle run through

the narrow passageway. Measured against the timelessness of the rock and the power of the boiling tidal current, man's great structural achievement of concrete and steel seems fragile indeed.

The entrance to Deception Pass was charted by early Spaniards, but it was British sea captain George Vancouver who first explored it in 1792. Vancouver named it to express his feeling of deception, for he originally thought the pass was the mouth of a large bay indenting the peninsula that is now known to be Whidbey Island. Before the days of marine engines, large sailing ships, unable to maneuver in the quirky wind and current of its confines, avoided the pass, choosing instead to sail southward along the outside shore of the island. Captain Thomas Coupe, who settled near Penn Cove in 1852, was the first man to brave the pass in a square-rigger. Coupe, a mariner noted for his exceptional courage and skill, challenged the pass under full sail in his three-masted bark, *Success*.

The Deception Pass Bridge

As early as 1907, a land link to Whidbey Island was urged in order to support the military garrison at Fort Casey and assist the agricultural industry on Whidbey Island. Blueprints were prepared, but time and again hopes were dashed as the government failed to appropriate funds for the project.

Finally, in 1933, the bridge appeared about to receive approval in the state legislature; Skagit and Island Counties earmarked $150,000 in local funds and work began on the approaches to the span. However, once more the state legislature balked, and it was not until the following year, after some fast footwork by local politicians, that the money was finally approved, along with some matching funds from the federal Public Works Administration. In August the excavation of solid rock for the first pier of the bridge was begun.

A highline with 4-ton capacity was rigged to Pass Island to transport the derrick for structural steel work, waterlines were laid from Cranberry and Pass Lakes for mixing the concrete, and a month was spent building an aggregate bunker and a cement warehouse. Month after month the steel fretwork grew against the sky until in July 1935, slightly less than a year from the beginning of the first excavation, the cantilevered spans stretching outward from Fidalgo, Pass, and Whidbey Islands were ready to be joined. Steelworkers clambering on the bridge under the hot summer sun were unable to align the sections. However, in the cool of the following morning when the metal had contracted enough to allow proper matching of the diagonals, the final joining was completed. Deception Pass was bridged!

Opposite: *The Deception Pass Bridge is dramatic, whether viewed from above or from the water.*

A winding set of stairs leads from the bridge deck to more sensational viewpoints.

The rock-walled main channel of Deception Pass itself is scarcely 500 feet across, and Canoe Pass, on the north, is a claustrophobic 50 feet wide at its narrowest point, with a sharp dogleg along the way. It is, however, the current pouring through the channels and its associated churning eddies that are the concern of most skippers, for it reaches a velocity of up to 8 knots as the granite spigot of the pass performs its twice-daily task of filling, and then draining, and then refilling Skagit Bay. Very experienced kayakers use the pass as an area to practice running strong currents.

✻ Skippers are advised to consult local tidal current tables and enter the pass during slack water, when the velocity of the current is at its minimum. Although fast boats do make the trip through the channel at other times, boating skill and knowledge of the local waters is advisable. High-powered boats should stay well away from other boats in the waterway so their wake does not cause the less-powerful vessels additional problems.

Deception Pass Bridge • The Deception Pass Bridge, which was begun in 1934 and completed the following year, spans the gulf between Fidalgo and Whidbey Islands, utilizing little Pass Island for its central pillars. Nearly thirty years of effort in state and national government were needed to bring the bridge into being. The bridge is part of SR 20, reached from the north via Anacortes and from the south via Whidbey Island.

Pass (Canoe) Island • Parking areas at either end of the bridge and a small disabled-accessible parking lot on Pass Island allow sightseers to leave their cars and walk along the span for an overlook of the pass that Captain George Vancouver never enjoyed. A view platform is on Pass Island.

Trails eastward from the view platform traverse Pass Island's rocky meadowland of grass, sedges, wildflowers, and gnarled, weather-twisted trees. The wildflower diversity here was once famous, but heavy visitor traffic has tramped most to oblivion. Please treat any remaining plants and flowers with care—take photos, not blossoms. Use extreme care and keep a tight hand on small children because the bluffs drop off steeply into the churning water. At the far eastern tip, the slope gentles enough to enable hikers to reach the water's edge.

A magnificent display of underwater life on the walls of Goose Rock and around Pass Island rewards venturesome scuba divers, but the treacherous tidal current makes this an area only for experts.

Prison Camp • Looking from the east end of Pass Island north to the cliff wall of Fidalgo Island, a gaping cave and an outfall of rock debris can be spotted. This is the remainder of a rock quarry that was operated in conjunction with a state prison camp through Walla Walla State Penitentiary from 1909 until 1914. A large rock crusher was built below the quarry, stretching down the cliff to water's edge. Rock dug from the quarry was put into the crusher, then mechanically sorted into bins and eventually loaded via chutes onto barges that were brought into Canoe Pass.

The penal colony, where up to forty prisoners lived at a time, was on a small bay due north of the eastern end of Pass Island. Park rangers discourage hikers from climbing on the cliffs in the quarry's vicinity because they are extremely dangerous. Be content to view it from the water or Pass Island.

Strawberry Island • Perhaps Strawberry is the perfect island; its 3 acres are just enough to assure visitors a measure of solitude in the middle of a busy freeway, while its mossy granite slopes are an insular rock garden bedecked with wind-shredded junipers, sedums, and wild strawberries. To this, add the crowning touch: a stupendous view into the jaws of Deception Pass.

Salmon anglers sometimes anchor offshore, but the island itself is accessible only to kayaks and other boats small enough to be drawn up on the rocky beaches. ✿ Boat-handling skill and experience are necessary to reach the island. Landing is easiest on the south and east sides, where the slopes flare more gently into the water. Small boats should approach on a rising tide, when the flow will push the craft eastward into quieter water, rather than draw it into the pass, less than 1/2 mile away.

Although the island is part of the state park, there are no camping amenities onshore. Please take any trash back home with you and leave the island as pretty as when you arrived.

Cornet Bay and Hoypus Point Area   Map 30

Fishing • Boating • Paddling • Bicycling • Scuba diving • Hiking • Horseback riding • Beachcombing • Clamming • Nature trail

Facilities: Hiking, bicycling, and equestrian trails, nature trail. *State park marina:* Dock with float, offshore mooring floats, launch ramps with boarding floats, picnic tables, fireplaces, restrooms, showers. *Commercial marina:* Dock with floats, boat launch hoist, diesel, gas, groceries, snack bar, laundry, restrooms, showers. *ELC:* Cabins, kitchen, dining hall, infirmary, recreation hall, swimming pool, playing fields, campfire circle

🚗 At a stop light 1 1/2 miles south of the Deception Pass Bridge, (8 1/2 miles north of Oak Harbor) turn east on Cornet Bay Road to reach the park boating facilities in 1 1/4 miles.

🛥 Cornet Bay is at the east entrance to Deception Pass, just south of Ben Ure Island. A park dock and float, 2 offshore mooring floats, and the park launch ramps are at the east side of the bay. The marina is reached by following daymarkers in the channel to the west.

Just a watery mile east of Deception Pass, Cornet Bay is a placid refuge from the often-turbulent waters of the pass. For boaters heading east to cruise the quiet of Skagit Bay, or those waiting for slack tide to enable them to run the pass, Cornet Bay offers both launching for trailered boats and mooring facilities for larger ones that arrive by water. ❈ Boaters unfamiliar with the area should not attempt to enter Cornet Bay on the west side of Ben Ure Island as a shoal extends west from the island.

A wide grass strip along the beach of Cornet Bay is dotted with picnic

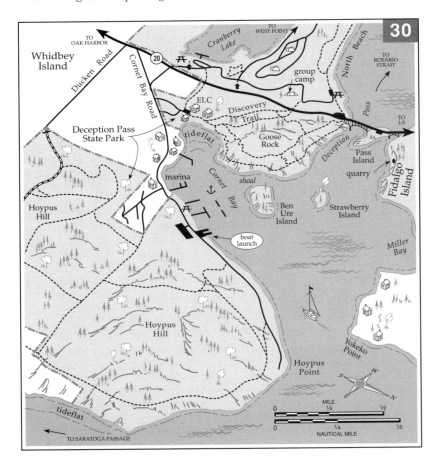

tables and fire braziers. The park dock drops to a 250-foot-long float, and two more 50-foot floats are anchored to offshore piles, parallel to the inshore float. A dock and float to the west are for state park service boats.

Four launch ramps, with loading piers between, drop into the bay. Parking is in a nearby lot or in a larger area across the road to the south. A commercially operated marina that is slightly farther into the bay has fuel, a float with overnight moorages, a launching lift, and supplies.

Traffic is generally light on Cornet Bay Road, making it an excellent bicycle detour from busy SR 20. The blacktopped run is downhill or level all the way to road's end at Hoypus Point, with a 100-foot climb back to the highway intersection on the return.

Ben Ure Island • Ben Ure Island, lying in the mouth of Cornet Bay, was named for an Anacortes businessman-turned-smuggler who lived there with his Native American wife during the late 1800s. The story goes that when planning to be away on a "business" trip, Ure would instruct his wife to build an evening campfire on the northern tip of the island. If Revenue agents were lying in wait in Cornet Bay, she would signal her husband by standing in front of the fire to block the light. If all was clear, she sat to the side and its beacon would guide him home. Today, a navigational light is near the spot where Ben Ure's wife maintained her navigational aid. The island is state park property and is open to dinghy and kayak explorations.

ELC and Goose Rock • The state park's ELC on Cornet Bay provides a base of operations for visiting environmental-education groups, by reservation.

Trails on Goose Rock provide a wooded perspective of the park. In spring, wildflowers abound.

The state park has mooring and launching facilities on Cornet Bay.

Camp facilities at the head of Cornet Bay are reached via the turnoff road, 1/2 mile east of the intersection of SR 20 and Cornet Bay Road.

Towering nearly 500 feet above Cornet Bay, Goose Rock is a small echo of Mount Erie to the north on Fidalgo Island, with its glacier-scoured north slope reflecting the southbound course of an ancient ice field, and its near-vertical south face, to the lee of the glacier, exhibiting little evidence of such wearing.

Trails on the rock interweave, merge, and sometimes end abruptly. Most lead to spectacular views. Trailheads are at the ELC or North Beach parking lot. The Discovery Trail, which runs from the ELC to SR 20, has numbered stations that identify flora and unique geological features along the way. A wide choice of other side paths and alternate destinations permits an interesting variety of trips and scenery. Total distance for an average loop hike is about 3 1/2 miles.

Low tide bares acres of eelgrass-coated mudflat in Cornet Bay—a marked contrast to the wave-scrubbed beaches on the west side of the park. Muck about and examine the variety of tiny marine life that inhabits the intertidal zone. The 1/2-mile section of property to the east, between the ELC and state park dock, is privately owned, so do not trespass.

Hoypus Point and Hoypus Hill • Cornet Bay Road continues northeast from Cornet Bay along the shore to Hoypus Point, passing a gated side road and a borrow pit that are starting points for the 3 1/2-mile hike that loops around the north slopes of Hoypus Hill. This area has been designated as Natural Forest Area, which means it is open to foot travel only—bicycles and horses are prohibited.

The road drive is scenic enough, with glimpses through a fringe of trees and brush of boating traffic in the channel, but walking the beach provides a more pleasant activity, with unobstructed views of Mount Erie due north and Mount Baker rising above Similk Bay to the northwest. The beach is narrow but passable during all but the highest tides. When high water forces the route inland, the low bank can easily be scrambled and the road walked for a distance. Hoypus Point, at road's end, is reached in slightly more than a mile from the marina.

From 1912 until the Deception Pass Bridge was completed in 1935, a ferry operated between Hoypus Point and Dewey Beach, linking Whidbey and Fidalgo Islands. A concrete bulkhead, a remnant of the old ferry landing, can still be seen at the road end. Old newspaper accounts tell of the crowded ferry conditions on Sundays (even then!), when carloads of tourists made springtime excursions to the park to picnic and view the pink masses of wild rhododendrons. Although the ferry has long since ceased operating, the flowers are still a spring attraction.

Beyond the point, the walking is even better, with a broader beach and views across the channel to Skagit, Kiket, and Hope Islands. In about a mile, the park boundary is reached; the tideflat continues on for yet another mile to Ala Spit, county property that is a CMT campsite. The trip from Cornet Bay to the park boundary and back is about 4 miles.

On the south of Hoypus Hill, 400 acres were acquired from the DNR in order to preserve one of the last vestiges of lowland old-growth fir forest in the region. Primitive trails in this area are open to hikers, bicyclists, and equestrians. Turn east off SR 20 on Ducken Road, the first road south of Cornet Bay Road, and reach the gated trailhead in 1 mile.

Skagit Bay Map 29

Camping • Picnicking • Fishing • Canoeing • Crabbing • Clamming • Scuba diving • Beachcombing

Facilities: Mooring buoys, campsites, CMT campsites, picnic tables, fireplaces, toilet, no water
Area: Hope Island, 166 acres; Skagit Island, 21 acres

Hope and Skagit Islands • Stretched across the middle of the channel between Whidbey and Fidalgo Islands, Hope Island and Skagit Island frame Kiket Bay, a small inlet of Skagit Bay. Hope and its smaller neighbor, Skagit Island, are undeveloped outposts of Deception Pass State Park. The north side of Hope Island holds the meager indentation of Lang Bay, where three mooring buoys are nestled. Ashore, a few picnic tables with fire grates can be found in clearings above the beach; drinking water is not available. Raccoons, porcupines, crows, and other scavengers often scatter trash. To minimize the problem, take your garbage home with you. The remainder of the island was traditionally used by the Samish tribe, and is a Natural Area Preserve; public access is limited to the small camping area at Lang Bay.

Less than a mile to the north, Skagit Island is a small version of Hope Island, duplicating its open, grassy bluffs on the southwest side and thick forest on the remainder. A 6-foot-high rocky bank circles the island, except on the northwest side where a shoal reaches out to Kiket Island. Two buoys off the northeast shore provide a place to hang a boat while dinghy-exploring nearby shallow waters or waiting for favorable tidal current to go through the pass. Shore adventurers can hike the trail that rings the island along the top of the embankment. On the northeast end of the island are two primitive CMT campsites. Another CMT site is directly across the channel on Ala Spit. Although it is outside the park boundary, it is on county property.

❄ The water around the islands, west to Hoypus Point, and north to the shallows of Similk Bay offer splendid small-boat excursions; however, the tidal current is quite strong in some areas and a paddle-propelled or underpowered craft might end up going in a different direction than intended. Use care, watch for tide rips, and stay well away from large, moving boats.

Skagit Island is said to have been a hideout for smugglers and all sorts of ruffians on the run from justice at the turn of the last century. Its strategic location, at the bend of the channel with views into Deception Pass and up-channel into Skagit Bay, made any stealthy approach by law boats quite difficult.

Deadman and Little Deadman Islands • Two tiny islands that sit on the fringe of the low-tide mudbanks of Skagit Bay, about 1½ miles southeast of Hope Island, are undeveloped state park property. Deadman and Little Deadman Islands are shown as Tonkon Islands on some charts. Their names come from the local Native practice of interring the dead in canoes fastened to high branches of trees on the islands.

These two islands lie in such shallow water, 0 to 6 feet at mean lower low water, that only kayaks or other shallow-draft craft can safely visit them. There are no shoreside facilities on either island, and camping and fires are prohibited.

Bowman Bay and Rosario Beach   Map 31

Camping • Picnicking • Boating • Paddling • Hiking • Fishing • Scuba diving • Tidepools • Windsurfing

Facilities: 2 RV sites (EW), 18 standard campsites, 8 CMT campsites (on Bowman Bay), picnic tables, fireplaces, picnic shelters, kitchens, restrooms, showers, boat launch (ramp), dock with float, offshore mooring float, mooring buoys, CCC Interpretive Center, fishing pier, underwater park, children's play equipment

🚐 From SR 20 at the west end of Pass Lake, head northwest on Rosario Road, and in 50 feet turn southwest on a road signed to Bowman Bay. The road drops steeply downhill to an intersection. The branch to the left goes to the launch ramp parking lot. The right branch leads to the campground, the CCC Interpretive Center, and picnic shelters. For Rosario Beach, continue northwest on Rosario

Road for 1 mile. Take the signed road to the south, which ends in the day-use area at the beach.

Bowman Bay indents the south side of Fidalgo Island at the west entrance to Deception Pass. There are five mooring buoys offshore, a mooring float on the south side of the bay, and a launch ramp at the center of the bay. A short dock and float are available in Sharp Cove. ❀ Care must be used on entering the bay because numerous rocks foul the north side of the entrance along the west side of Sharpe Cove.

Yet another facet of this diverse park: Here, rounded bays facing away from the swirling current of the pass enable sea life to grow in profusion on rocks and beaches. Offshore, salmon runs attract commercial and sport anglers.

Bowman (Reservation) Bay • Some nautical charts still designate Bowman Bay as Reservation Bay, a holdover from World War I when a military reservation was located here. Nearby residents, agreeing with the U.S. Geological Survey, prefer the name of Bowman Bay, honoring Amos Bowman, the Fidalgo Island pioneer who had a summer cabin on the shore.

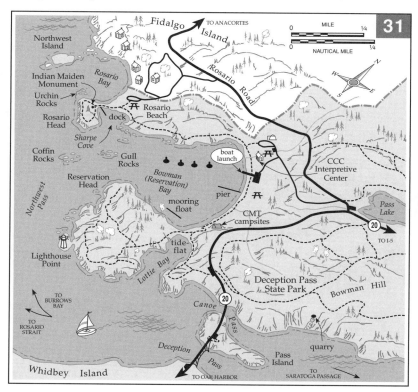

The bay offers some anchorages, and five mooring buoys and a mooring float in the bay (no land access) provide tie-ups for visiting boaters. The long stationary pier is the remains of a defunct fish hatchery. While the pier is a fine place from which to drop a fishing line, it is unsatisfactory for mooring boats because the vertical piles are widely spaced, and the dock level is so high above the water that disembarking is impossible. On the south side of the end of the pier is a small dinghy float. The brush above the beach south from the pier holds eight CMT campsites.

Although much smaller than Bowman Bay, Sharpe Cove to the north, tucked behind Rosario Head, is usually a better spot for a layover. There is a small dock with a float on the cove, along with space for several good anchorages.

CCC INTERPRETIVE CENTER. The strong, road-edging guardrails of rock and logs, sturdy stone-walled restrooms and kitchen shelters, and rustic picnic shelters that the state park boasts are all products of the Depression-era Civilian Conservation Corps (CCC). The CCC was one of the "New Deal" programs instituted by President Franklin D. Roosevelt to break the country free of the Great Depression. Across the nation, unemployed young men were enrolled in the Corps and sent on minimum six-month tours of duty to camps where they worked on projects to conserve natural resources. They constructed trails to fire lookouts, fought forest fires, felled snags, planted trees, and built parks. A number of Washington's older state parks owe their facilities to the CCC.

At Bowman Bay, between the campground and the boat launch area a rock-walled building that was constructed by these men now houses displays telling the story of the CCC. Panels describe camp life, display cases contain photos and memorabilia from the camps, and in a video program, a veteran of the Deception Pass CCC Camp tells of his experiences. The volunteer-staffed center is open Thursday through Monday during summer months, or at other times by appointment.

RESERVATION HEAD. The path south along the shore of Bowman Bay leads to hiking trails that traverse Reservation Head and a smaller, unnamed headland lying east of Lottie Bay. Climbing high on exposed, grassy bluffs, the trails offer views into Deception Pass, across to Cranberry Lake, and out to the inviting blue-green islands of the San Juans. Shallow Lottie Bay separates the two cliffy headlands. Long ago, Bowman and Lottie Bays were joined as a continuous waterway; over the years, wave action built

Marine invertebrates such as starfish live on Deception Pass beaches. This is a marine preserve, so any marine life seen should not be handled.

the sand neck linking Reservation Head to Fidalgo Island that created the two bays. At extreme low tide, Lottie Bay is nearly drained.

Rosario Beach • The state park shares choice Rosario Bay with a university marine research facility and a number of private homes. The spacious picnic area faces on Rosario Bay and Sharpe Cove. Restrooms have outside showers for rinsing saltwater from swimmers and scuba divers. Trails from the picnic area lead upward to the modest heights of Rosario Head or around Sharpe Cove and on to Bowman Bay. Lanky firs along the trail extend horizontally out over the water, supported by but a few roots. Possibly the next storm will see their demise, or perhaps they will still be stubbornly clinging there when your grandchildren hike the trail.

The bay itself is suitable for snorkelers and divers with beginning skills; greater experience is needed to venture out of the bay into deeper, swifter water. At low water, tidepools give land-bound sightseers a glimpse of what lies beneath the water. The underwater park is legendary among divers and marine biologists for its extravaganza of sea life. Beneath the water is a rococo world of flamboyant anemones, sea pens, nudibranchs, sponges, and a large concentration of purple and green sea urchins. The rocks lying just off Rosario Head are well named as Urchin Rocks. This is a marine preserve; the taking or destruction of any marine life is prohibited.

The territory from Deception Pass eastward belonged to the Samish tribe, who harvested the vast runs of salmon that swarmed through the channels. The pass obviously impressed early Native Americans as much as it does people today, for it is mentioned in several of their legends. One tells of an Indian princess named Ko-kwal-alwoot who lived at Deception Pass and who became the bride of the king of the fishes, going to live with him in his underwater kingdom. Her long, flowing hair, turned green from its long exposure to water, can still be seen drifting in the current—although unimaginative people see it only as seaweed.

A monument representing this legend has been placed near the beach on Rosario Head. The 24-foot cedar log, carved in the traditional style of the Samish Indians, shows Ko-kwal-alwoot on one side as an Indian maiden and on the other as the sea spirit she became.

NORTHWEST ISLAND. Northwest Island, ½ mile northwest of the Rosario Beach picnic area, is yet another of the park's small undeveloped islands. The grassy, 1-acre rock is visited mainly by gulls and scuba divers. Although it lies temptingly close, divers are advised to

A monument at Rosario Head commemorates a Native American legend.

take a boat to the island rather than attempt to swim the distance because of the strong tidal current.

Cranberry Lake Vicinity Map 32

Camping • Picnicking • Boating • Paddling • Fishing • Hiking • Beachcombing • Swimming

Facilities: 83 RV sites (EW), 147 standard sites, 5 hiker/biker sites (at Cranberry Lake), 3 group camps (near North Beach), picnic tables, fireplaces, picnic shelters, kitchens, restrooms, RV pumpout station, bathhouse, showers, swimming beach, amphitheater, boat launch (ramp on Cranberry Lake), fishing dock, paddlecraft rentals (concession)

🚗 Cranberry Lake and North Beach can be reached from the main park entrance 1 mile south of the Deception Pass Bridge.

South of the Deception Pass Bridge, just inside the park's main entrance, a large information board directs visitors to Cranberry Lake, North Beach, and West Beach, and shows their various attractions. A ¼-mile nature walk begins here. This is one of the best bicycling areas in the park, with smooth and level roads first wending through cool forest, and then edging the lakeshore. Tent sites for late-arriving bicyclists are usually available at Cranberry Lake Campground, even if the campground is filled with car campers.

North Beach • Whether seen from the forest trail that traverses it or from the water's edge, North Beach is one of the most popular areas in the park.

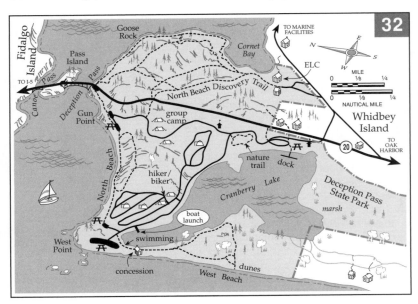

A trailhead can be found on the outside loop of the lower Cranberry Lake Campground, or head east on any of several well-beaten paths from the West Point parking lot. The nearly mile-long curve of the beach is broken by three rocky headlands. The most prominent of these, Gun Point, was the location of 3-inch rapid-fire guns that guarded the pass during World War II.

At low tide, the beach is easily walked from West Point to the base of the vertical cliffs below the Deception Pass Bridge. Higher tides force the route inland at times for easy scrambles over rocky bluffs or a retreat to the trail higher up in the forest. From the North Beach picnic area, the trail continues east beneath the bridge and on to Goose Rock. East of Gun Point, hikers enjoy ant's-eye views of the bridge and, at slack tide, the parade of boats through the pass.

The picnic area lies at the end of the first spur road inside the park entrance. From a parking lot in ¾ mile, a path leads across a rustic wooden bridge over a marsh to the sandy beach area with a picnic shelter, picnic tables, and fire braziers.

Along the side of the road leading to the North Beach picnic area are group camps with Adirondack shelters in a wooded setting. Two of the camps can accommodate thirty-two persons, and the third can accommodate sixty-four; they are available by reservation.

Cranberry Lake • Had the ancient glacier that carved Deception Pass not left a pile of debris in its wake, Cornet Bay probably would have reached through to Rosario Strait, Goose Rock would have been an island, and Cranberry

Shallow Cranberry Lake is ideal for swimming, paddling, and small boat sailing.

Lake never would have come into being. As it was, it appears that a neck of land remained, joining Goose Rock to the glacial outfall of Whidbey Island and forming the Cranberry Lake area merely as a shallow saltwater inlet of the sea. Over the centuries, wind and waves sweeping in from the Strait of Juan de Fuca built a sandbar that eventually joined to the rocks of West Point, forming a lagoon similar to those found in other places on the island. However, instead of the brackish seawater entrapped in other lagoons, here an underground spring filled the sºhallow depression and changed the environment from saltwater to freshwater marsh, with cattails, willows, skunk cabbages, lily pads, muskrats, beavers, river otters, ducks, and fish.

Cranberry Lake is only about 10 to 20 feet deep throughout, with its deepest point a 40-foot "hole" near the north shore. It continues to be filled in with sediment; the closing-in of the lake margins is quite evident in photos taken over a period of years. In perhaps just a few decades the lake will be completely filled in and overgrown with vegetation.

The trout-stocked lake is inviting for either fishing or quiet-water paddling; boats with gasoline motors are not permitted. Muskeg bogs on the southwest can only be reached by water; there, the observant might spot beaver and muskrat lodges at the edge of the marsh. A gravel launch ramp is on the north shore of the lake between the campground entrance and the day-use area. Lightweight boats can be put in from the picnic area by carrying them the short distance to the water.

On the southeast corner of the lake is a picnic area in shaded grass. Paths lead from the parking lot down to a long fishing dock that parallels the shoreline. The massive CCC-built kitchen shelter above the dock is on the site of an old Native American longhouse; apparently the early members of the Samish tribe enjoyed the spot as much as visitors do today.

Mama and the kids enjoy an outing on Cranberry Lake.

Severe winds off the Strait of Juan de Fuca deposit piles of driftwood and other sea treasures on West Beach.

West Point and West Beach • Contained in this small area is probably the greatest diversity of environment within the park: forest, lake, cattail bogs, rocky headland, ocean surf, and one of the finest sand beaches and dunelands on Puget Sound, all enhanced by views back to Mount Erie and out across the Strait of Juan de Fuca to Olympic peaks. The downside of its attractions, however, is seen on sunny spring and summer weekends or on holidays when the area draws crowds, and park rangers become traffic cops attempting to handle the throngs.

On hot summer days, visitors can bathe in the roped-off swimming area on the northwest beach of bathwater-warm Cranberry Lake or dash across the sandbar for a bracing dip in frigid Puget Sound. Prospective clam diggers will find slim pickings on West Beach—waves sweeping in from the strait constantly shift the sand, making it an impossible environment for sea life. The beauty of the shore lies in its pristine, unbroken sweep, and in the dunes that back it. A blacktop path leads into the dunes, which are now anchored by vegetation. A small platform provides an overview of the marsh.

In winter, when storm winds howl in from the ocean, sending waves crashing against the rocks at West Point, hardy souls who savor the excitement of marine pyrotechnics will enjoy a visit to West Beach. Such storms are literally breathtaking; at times, they are so severe it is impossible to stand against the force of the wind. Post-storm beachcombing might yield driftwood, agates, interesting flotsam, and seafoam to play in.

Deception Island • Lying less than ½ mile northwest of West Point, rugged Deception Island is a far outpost of the state park. ✥ Eastern approaches to the island are shallow and rock-riddled and the current can be strong; boaters should use great care. Immediately to the west, the underwater shelf drops off quickly, making for excellent fishing and scuba diving just offshore.

Small boats can be beached on any of several rocky coves; the largest bay on the northwest side of the island is probably the easiest. Due to its difficult access and limited use, the island has not been developed by the park and has no onshore amenities.

Pass Lake Map 33
Fishing (freshwater) • Paddling • Birdwatching
Facilities: Launch ramp

Water holds its own special fascination, whether as ocean swells surging through narrow rocky channels, as placid waves lapping on sandy beaches, or in brackish marshes choked with cattails. Here the state park offers 100 acres of crystal-clear lake water for trout fishing or still-water canoeing. A gravel public boat ramp and parking lot adjoin the intersection of SR 20 and Rosario Road. Where SR 20 parallels the lakeshore, some pulloffs provide spots to put in hand-carried boats or to have a waterfront picnic.

The trout-stocked lake is open to fly fishing during fishing season; gasoline motors are not permitted. It offers good catches of rainbow trout and Atlantic salmon, but is under catch-and-release regulations. A favorite means of fishing the lake is with a float tube and waders. Canoeists find paddling

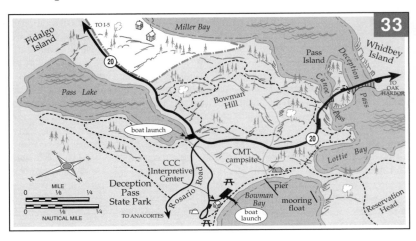

Pass Lake is a favorite for catch-and-release fishing or still-water canoeing.

the length of the lake and along the brushy shoreline to be idyllic. Deer, muskrat, skunk, fox, and other small wild animals might be seen onshore, especially at dusk. In winter, migratory ducks take a rest stop on the lake, floating together in convivial rafts. A boot path wanders along the northwest shore and connects to other primitive trails through the woods that reach Rosario Road ¼ mile west of SR 20.

Bowman Hill, south of the lake, is a densely wooded, undeveloped section of the park. About 2 miles of unimproved trails loop over and around the hill, leading to stunning panoramas from bald viewpoints. The trails are recommended only for hikers experienced in routefinding. The south slope of Bowman Hill is extremely cliffy; hikers are warned to stay well away from the edge. Trails begin at the pullout just north of the bridge.

chapter six

Whidbey Island

🚌 Access to Whidbey Island is by the SR 20 bridge at Deception Pass at the north end of the island, or at the south end by ferry from Mukilteo, on the mainland, to Clinton. To reach the ferry, leave I-5 at Exit 189 (SR 526W, Paine Field, Whidbey Island Ferry) and follow signs for 2 1/2 miles to the terminal at Mukilteo. One main thoroughfare traverses the length of Whidbey Island—SR 20 from the northern end becomes SR 525 in the southern part of the island. Midway on the island, at Keystone, a second ferry gives access to and from the Olympic Peninsula via Port Townsend.

⛵ The 45-mile-long island offers numerous spots for boat access. Most are on the sheltered east side. From Everett, via Saratoga Passage, Langley is 8 n.m., Coupeville 25 n.m., and Oak Harbor 26 n.m..

THE 45-MILE-LONG RIBBON OF LAND that is Whidbey Island averages a mere 3 miles in width. From some vantage points, it is possible to see both bodies of water that flank it at once—Saratoga Passage on the east and the Strait of Juan de Fuca or Admiralty Inlet on the west. Whidbey holds the honor of being the longest island in the United States; for many years, New York's Long Island was considered to be the longest, but in 1985 the U.S. Supreme Court, ruling in a boundary dispute case, determined that Long Island is actually a peninsula.

The western edge of the island is frequently buffeted by winds and heavy seas sweeping in from the strait. ❀ Boaters will find no protection along the long, smooth windward shoreline or in its few broad, open bays. Whidbey's leeward eastern shore is deeply indented by several snug coves, providing welcome protection in foul weather. Much of the island's population and its few small towns are concentrated along this east side.

The central section of Whidbey Island is markedly historic, with pioneer relics around nearly every bend of the road. Eight separate vicinities, commemorating more than one hundred years of rural settlement and coastal defense, are included in Ebey's Landing National Historical Reserve.

A second industry, the military, has also left its mark on the island. Admiralty Head was the site of Fort Casey, one of the World War I forts that guarded Puget Sound. Although the Army post at Fort Casey is closed and the site is currently a state park, the military influence is now felt in the

Opposite: *Libbey Beach County Park gives access to wild and wonderful beach walks along the west side of Whidbey Island.*

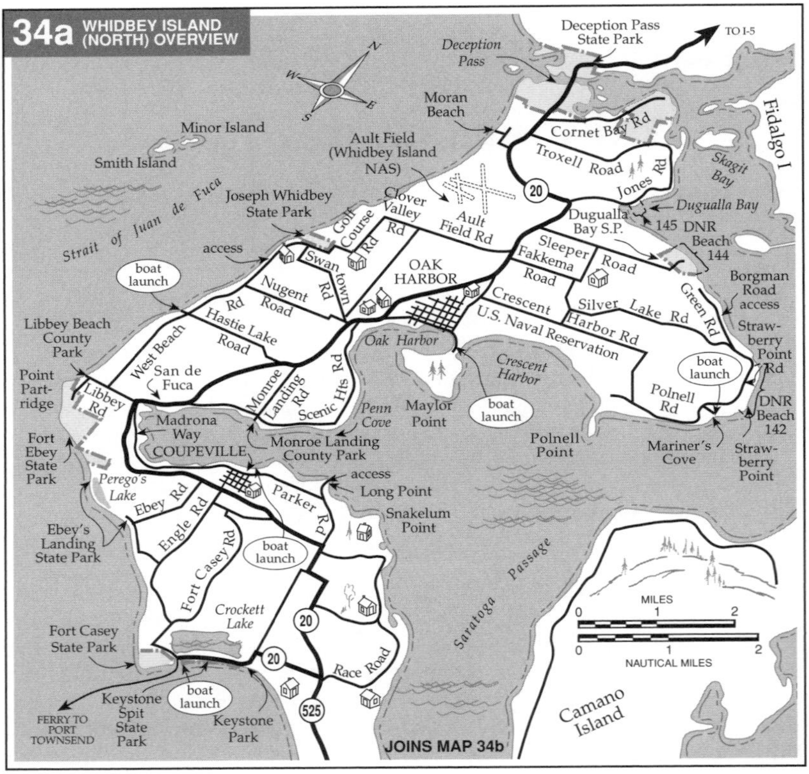
34a WHIDBEY ISLAND (NORTH) OVERVIEW
Deception Pass State Park
TO I-5
Deception Pass
Moran Beach
Fidalgo I
Minor Island
Smith Island
Ault Field (Whidbey Island NAS)
Cornet Bay Rd
Troxell Road
Jones Rd
Skagit Bay
Strait of Juan de Fuca
Joseph Whidbey State Park
Clover Valley Rd
Golf Course Rd
Ault Field Rd
Dugualla Bay
Dugualla Bay S.P.
145 DNR Beach 144
access
boat launch
Swantown Rd
OAK HARBOR
Sleeper Road
Fakkema Road
Borgman Road access
Nugent Road
Rd
Hastie Lake Road
Crescent Harbor Rd
Silver Lake Rd
Green Rd
Libbey Beach County Park
West Beach
U.S. Naval Reservation
Strawberry Point Rd
Oak Harbor
Crescent Harbor
boat launch
Point Partridge
San de Fuca
Libbey Rd
Monroe Landing Rd
Scenic Hts Rd
Penn Cove
Maylor Point
boat launch
Polnell Rd
DNR Beach 142
Madrona Way
COUPEVILLE
Monroe Landing County Park
Polnell Point
Mariner's Cove
Strawberry Point
Fort Ebey State Park
Perego's Lake
access
Long Point
Parker Rd
Ebey Rd
Engle Rd
Snakelum Point
Ebey's Landing State Park
boat launch
Fort Casey Rd
Saratoga Passage
Crockett Lake
20
MILES
0 1 2
0 1 2
NAUTICAL MILES
Fort Casey State Park
Race Road
Keystone Spit State Park
boat launch
Keystone Park
525
Camano Island
FERRY TO PORT TOWNSEND
JOINS MAP 34b

form of the huge U.S. Navy air base on the north end of the island. Military planes are so commonplace that a jet screaming overhead attracts less attention than the presence of a soaring bald eagle. Navy personnel, civilian employees, and their families account for nearly half of Whidbey Island's population.

STRAIT OF JUAN DE FUCA

Map 34a

Smith and Minor Islands • The extreme eastern end of the Strait of Juan de Fuca is marked by Smith and Minor Islands, the islands' navigational light serves as an important guide for boats traveling between Puget Sound and the San Juan Islands. The islands are not a place to visit, but certainly are of interest as you pass by.

The two islands lie 4 n.m. off the northwest shore of Whidbey Island. At low tide, Smith joins the much smaller Minor Island. ❄ West of Smith Island, a large kelp bed that extends for 1½ miles and a rock that bares at extreme low tides are boating hazards. Smith and Minor Islands are designated as a

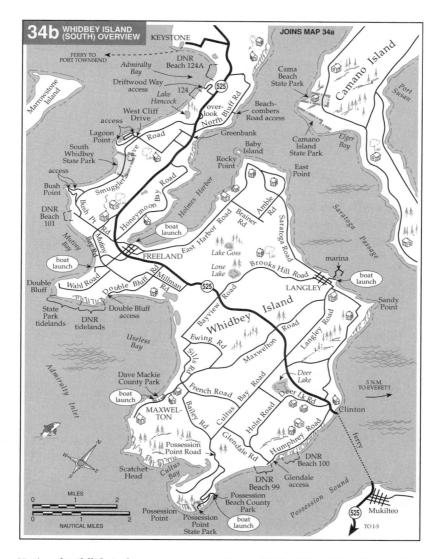

34b WHIDBEY ISLAND (SOUTH) OVERVIEW

National Wildlife Refuge to protect nesting seabirds. Minor Island is a major breeding site for harbor seals.

In the mid-1800s Smith Island, along with points on Cape Flattery, New Dungeness, and Admiralty Head, was noted as a critical navigational point and was selected as a site for a Coast Guard light. Construction on the Smith Island light began in 1857, and it was first lit in October 1858. The beacon was manned continuously until it was automated in 1976. Life on this remote rock was hardly exciting. Generally two men, with their families, were assigned to Smith Island. When not tending the light, they raised food in their garden or hunted the rabbits that overran the island (undoubtedly introduced to the island by an early lighthouse keeper). When seas were calm, they could row their small boat 8 miles to the closest civilization—Richardson, the tiny general store on the southern tip of Lopez Island. The "metropolis" of Port Townsend was 13 miles south.

Battering by wind and waves from the strait has caused extreme erosion of the islands—sometimes as much as 5 feet in a single year. In 1860, Smith Island was about 50 acres in size; today, it is less than 12. The light was originally on a frame building, but erosion endangered the old structure, necessitating relocation of the light to a tower farther inland. The buildings were so badly undercut by erosion they collapsed into the sea.

Joseph Whidbey State Park   Map 34a

Picnicking • Beachcombing • Birdwatching

Facilities: Picnic tables, fireplaces, picnic shelter, toilets, CMT campsite, no water

Area: 112 acres; 3100 feet of shoreline on the Strait of Juan de Fuca

🚗 *From the north:* From SR 20, 7 miles south of the Deception Pass Bridge, turn west on Ault Field Road, which becomes Clover Valley Road in another 2 1/4 miles. In 3/4 mile, the road heads south as Golf Course Road, which Ts into Crosby Road in 1 mile. Turn west on Crosby Road, which reaches the park in 1 1/4 miles. *From the south:* At the south side of Oak Harbor, turn northwest from SR 20 on Swantown Road, and reach the park in 3 miles.

Joseph Whidbey State Park has a wide beach for wading or sand digging, as well as driftwood to climb on.

🔽 The park is on the Strait of Juan de Fuca, 6¾ n.m. north of Point Partridge and 1 n.m. south of Rocky Point, just north of a string of beachfront homes. The nearest launch ramps are 4 n.m. north at Deception Pass State Park, or 6½ n.m. south at Hastie Lake Road, north of Point Partridge.

One of the most glorious beaches on Whidbey Island lies just south of the Naval Air Station. Here, land acquired from the Navy is a popular day-use park. Nice picnic sites are scattered throughout the park, some shaded by trees. The lower beachside area boasts a picnic shelter and grassy playfield as well. A CMT campsite is hidden in the brush at the northeast end of the playfield. Waves from the Strait of Juan de Fuca toss silvered driftwood onto the long sandy beach. Smith and Minor Islands can be seen directly offshore, 4 miles away.

Trails through the beach grass just above the driftwood line follow the beach north out of the park property and continue for more than a mile to the Navy's Rocky Point Picnic Area. Just before leaving the park, the beach-side trail passes an inland marsh area—an excellent spot for birdwatching. Waterfront homes of Swantown delineate the southern end of the park. A less-obvious access to the park is on the south, immediately next to the first residence. Here is a graveled parking space for a few cars and a trail that leads directly to the beach.

Point Partridge Launch Ramp (Island County) Map 34a
Boating • Paddling

Facilities: Launch ramp

🚗 From SR 20 6 miles north of Coupeville or 3 miles south of Oak Harbor, turn west on Hastie Lake Road. At the intersection of West Beach Road and Hastie Lake Road is a parking lot and launch ramp between private homes.

🔽 The ramp lies 2½ n.m. north of the Point Partridge light.

A 1-lane paved launch ramp near the south end of the parking lot off West Beach Road leads to a cobble and boulder beach. The paved lot has space for a half dozen boats with trailers. Launch ramps have a hard life on this side of the island. Putting in at this one can be difficult, as sand, logs, or debris might choke the access. Winds off the strait frequently cause additional problems, and launching large or heavy boats in the incoming wave surges is a problem.

A park bench at the head of the launch ramp offers grand vistas of pleasure boats at play in the Strait of Juan de Fuca.

Libbey Beach County Park (Island County) Map 34a
Beachcombing • Picnicking • Paddling

Facilities: Picnic tables, fireplaces, picnic shelter, toilets, no water
Area: 3 acres; 300 feet of shoreline on the Strait of Juan de Fuca

From SR 20 3 miles north of Coupeville or 6 miles south of Oak Harbor, turn west on Libbey Road, and reach the park at road end in 1½ miles.

The park is ½ mile north of Point Partridge. It is suitable only for paddlecraft launching or landing.

A very small day-use county park just north of Point Partridge gives access to some wild and wonderful beach walks below the steep, eroded cliffs on the west side of the island. Picnic tables in a grassy pocket away from the beach are well protected from wind, but do not provide a view of the water; a picnic table near the beach bulkhead has better views.

An opening between a pair of overlapping, 10-foot-high, log-pile bulkheads permits access to the beach. Beach walks south around the point lead to connecting trails from Fort Ebey State Park, ½ mile away. To the north lie 6 magnificent miles of public tidelands beneath sandy bluffs that soar to a height of 200 feet. Use care not to become trapped by incoming tides.

Fort Ebey State Park   Map 35

Historical display • Camping • Picnicking • Bicycling • Hiking • Beachcombing • Surfboarding • Paragliding • Parafoiling • Glider flying • Viewpoints • Fishing (freshwater and saltwater)

Facilities: 4 RV sites (EW), 46 standard campsites, CMT campsite, 3 primitive bicycle sites, group camp (50 persons), picnic tables, fireplaces, picnic shelter, restrooms, showers, 3 miles of hiking/biking trails, abandoned coast artillery fortification
Area: 644 acres; 8000 feet of saltwater shoreline on Admiralty Inlet; 1000 feet of freshwater shoreline on Lake Pondilla

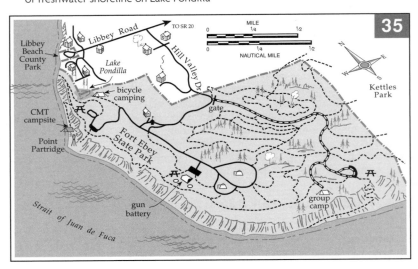

The 250-foot-high bluff between Fort Ebey State Park and Ebey's Landing is a spectacular example of glacier-deposited till.

From SR 20 3 miles north of Coupeville or 6 miles south of Oak Harbor, turn west on Libbey Road, and in 1 mile, turn south on Hill Valley Drive to reach the park in 1/2 mile.

As you stand on the heights above the Strait of Juan de Fuca you'll find it easy to see why the Army chose this site for a fort to protect the inland waters. From here, there is a vast panorama out to Point Wilson and Port Townsend, south down Admiralty Inlet, and north to Vancouver Island and the San Juans. This park does not have as fine a display of old military equipment as does Fort Casey to the south, but there is enough to keep inquisitive youngsters busy for a day, and the campground is much nicer.

Near the contact station, the road splits at a T intersection. Picnicking is to the north; car camping is to the south. By following the road north you reach trails, a picnic shelter, and picnic tables. A short trail from the north parking lot goes to Lake Pondilla, which has a bicycle camping area on its shores. Drinking water is available at the south end of the lake, but campers must hike the short distance back up the hill to use the restrooms. Bass fishing is rumored to be good in the 3.5-acre pond. A fishing license is required.

An extensive hiker/biker trail system laces the woods between the group camp road and the campground road. Trails follow the top of the steep bluff; a few drop down to the beach. A map is available at the park office, and trails are identified where they cross park roads. Several of the trails tie into an even more elaborate Island County trail system at Kettles Park, adjacent

Pink rhododendron blossoms brighten Fort Ebey State Park in the spring.

to the east. The wide, bay-head beach north of Point Partridge, reached by trail from the north parking lot, holds a layer of silvered driftwood above its gently sloping sand. A CMT campsite is in the brush near Point Partridge.

This coast artillery fort was established in 1942, a world war later than Fort Casey. Fort Ebey was manned during World War II but was surplused soon after its end. The pair of armored 6-inch rapid-fire guns placed here were designed as backup for the large guns on the emplacements built farther out on the Strait of Juan de Fuca at Point Flattery, Point Angeles, and Striped Peak west of Port Angeles.

No guns remain here, but youngsters delight in prowling through the old battery shell rooms, spotting room, plotting room, and switchboard room, or climbing a metal ladder down a concrete shaft to a fire-control center located lower on the bluff, overlooking the strait. From the fire-control center, observers directed the fire of the two 6-inch guns located in the battery. Picnic sites on the grassy bluff just north of the battery have excellent views across Admiralty Inlet to the snow-clad peaks of the Olympic Range.

Campsites with picnic tables and fireplaces are along two forested loops at the end of the road. Four have RV power and water hookups. Rhododendron bushes scattered throughout the timber promise a blaze of beauty in the spring.

A gated road heading south near the state park entrance ends at a former DNR Recreation Site that has been incorporated into the state park. A spur road near road end leads up to the park's group camp area. Here, a wide grass field spreads atop the 250-foot-high bluff. Amenities are only toilets, a picnic shelter, and campsites, but the view is unparalleled. At road's end, a trail leads steeply downhill past picnic tables, each on its own terraced platform, giving picnickers "balcony views." The trail breaks out onto a windswept slope 150 feet above the water. Wide views encompass Perego's Lake, a saltwater lagoon at the end of a sweeping crescent of beach. Across Admiralty Inlet are Marrowstone Island and Port Townsend, and north of it Protection Island and Discovery Bay. The trail continues diagonally down the soft glacial-till bluff to the beach, which can be walked south all the way to Ebey's Landing State Park.

SKAGIT BAY AND NORTH SARATOGA PASSAGE
Map 34a

Dugualla Bay State Park (undeveloped) and DNR Beaches   Map 34a
Hiking • Nature Study • Beach Walking

Area: 586 acres; 6865 feet of saltwater shoreline on Skagit Bay

🚗 *State Park and Beach 144:* Take SR 20 5¼ miles south from Deception Pass State Park. Turn east on Sleeper Road and follow it to its end at the park gate in 2½ miles. *Beach 145:* About 3¾ miles south of Deception Pass State Park, turn east off SR 20 on Jones Road. In 1 mile, head south on Dike Road to reach the dike at the head of the bay in 200 yards.

🛥 The property lies southeast of Dugualla Bay on Skagit Bay, just southwest of Goat Island. The shallow beach can only be approached by shallow-draft beachable boats or paddlecraft. The nearest launch ramp is at Cornet Bay in Deception Pass State Park, 6 n.m. northwest.

An undeveloped section of park property faces on Dugualla Bay. It has a few deteriorating old logging roads that penetrate dense second-growth forest to the east of the entrance gate; one ends in a crude, steep trail down to the beach on Skagit Bay. To reach the beach trail, when the road splits about 700 feet from the park gate, follow the southwest branch for ¼ mile to a Y. Head east, avoiding obscure spurs, for another ½ mile to the beach trailhead. The slick, muddy trail starts steep and gets steeper before it switchbacks down to the beach in ½ mile. The shore, which is designated as DNR Beach 144, is an unappealing 500-foot-wide mudflat at low tide, and virtually nonexistent at high tide. Someday the upland portion of the property could become a magnificent campground.

DNR Beach 142 • Two more sections of DNR public tidelands lie along the northeast shore of Whidbey Island. The first, Beach 142, at the tip of Strawberry Point is a 4800-foot strip of tidelands accessible only by boat. There is good clamming here during low tides, and good beach walking beneath towering bluffs when tides permit.

DNR Beach 145 • Near the head of Dugualla Bay, along its north shore, is an 800-foot-wide chunk of rocky tideflat below steep, wooded headlands. Although the uplands are private, the beach is easily reached from the dike at the end of the bay. For beachgoers, the beach itself has little appeal, and the shore east of the dike dries to a ¼-mile-long mudflat at low tides. Birds, however, love it. Birdwatchers will spot herons, shorebirds, and wintering waterfowl. Hedgerows and brush along the dike harbor a variety of passerines.

Strawberry Point Boat Launch (Island County) Map 34a

Boating • Paddling

From Oak Harbor, head north out of town on the road that follows the boundary of the Navy base, SE Regatta Drive. Turn east on Crescent Harbor Road, following the road along the north edge of the reservation. Follow the road as it becomes first Reservation Road and then Polnell Road. In 7 miles, at a T intersection, turn right (east) into the Mariner's Beach subdivision on Mariner's Beach Drive. Follow the road downhill for ½ mile to a small parking area above a 1-lane paved launch ramp.

The ramp is 6 n.m. east of Oak Harbor and 2 n.m. northwest of Utsalady Point on Camano Island

An obscure, unmarked, but nevertheless public boat ramp on Strawberry Point gives access to Skagit Bay and several nice DNR beaches. The ramp is sandwiched between two private homes, and parking in the vicinity is minimal. All surrounding property, as well as the dredged lagoon housing a small yacht club, is private. Boaters can explore the shoreline north along Strawberry Point and on to Dugualla Bay.

Oak Harbor Map 36

Shopping • Picnicking • Beach walking • Boating • Paddling

Facilities: *Oak Harbor:* Restaurants, lodging, stores. *Marina:* Guest moorage with power, water, wireless broadband, 4-lane launch ramp with boarding float, boat launch hoist, gas and diesel, marine repairs and chandlery, boat pumpout station, restrooms, showers, laundry, ice, picnic tables, children's play equipment

From the Clinton ferry terminal: Drive north for 26 miles on SR 525, which becomes SR 20 midisland. *From the north:* Follow SR 20 over the Deception Pass Bridge and continue south for 9½ miles. To reach the marina, from the corner in downtown Oak Harbor where SR 20 turns northwest, head east on SE Pioneer Way and arrive at the marina in 1¼ miles.

Oak Harbor lies on Saratoga Passage near the north end of Whidbey Island, 23 n.m. from Port Gardner in Everett and 18 miles from Deception Pass. To reach the marina, closely follow the channel, marked by day marks and buoys, as it bends northwest and then north at the entrance to Oak Harbor. The marina is at the far north end of the channel. ☸ Markers on the dogleg channel leading into the marina should be followed scrupulously; shoals lie immediately outside the dredged channel, and several rocks lurk just off the end of the point.

Whidbey Island's largest town, Oak Harbor, strongly feels the effects of the nearby naval air base. Instead of cluttering the waterfront with high-priced restaurants and privileged businesses, Oak Harbor has devoted most of its shoreline to parks, ranging from the tidy little picnic area overlooking the marina to the multiuse City Beach Park on the west end of the shore. For visitors approaching by water, the city is nicely wrapped in green.

The town does not have the "quaint" aura that Langley and Coupeville have—most of the stores are modern, and the main highway is lined with fast-food restaurants, car dealerships, and service stations. Despite the occasional jet streaking overhead, life here is still relatively sedate, with both townsfolk and tourists on hand to take part in its "Holland Happening" festival the last week of April and its "Old Fashioned Fourth of July."

Oak Harbor has a distinctive Dutch flavor, with Dutch names on some streets and businesses. Back in 1894, a land company made a concerted effort to attract Dutch settlers to the island, touting the rich farmland and temperate climate, quite similar to their homeland. More than 200 Hollanders came to Whidbey Island; most settled on the northern end. Their farming skills turned much of the rich soil, and even some of the poorer, into productive farmland.

Oak Harbor Marina • Oak Harbor's city-operated marina ranks with the best to be found anywhere on Washington's inland waters. The harbor itself is a 1½-mile-long curving arm tucked behind Maylor Point. Moorage for about 115 visiting boats is in slips behind the breakwater, or along the outside of the main float leading to shore. Some permanent slips might be available when owner vessels are out; check with the marina office. Part of the breakwater's wave-canceling design includes a series of 18-foot-square concrete floats on the outboard side of the walkway. For the slips behind it, these make an excellent "front porch" for picnicking or sunbathing.

✵ When approaching the moorage areas on the north side of the marina, beginning at the entrance light, stay close to the breakwater and inside the shoal water markers; this dredged channel is the only safe route. A key

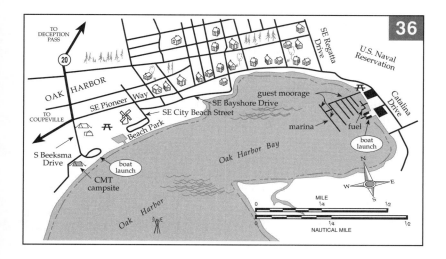

The marina operated by the Port of Oak Harbor is one of the best on the sound.

card, obtained at the marina office, is needed to open the main gate and restroom doors after hours.

The boat launching area is immediately to the south. Here, a former Navy seaplane ramp has been converted into a 4-lane ramp, with an adjoining float for loading. A sling hoist is at the head of the fuel dock.

The marina is about ½ mile from downtown stores—an easy walk, but taxi service is available. The town offers a full range of services and boating supplies.

Oak Harbor City Parks Map 36

Camping • Fishing • Paddling • Swimming • Field sports • Beach walking

Facilities: 56 RV sites, 26 tent sites, CMT campsite, picnic tables, fireplaces, kitchen shelters, restrooms, showers, RV pumpout station, sports fields, children's play equipment, wading pool, swimming beach (saltwater lagoon), launch ramp
Area: 28.5 acres; 2100 feet of shoreline on Oak Harbor

🚐 Follow SR 20 into downtown Oak Harbor. Where it makes a sharp turn northwest, either head south on S Beeksma Drive to reach the camping area, or head east on SE Pioneer Way to SE City Beach Street, which leads south to the park.

⛵ The park is 1 n.m. southwest of the Oak Harbor marina. ❊ Because the offshore water is very shoal, only shallow-draft craft should approach by water.

On the south side of the city, the shore is devoted to City Beach, a large, multiuse park with two entrances; the entrance at the east end of SE City Beach Street leads to the day-use area; a second road farther west, S Beeksma Drive, goes to the RV campground. A 1-lane paved launch ramp is on a loop at the end of the latter road, just past the campground. Because the park faces on a long tideflat, the ramp is best suited for hand-carried boats; it might not be usable for launching from vehicles during moderate to low tides. A CMT campsite sits at the extreme west end of the beach, behind a low dirt berm.

The park's centerpiece, a full-size replica of a windmill, pays homage to the city's Dutch heritage. Near it are a saltwater lagoon swimming beach, wading pool, and play paraphernalia. Views from the park are down the length of Saratoga Passage.

A second city park, Flintstone Park, is east of City Beach at the end of Southeast Bayshore Drive, which parallels the shore. The small waterfront site holds tables and grass for spreading out picnic goodies. Another very nice little park, this one next to the marina, has picnic tables, a barbecue pit, volleyball courts, and a view of downtown Oak Harbor—very pretty at night. It is popular with marina visitors.

PENN COVE

Map 37

The east shore of Whidbey Island bends around two major bays: Holmes Harbor on the south and Penn Cove on the north. Penn Cove runs westerly from Saratoga Passage for 3½ miles. A ½-mile-long sandspit extends north from Snakelum Point, the southernmost point at the entrance to the cove. ☸Boaters entering the bay from the south should stay well outside the buoy marking the end of the spit.

Mussel-raising farms are a recent commercial venture on Penn Cove. Seed mussels are attached to ropes suspended from floats or rafts, where they

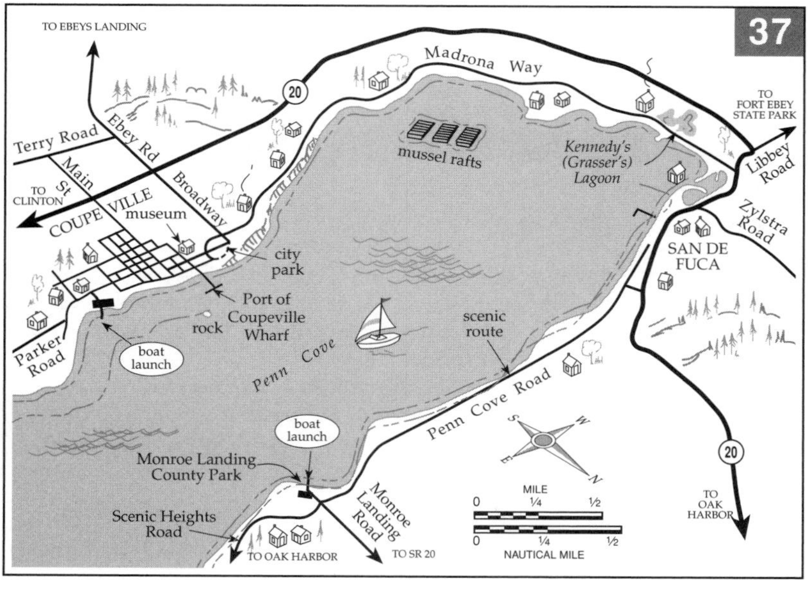

If You Dig It, Will They Come?

At the turn of the nineteenth century, a syndicate had plans to dig canals through Whidbey Island at points where the land was constricted to a mere mile in width. One canal would have gone from Penn Cove through to West Beach, in the vicinity of Libbey Road. The second canal would have been built from the northeast shore of Holmes Harbor through to Lake Hancock. It was reasoned that shipping traffic would take advantage of the canals as a short-cut between the Strait of Juan de Fuca and the growing port of Everett. The passages, of course, were never dug, and one can only imagine what Whidbey Island would be today if they had come into being.

grow in the nutrient-filled water. After two years, the bivalves are harvested and shipped to restaurants and lucky gourmets throughout the United States. Most of the floats lie along the side of the cove, between Coupeville and the head of the bay, and do not present a navigational hazard.

A scenic drive or bicycle route follows the shoreline of Penn Cove, with views of the cove, Saratoga Passage, and Skagit Bay. Follow the shore south out of Oak Harbor on Scenic Heights Road. About ¾ mile south of Oak Harbor, a portion of Scenic Heights Road along the bluff has slipped away, necessitating an inland detour via Balda and Miller Roads before Scenic Heights can be rejoined. At the junction with Monroe Landing Road, Scenic Heights Road becomes Penn Cove Road. At San de Fuca, turn right (north) on Holbrook Road to reach SR 20. Follow SR 20 southwest for ½ mile, and turn left on Madrona Way and follow it for about 11 miles into Coupeville.

Monroe Landing County Park (Island County) Map 37
Boating • Beachcombing • Historical site

Facilities: 1-lane launch ramp, interpretive displays, no water
Area: 0.5 acre

From SR 20, 1¼ miles west of Oak Harbor, turn south on Monroe Landing Road, and in 1¾ miles reach the Penn Cove Road intersection and the park. A parking area is next to the launch ramp; a large gravel lot for boat trailers is on the opposite side of Penn Cove Road

Monroe Landing Park is on the north side of Penn Cove, due north of Coupeville, and at the west end of an obvious high bluff above the cove. The nearest mainland launch ramps are at Utsalady on Camano Island, 9 n.m. northeast, and Everett, 26 n.m. southeast.

The beach at Monroe Landing holds a pretty assortment of sand-edged driftwood and beach grass, nice enough for a pause from bicycling, driving, or paddling. It is one of eight sites included in Ebey's Landing National

Historical Reserve. Ship's Master Joseph Whidbey found a large village of Indians here in 1792, while he was conducting explorations for George Vancouver. The park's interpretive displays tell of the Skwdab subgroup of the Skagit tribe, which had numerous villages around Penn Cove, Oak Harbor, Dugualla Bay, and the lower Skagit River. A potlatch house stood here until about 1910. Indian canoe races and athletic competitions took place on Penn Cove each summer through the 1930s.

Coupeville   Map 37

Boating • Kayaking • Picnicking • Fishing • Shopping • Beach walking • Museum

Facilities: *Coupeville:* Restaurants, shopping, lodging, museum. *Wharf:* Guest moorage *(no power or water)*, 4 mooring buoys, gas, diesel, deli, shops, marine supply, kayak rentals, restrooms with showers. *Captain Thomas Coupe Park:* Launch ramp, picnic tables, RV pumpout station, restrooms. *City Park:* Picnic tables, picnic shelter, restrooms, children's play equipment, tennis courts, bandstand. *Museum:* Restrooms, gift shop

🚐 Turn off SR 20 at the intersection signed to Coupeville and follow the road ½ mile into town. It also can be reached from the north via the scenic route from Oak Harbor (see Penn Cove, described previously). *Museum:* On Alexander Street between Front Street and 9th, immediately uphill from the Port of Coupeville wharf.

🛥 Coupeville is off Saratoga Passage, 23 n.m. from Port Gardner in Everett and 18 n.m. from Deception Pass.

Coupeville is, in many ways, the essence of Whidbey Island—at times salty, at times rural, and always conscious of its pioneer heritage. This earliest town on the island is one of the sites in Ebey's Landing National Historical Reserve. Signs on a number of homes tell the dates they were built and the names of their original owners. The residence of Thomas Coupe, the sea captain who founded the town, dates back to 1852.

All of the interesting old storefront buildings are along NE Front Street. Many of these stores now house antique shops, arts and crafts galleries, and other businesses catering to tourists. A guide for a historical walking tour of the town is available at the Island County Historical Society Museum (see below). During the summer, the museum conducts guided tours past these historic houses and businesses.

Port of Coupeville Wharf • The focal point of Coupeville is the long Port of Coupeville wharf that stretches into Penn Cove. Overnight moorage is available on a float off the head of the wharf; gas and diesel are available at the red, barnlike building on the end of the wharf. Mooring buoys are northwest of the fuel dock.

�֎ There is only 5 to 9 feet of water under the float at a zero tide, so deep-draft boats are advised to anchor out. Boaters should be wary of a large submerged rock that lies 300 yards northeast of the wharf.

The Coupeville Wharf is a Penn Cove landmark.

Island County Historical Society Museum • The historical museum in Coupeville is well worth a visit for its insights into Whidbey Island life from early Native American times through pioneer days. The beautifully carved wooden doors at the entry hint at the treasure trove the building holds. Fascinating, well-presented displays tell of such things as the ships and sea captains that sailed out of Whidbey Island ports and show models of early day vessels that plied north Puget Sound. Rooms and nooks are outfitted as a late-1800s schoolroom, a pioneer cabin, and a shipping office on the Coupeville Wharf. Displays change regularly.

The museum also houses a collection of historic artifacts and a reference library for researchers of local history. Adjacent to the museum is Alexander's Blockhouse, which was built to protect Penn Cove residents during the 1855–1856 Indian Wars, but was never used. Summer museum hours are Wednesday through Monday from 10:00 A.M. to 5:00 P.M.; winter hours are Friday through Monday from 11:00 A.M. to 5:00 P.M.

Captain Thomas Coupe Park and Coupeville City Park • A public launch ramp is in the small Captain Thomas Coupe Park on the east side of town at the corner of NE 9th and N Otis Street. The 1-lane paved launch ramp is somewhat the worse for the wear but still usable with caution. The large parking lot has space for a number of cars with trailers. Picnic tables and restrooms are nearby. At the entrance to the parking lot is an RV pumpout station.

After exploring the town, take time for a picnic in the city park sitting on a high grassy bluff immediately west of the Port of Coupeville wharf. The park has wide views out over Penn Cove. There is no access to the shore down the steep embankment; walk a barricaded road down the hill for beach access near the wharf.

ADMIRALTY INLET
Map 34a

Ebey's Landing National Historical Reserve

Colonel Isaac Ebey certainly did not intend to make history in quite the way he did—by being decapitated by some surly Canadian Indians. Ebey was already assured a place in Washington history as the first permanent settler on Whidbey Island and as a political leader. As it was, this very leadership quality brought him to the attention of the Indians who, in August 1857, were looking for some kind of white "chief" on whom they could avenge the untimely demise of one of their chiefs a year earlier near Port Gamble.

The beach section of the late Colonel Ebey's homestead is now a state park; the upland portion of the farm, as well as the cemetery where he is buried, are a part of Ebey's Landing National Historical Reserve, a unique unit of the National Park Service. The purpose of Ebey's Landing National Historical Reserve is to "preserve and protect a rural community that provides an unbroken historic record from the nineteenth-century exploration and settlement in Puget Sound to the present time." The historical reserve is comprised of 17,400 acres on central Whidbey Island, about 90 percent of which is privately owned. Included are the town of Coupeville; Fort Casey, Ebey's Landing, and Fort Ebey State Parks; the state DNR's Rhododendron Park; Sunnyside Cemetery; Ebey's Prairie; Grasser's Hill and Lagoon (in the

The beachwalk at Ebey's Landing is one of the grandest walks on Puget Sound.

San de Fuca vicinity); Monroe Landing; Smith Prairie (south of Snakelum Point); and Crockett and Perego's Lakes. Three blockhouses dating from the 1850s, as well as dozens of other structures that are related to the history of central Whidbey Island, lie within the reserve.

Ebey's Landing State Park   Map 38

Historical displays • Hiking • Birdwatching • Beach walking • Paddling • Surf fishing • Glider flying

Facilities: Hiking trails, toilets, no water

Area: 45.8 acres; 6120 feet of shoreline on the Strait of Juan de Fuca

Park: From SR 20 on Whidbey Island, turn south on Ebey Road, 1/4 mile west of Coupeville. The park is reached in 1 3/4 miles. *Cemetery:* Turn northwest off Ebey Road on Cook Road and proceed 1/2 mile to the intersection of Cook, Cemetery, and Sherman Roads, and turn southwest on Cemetery Road.

Accessible only by paddlecraft or boats that can be beached, the park is on the west shore of Whidbey Island, midway between Admiralty Head and Point Partridge. Hand-carried craft can be launched from the beach.

Ebey Road travels through the finest farmland on all of Whidbey Island—a green and gold prairie that has seen human habitation for some 12,000 years. The National Park Service owns property at Ebey's Prairie, but it is leased for agriculture, assuring that its traditional use will remain unchanged.

A kiosk at the state park holds historical displays and information panels. A trail gradually ascends the 200-foot wind-blown Perego's Bluff, with glorious views out over Admiralty Inlet and down to the tawny beach below. It then descends to the north end of Perego's Lake, a brackish saltwater lagoon named for an eccentric recluse who once lived on the bluff above. From here, continue on by trail to Point Partridge or walk the beach back to the parking lot. The trip around the end of the lagoon and back is about 3 1/2 miles.

Sunnyside Cemetery, which lies on a slight hill on the northwest side of the prairie, offers a panoramic view of the plain. For headstone history, stroll

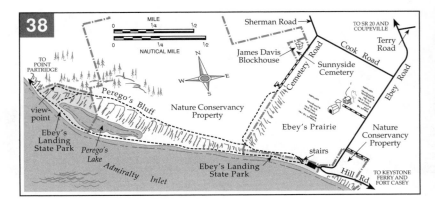

The historic James Davis Blockhouse is at Sunnyside Cemetery.

through the cemetery. Colonel Ebey is buried here, as well as a number of early pioneers. The James Davis Blockhouse, dating from the 1855 Indian uprising, is also seen here.

The Ebey's Prairie Trail to the state park starts from the west end of Cemetery Road at an overlook. Three display panels found here describe geological history of the prairie and cultivation of the central Whidbey prairies by Indians, and later farming by settlers. Near the edge of the bluff, the trail intersects the trail rising from the state park. Watch for hawks and eagles soaring above. Sights and sounds fill the senses: peaks of the Olympic Range piercing the horizon, the ghostly white cone of Mount Baker at your back, the muted booming of waves breaking on the long curve of beach.

Fort Casey State Park Map 39

Historical displays • Camping • Picnicking • Scuba diving • Hiking • Beach walking • Clamming • Fishing • Boating • Interpretive center

Facilities: 35 standard campsites, hiker/biker sites in the picnic area, picnic tables, fire grates, restrooms, showers, lighthouse, interpretive center, gift shop, hiking trails, interpretive signs, 2-lane launch ramp with boarding floats, underwater park
Area: 142.07 acres; 8305 feet of shoreline on Admiralty Inlet

🚙 *From the north:* From SR 20 on Whidbey Island, turn south on Engle Road at Coupeville and reach the park in 3¼ miles. *From the south:* 6 miles south of Coupeville, where the main north/south road changes from SR 20 to SR 525, follow SR 20 west and reach the park in 3½ miles.

The launch ramp is on the east side of Keystone Harbor (the ferry landing) on the north side of Admiralty Bay. Port Townsend is 4 n.m. southwest.

The kids will have so much fun they will never suspect they are getting a history lesson! Here are dozens of darkened corridors to explore and masses of concrete parapets to scramble over. Do not miss the searchlight emplacements below the rim of the bluff and the switchboard building to the east that controlled electrical power to the emplacements; take along a flashlight and use care exploring. Do not allow youngsters to become rowdy, and keep a tight hand on the younger ones. Falls from the bunkers and bluffs have caused serious injuries and even fatalities.

After curiosity with the Army fort is satisfied, there are still a beach and several miles of trails to wander. Footpaths lace the bluff below and around the gun batteries. Reach the shore from the campground or from the northernmost battery; this can be the start for a 5-mile beach walk beneath the wildest bluffs on the island, all the way north to Point Partridge. Keep an eye on incoming tide.

The picnic area and overnight hiker/biker camping are in trees on the hillside above the emplacements. The old barracks, passed on the way into the park, are now a part of a Seattle Pacific University facility used to house educational group camps. On the east side of the park, below the bluff, is the overnight camping area. The campsites lie in rather cramped quarters on a beach formed by material dredged from the Keystone channel. Due to

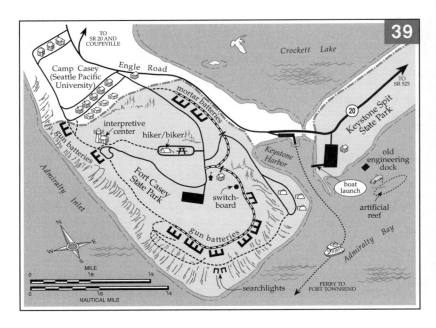

This 10-inch disappearing carriage gun at Battery Worth is similar to those used at the fort during World War I. It was brought to the park from the Philippines.

the popularity of the park, the thirty-five sites are usually claimed by mid-day in the summer. Reservations are not accepted. A trail leads from the end of the campground up the bluff to the emplacements, or the road can be walked to the upper portion of the park.

On the east shore of Keystone Harbor, behind a pile breakwater, are the two paved ramps of the state park boat launch, framed by boarding floats. This is one of the best launch ramps on the island, with a good drop-off and excellent protection by breakwater and rock jetty. ❋ Launching can be difficult during the comings and goings of the Keystone–Port Townsend ferry.

Keystone Spit   Map 34a and 39
*Picnicking • Beach walking • Birdwatching • Surf fishing • Kite flying •
Windsurfing • Scuba diving • Interpretation*

Facilities: *Keystone Spit State Park:* Interpretive displays. *Keystone Park:* Picnic tables, fire braziers

Area: *Keystone Spit State Park:* 279.8 acres; 7330 feet of saltwater shoreline on Admiralty Bay, 7000 feet of freshwater shoreline on Crockett Lake. *Keystone Park:* 0.2 acre; 500 feet of saltwater shoreline on Admiralty Inlet

🚗 *Keystone Spit State Park:* See directions to Fort Casey State Park, described previously. Keystone Spit is immediately east of Fort Casey. SR 20 runs the length of the spit, between the beach and Crockett Lake. A couple of small parking areas along the south side of this road are public accesses. *Keystone Park:* As SR 20

Guns Along the Inlet

Fortification was not the initial government use of Admiralty Head. A lighthouse reservation was acquired here in 1858, and the first light, which stood west of the present emplacements, was shown in 1861. When Admiralty Head was chosen as one of three sites for primary defense of Puget Sound, the lighthouse was moved to its present position. In the 1920s, the light was determined to be obsolete and the beacon was removed in 1927. During World War II, the lighthouse building was used as a training center and kennel for the dogs of the military K-9 Corps. It was finally refurbished and converted to an interpretive center when the fort became a state park.

The first gun emplacements at Fort Casey were completed in 1899, and by 1907 the fort complement included ten batteries with nineteen guns ranging in size from 3-inch to 10-inch, sixteen 12-inch mortars, and a garrison of more than two hundred men. The most lethal of the armaments were the seven 10-inch guns mounted on disappearing carriages that withdrew behind a thick protective wall after each round was fired. The batteries at Fort Casey, along with those at Fort Worden near Port Townsend and Fort Flagler on Marrowstone Island, formed a "Triangle of Fire" designed to guard Puget Sound and the vital Navy shipyards at Bremerton.

In 1917, when the United States entered World War I, the fort was placed on twenty-four-hour alert and activities were expanded to provide training for harbor defense companies headed for Europe. At the end of the war, the fort was placed on caretaker status and then used as a training center by the National Guard, Reserve Officers Training Corps, and Citizen's Military Training Corps. Some of the guns had been removed during the war for use on the European front, and by 1933 all the remaining original armaments had been taken away to be melted down. However, a few new anti-aircraft batteries were placed in recognition of that new style of warfare. With the outbreak of World War II the fort again served as a training site, and for five years after the war was a satellite camp for engineering troops stationed at Fort Worden. The property was eventually surplused, and in 1956 was acquired by Washington State Parks.

Fort Casey's emplacements, which are the best preserved in the state, include four guns in place; the two 3-inch rapid-fire and two 10-inch disappearing carriage guns were procured from Fort Wint in the Philippines in 1968 for display here. Several information boards explain the history of coastal fortification. The interpretive center in the lighthouse exhibits some of the ammunition used in the guns and other informative displays. Stairs inside the lighthouse tower can be climbed for views of the huge water highway that the fort guarded. The interpretive center is open daily from 11:00 A.M. to 5:00 P.M., from April through October, and other times by appointment.

bends north at the east end of Keystone Spit State Park, continue straight ahead on Keystone Avenue to reach the park in a few hundred feet.

🛶 See directions to Fort Casey State Park, described previously. Only beachable boats can access the spit itself.

Keystone Spit, just east of Fort Casey, has several recreational attractions, as well as being the terminal for the Port Townsend ferry and holding the launch ramp for Fort Casey State Park. Crockett Lake, the 250-acre marsh formed by the sandbar at Keystone, is a prime birdwatching area, especially during migratory season. Look for hawks and passerines around the edges of the lake, and herons and transient waterfowl in the water. The saltwater side of the sandbar is good for birdwatching too, as well as beachcombing.

Keystone Spit State Park (Undeveloped) ● The two shores, one freshwater and one saltwater, are open for day use. But the state park's offerings do not end at the waterline. Keystone's rock jetty and piles of the old Army engineering dock immediately to the east are designated as an underwater park. This marine habitat is the most popular diving spot on Whidbey Island for both snorkeling and scuba diving. Beneath the surface is a kaleidoscope of sea life—lacy white sea anemones, brilliant purple plume worms, swarms of kelp greenlings, shy octopus hiding in dark niches, rockfish, and large lingcod. Because this is a protected sanctuary, many of the fish are quite tame and can easily be approached.

A small ferry runs between Keystone and Port Townsend.

Keystone Park (Island County) • This small, austere park lying off SR 20 just east of Keystone Spit State Park offers a pair of picnic tables and a fire brazier overlooking Admiralty Bay. Stop for a snack, let sea breezes ruffle your hair, and watch offshore for maritime traffic.

DNR Beaches 124A and 124 • Two public DNR beaches stretch beneath steep cliffs on Admiralty Bay south of Keystone. Beach 124A is a 4200-foot strip south of the Admiral's Cove subdivision. Beach 124, which is 2400 feet long, lies a mile farther south. Neither have land access—they must be reached by boat. The public beach is below the mean high water level.

South Whidbey State Park Map 40

Camping • Picnicking • Fishing • Clamming • Beach walking • Hiking • Crabbing • Birdwatching

Facilities: 9 RV sites (EW), 37 standard campsites, 6 primitive sites, group camp, picnic tables, fireplaces, picnic shelter, restrooms, showers, RV pumpout station, amphitheater, nature trail, hiking trails

Area: 374.08 acres; 4500 feet of shoreline on Admiralty Inlet

🚗 From the ferry landing at Clinton on Whidbey Island, take SR 525 northwest for 9 miles. Turn west on Bush Point Road, which in about 3 miles becomes Smugglers Cove Road. Continue north for another 1½ miles to the park entrance.

🛶 The park is accessible only by paddlecraft or beachable boats. The beach is midway between Lagoon and Bush Points. The launch ramp at Keystone Spit is 5 n.m. north.

Here are both greenly forested uplands and open, wave-washed beach in what is probably the prettiest park on all of Whidbey Island. The forest is wonderful old Douglas-fir and massive western red cedar, with a thick

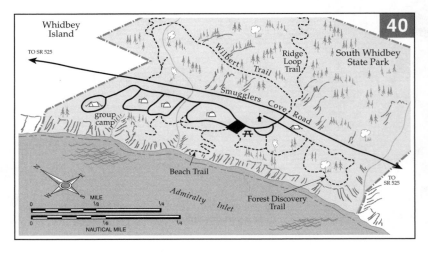

Sunshine and sand are popular attractions at South Whidbey State Park.

understory. Trails are edged by ferns, red elderberry, salmonberry, and a goodly amount of stinging nettles (don't stray off the trail!). The shore is gently sloping sand, giving way to cobbles and rocks at the low-tide level. At high tide, the strip of exposed beach is quite narrow. A northerly breeze sweeping down from the Strait of Juan de Fuca cools the shoreline much of the time, so swimming is usually chilly, even in warm weather.

Trails lead from the campground and parking area down the high bank to the beach. Another trail loops through the dense forest in the southern section of the park. A 255-acre section of the park, lying on the east side of Smugglers Cove Road, includes a stand of old-growth forest, with some giant Douglas-firs and red cedars more than 250 years old. A pair of trails through this magnificent forest start immediately across the road from the park entrance and return to the road near the group camp area. The Wilbert Trail is the lower section with the least elevation gain, while the steeper Ridge Loop Trail climbs along the east perimeter of the park. Walk quietly and possibly see black-tailed deer, squirrels, and other forest creatures; look up for bald eagles, ospreys, and pileated woodpeckers.

Mutiny Bay Launch Ramp   Map 34b

Boating • Paddling

Facilities: Launch ramp

🚗 From the Clinton ferry terminal, head east on SR 525 for 9 miles. Turn west on Bush Point Road, in 1/2 mile turn south on Mutiny Bay Road, and in 1 3/4 miles turn south on Robinson Road to reach the launch ramp in another 1/4 mile.

🚤 The ramp is on the west side of Whidbey Island, roughly in the center of the Mutiny Bay shoreline, about 3/4 mile north of Double Bluff

Why Mutiny Bay? The stories vary—one tale is that British sailors jumped ship here to become settlers; another story claims that local Native Americans serving as crew on a ship carrying whiskey mutinied here and seized the cargo. Although the name is intriguing, the bay is not much—just a slight inward curving of the shoreline, as bays along this side of Whidbey Island are inclined to be. The only public area on Mutiny Bay is the launch ramp at the end of Robinson Road.

On the north side of the road is a gravel and grass lot with parking space for a dozen cars with trailers. The 1-lane paved ramp is straight ahead, between private homes. This ramp, like others on this side of the island, is subject to considerable wave action, and the access might be choked by sand or debris. Watch for mergansers swimming offshore. This adaptable duck usually breeds and nests in a freshwater habit but often takes to the sea for the summer.

Double Bluff Beach Access (Island County) and DNR Tidelands
Map 34b

Beachcombing • Swimming • Paddling • Clamming • Birdwatching

Facilities: *At the county beach access:* Disabled-accessible toilets, picnic tables, information kiosk

Area: 21,120 feet of saltwater tidelands on Useless Bay

From the Clinton ferry landing, take SR 525 northwest for 8¼ miles. Turn south on Double Bluff Road, and follow it to the county park at road end in 2¼ miles. The state tidelands extend west from here to Double Bluff.

The tidelands are on the south shore of Whidbey Island on Useless Bay, between Double Bluff and the residential community to the east. Useless Bay is not whimsically named, and the tidelands can only by approached by a beachable boat.

The beach area on Useless Bay along the shore north of Double Bluff is owned by the state but is undeveloped except for the blacktopped parking lot at the end of the road and a small adjacent county park. One could certainly argue that nature has done all the development necessary on this shore, and any further refinement by man would be sacrilegious. This is just the place for the serious beach fanatic, with acres of sand for wandering at low tide and piles of driftwood providing private little niches for an afternoon of daydreaming. Rustling beach grass, slapping waves, and the plaintive cries of seabirds create a salty symphony.

A sandbar in the long tideflat traps shallow ponds of water at low tide for toddlers to dabble bare toes. At the far end of the beach is a glacial-till bluff—at 367 feet high one of the tallest and sheerest precipices on the island. The bands of glacial till visible in the face of the bluff were contorted about 100,000 years ago by a major earthquake. The beach can be walked west all the way around the point to the homes of Mutiny Bay.

Sailors call this Useless Bay because its widespread arms offer scant protection against wind and waves, and the shallow bottom reaches up to grab unwary keels. For kayakers, though, when the weather is calm, the bay offers interesting exploration along its shores and south around the corner

Double Bluff Beach Access on Useless Bay is spectacular.

to Cultus Bay. Here are two bays, side by side, with identical names, albeit in different languages—Cultus is Chinook jargon for "useless." Except for a dredged basin, most of Cultus Bay dries at low tide and becomes useless, even for canoes.

Dave Mackie County Park (Island County) Map 34b

Boating • Paddling • Swimming • Clamming • Sports field

Facilities: Picnic tables, picnic shelters, fireplaces, restrooms, children's play area, baseball field, 2-lane paved launch ramp
Area: 4 acres; 400 feet of shoreline on Admiralty Inlet
🚗 From the Clinton ferry landing, follow SR 525 northwest for 3¼ miles and turn southwest on Maxwelton Road. In 5 miles, reach the small community of Maxwelton and the park.
🚤 The park is on the southeast side of Useless Bay, 1½ n.m. north of Scatchet Head. The launch ramp is usable only at high tide.

With its ball diamond and bleachers, Dave Mackie County Park is obviously meant for the use of residents, not necessarily tourists. But residents (who know a nice beach when they see one) probably won't object to an outlander or two dropping by to share it.

The park lies on a low grassy bank above Useless Bay; a boulder bulkhead lines the high-water level. Two roads reach into the park—the one on the south leads to the 2-lane paved launch ramp. Mooring buoys offshore are private. Because the ramp faces on a long tideflat, launching is possible only at moderate to high tide, and with boats that are small enough to be at least partially carried or dragged.

Water flowing over the gently sloping bottom warms to temperatures bearable for wading and swimming. Picnic tables here offer lunchtime views of the beach and boating activity, as well as impressive views across Useless Bay to the rapidly rising cliffs at Double Bluff.

SOUTH SARATOGA PASSAGE AND POSSESSION SOUND
Map 34b

Holmes Harbor and Freeland   Map 41

Boating • Paddling • Beachcombing • Clamming • Picnicking • Hiking

Facilities: *Freeland:* Groceries, cafés, marine supplies, shopping. *Freeland County Park:* Picnic tables, picnic shelters, fireplaces, benches, children's play equipment, disabled-accessible restrooms, trail, 2-lane paved launch ramp with boarding float

Area: 7 acres; 1500 feet of shoreline on Holmes Harbor

🚙 From the Clinton ferry landing, take SR 525 northwest for 9 miles to reach Freeland. At a stoplight, turn north on Main Street, which heads east in one block. In two more blocks, at a stop sign, turn north on E Harbor Road. As E Harbor Road bends east, continue straight ahead on Stewart Road, which makes a sharp turn to the west along the head of the bay and reaches the shore of Holmes Harbor and the park in 1/4 mile.

🛥 *Freeland County Park:* The park is at the south end of Holmes Harbor in the center of the shoreline. Everett is 19 n.m. away, around Rocky Point.

The largest cove indenting Whidbey Island, Holmes Harbor runs southward off Saratoga Passage, penetrating the shoreline for more than 5 miles. There are no public docks or moorages on the bay; the only public facilities are the launch ramp and park at Freeland, the small town at the head of the bay. Holmes Harbor is large enough that boaters can spend a full day here—anglers trying the traditional "hot spots," sailors enjoying long tacks across the mile-wide bay, and pleasure cruisers drifting along the scenic shoreline.

❄Anchorages can be found in the bay along the northwest shore by Greenbank. The head of the bay offers good holding ground for a hook in a mud bottom at 17 fathoms; however, there is little protection here from either northerly or southerly blows because the land at the head of the bay is very low.

After its 5-mile flow southward, Holmes Harbor peters out in a mudflat at the village of Freeland. The shopping center sits on the hillside 1/2 mile above the harbor. One of several utopian cooperative communities founded on Puget Sound in the late 1800s, Freeland was established in 1900 by a group of defectors from Equality, a socialist colony south of Bellingham on Samish Bay.

Freeland County Park (Island County) • The small county park at the head of the bay has a launch ramp next to the park restroom. Do not mistakenly try to use the wide ramp farther west by the shipyard; that one is private.

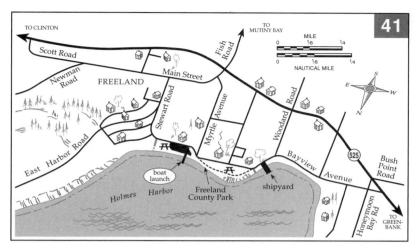

Launching or landing at moderate to low tide or with large trailered boats might be difficult, due to the gentle slope of the tideflat. The day-use park has a nice beach and facilities for picnicking or playing. On a slight knoll to the west are a picnic shelter and a woodland trail that can be jogged or sauntered, depending on whether your interest is fitness or relaxation.

Langley   Map 42

Boating • Paddling • Fishing • Crabbing • Picnicking • Shopping • Beach walking • Viewpoint

Facilities: *Small Boat Harbor:* Guest moorage with power and water, boat pumpout station, 1-lane paved launch ramp, fishing pier, restrooms, showers, picnic tables, fireplace. *Langley:* Fuel, lodging, groceries, restaurants, shopping
Area: *Seawall Park:* 1 acre; 1000 feet of shoreline on Saratoga Passage
From the Clinton ferry terminal, follow SR 525 northwest out of town. In 2½ miles, turn north on Langley Road and follow it for 3 more miles into town.

The town of Langley is in itself a good reason to visit Whidbey Island. The term "quaint" might well have been coined just to describe this village by the sea. Although local merchants do like to capitalize on the town's particular aura, it is authentic—most of the weathered little storefront shops have been soaking up history along with the salt air for nearly one hundred years. For shopping addicts, the town is pure heaven, with marvelous little art galleries, crafts shops, antique stores, bookstores, and, when you need a rest, numerous purveyors of refreshments.

Langley Small Boat Harbor • Langley faces directly on Saratoga Passage, without the benefit of any natural land protection. The boat harbor on Wharf Street, at the east end of the town, once had a meager little guest float that

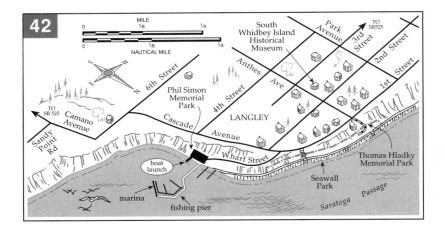

bobbed and rolled with every swell off the channel. Finally the old wharf and the guest float were replaced with a dandy little yacht basin behind a sturdy pile breakwater.

Here, there are slips for visiting boats as well as additional permanent berths. The moorages are quite short and narrow; it might be difficult to get boats over 30 feet long into them. A long fishing pier with cleaning stations and rod holders follows the outside of the west portion of the breakwater. A barge on the shore side of the moorage has a boat pumpout station. Boaters arriving at the yacht basin will find the town's shopping and dining district is just a block up the hill. Plans call for expanding the moorage, more than tripling its current size.

Phil Simon Memorial Park •

On-shore, immediately east of the yacht basin, Phil Simon Memorial Park has a 1-lane paved launch ramp. Parking space for a few cars with trailers is adjacent, as is a small picnic area and restrooms.

Seawall Park and Thomas Hladky Memorial Park •

The two-block-long business district of Langley sits above the water on a 100-foot embankment. Portions of some buildings extend out onto piles along the edge of the bluff. The town has made the most of its beachfront by turning it into pretty

Bas-relief designs decorate Langley's Seawall Park.

little Seawall Park, a 30-foot-wide grassy swath between a concrete bulkhead and the blackberry-covered embankment.

Picnic tables in the park provide vistas of boat traffic in Saratoga Passage and of the impressive bluffs of Camano Head, immediately across the channel. Bas-relief Northwest Indian designs decorate the bulkhead, and concrete steps interrupt the wall in three places, giving access to the beach below: boulder and cobble at the east end, becoming sand to the west. From above, near the east end of the shopping district, the park can be reached via a long set of stairs descending in tiers from an overlook. A charming bronze statue of a boy and his dog shares the viewpoint at the head of the staircase.

A second access to the beach leaves from a steep, blacktopped path at the intersection of 1st Street and Anthes Avenue. The path ends at one of the bulkhead-interrupting steps, framed by two tall totem poles. A grass strip along one side of the path ends at a viewpoint memorial to city father Thomas Hladky.

Columbia Beach (Clinton)   Map 34b

Fishing • Shopping

Facilities: *Ferry landing:* Fishing pier, float, restroom. *Clinton:* Stores, restaurants, fuel (service station)

🚗 At the Mukilteo–Clinton ferry landing

🛥 4 n.m. from Mukilteo, and 7½ n.m. from Everett

To most people arriving at Whidbey Island via the Mukilteo ferry, Clinton is just a blur as they leave the boat and whiz by headed for points north. Slow down a bit and you will find the small town has several places of interest. A walkway along the north side of the ferry landing leads to a public fishing pier. The elevated platform, which has a roofed shelter for inclement weather, is a nice place to observe ferry and boating activity or watch people catching fish.

The float below has space for day-use moorage for four or five small boats; it might be pulled out during stormy winter months. Parking is at the top of the hill in the ferry parking lot, ¼ mile south of SR 525 on Humphrey Road. The town of Clinton has a few stores; more are scattered along the highway.

Possession Point DNR Beaches   Map 34b

🛥 The nearest boat launches are at Mukilteo or Possession Beach County Park

Possession Point marks the extreme south end of Whidbey Island. Here, two public beaches can be reached by hand-carried boats put in the water at Clinton or at a Glendale road end just north of the intersection of Glendale and Humphrey Roads. An artificial reef, marked by buoys, has been placed just off Possession Point as an aid to fishing in the area. It lies west of the lighted bell buoy that marks shoals at the south end of the point.

DNR Beach 100 is a 2550-foot-long strip that lies beneath bluffs ½ mile north of Glendale. Beach 99 is 1160 feet of tidelands just north of the beach homes at Possession Point. The public lands are only the area below mean high water. Dungeness and red rock crabs can be caught in the area.

Possession Beach County Park (Island County)   Map 34b

Picnicking • Beachcombing • Birdwatching • Boating • Paddling • Hiking • Clamming

Facilities: Picnic tables, restrooms, 2-lane launch ramp with boarding float, hiking trail, interpretive displays

Area: 2 acres; 1500 feet of saltwater shoreline on Possession Sound

🚐 From the Clinton ferry landing, take SR 525 northwest for 2½ miles, and turn south on Cultus Bay Road. In 4¾ miles, where Cultus Bay Road makes a sharp turn to the west, continue south for another 1¾ miles to reach the entrance to the park.

🚤 The park is on the east side of Whidbey Island on Possession Sound, 1 n.m. north of Possession Point.

Possession Beach County Park, near the south end of Whidbey Island, not only offers a public launch ramp into waters renowned for their salmon and bottomfish catches, it also represents a valiant attempt to retain a rare and ecologically precious barrier beach berm and saltwater marsh environment.

The beachfront berm encloses a saltwater lagoon and marsh that alternately drains and fills with the tide, and is fed by freshwater from uphill streams. Beach grasses and a scattering of wildflowers anchor the soil of the berm. The habitat, ranging from beach to forest, hosts dozens of species of birds and mammals.

A ¾-mile-loop hiking trail probes the park's upland forest. Picnic tables, some shaded by stunted firs, are scattered along the start of the trail. The 2-lane launch ramp is paved. Artificial reefs at nearby Gedney Island and Possession Point provide a protected habitat for bottomfish such as lingcod and true cod—an alternative fishing challenge to the area's plentiful salmon.

Possession Point State Park   Map 34b

Paddling • Camping • Fishing • Shellfish • Scuba diving

Facilities: 3 CMT campsites, toilet, cabin, no water

Area: 25 acres; 1175 feet of saltwater shoreline on Possession Sound

🚐 See directions to Possession Beach County Park, described previously. Just west of the entrance to the county park, turn south on Franklin Road, and reach the park gate in ½ mile. Until a parking area is developed, there is only limited roadside parking outside the park gate (don't block driveways of adjacent residences).

🚤 The park is the first shoreline development north of the tip of Possession Point, and can be recognized by the two-story ranger residence surrounded by a picket fence. The county park launch ramp is ½ n.m. to the north.

The driftwood-strewn beach at Possession Point State Park is close to the fine fishing grounds off Possession Point.

This park is intended primarily as a CMT campsite, offering a sorely needed stopover point on the long paddle between the Seattle/Edmonds area and the nearest marine trail site to the north on Camano Island. Three campsites are along the grass strip above the beach to the north. The only amenity is a toilet beside a shed near the residence. State Parks plans to restore a tiny old fisherman's cabin at the north end of the property so that it can be used for refuge in inclement weather. The gentle cobble and sand beach drops away sharply about 200 feet offshore.

Whidbey Island Road Ends   Maps 34a and 34b

A number of road ends give access to beaches and water around Whidbey Island. Typically, these are 30- to 50-foot-wide strips of shoreline flanked by No Trespassing signs; parking nearby is usually minimal. All accesses provide a place to put in a hand-carried boat or kayak for exploration of nearby shores. Do not trespass on adjoining private property.

MORAN BEACH. This day-use parking area, on the northwest side of the island immediately north of the Naval Air Station, faces on the Strait of Juan de Fuca overlooking Smith and Minor Islands and the south ends of

Lopez and San Juan Islands. To reach it, turn west off SR 20 at Banta Road, 3 miles south of Deception Pass. In 1/4 mile, turn north on Moran Road, and in another 1/4 mile, head west on Powell Road. The beach access lies at the road end in another 1/4 mile.

WEST BEACH ROAD. Headed south from Swantown and the southern entrance to Joseph Whidbey State Park, West Beach Road parallels the shore. In about a mile from Swantown, just before the road heads uphill, park in pulloffs on the west side of the road near an overgrown house foundation. Walk the beach southward below towering bluffs (with due caution for tide levels).

DRIFTWOOD WAY. This gently sloping sand and gravel beach lies midway down the west side of the island. To reach it, 3 miles north of Greenbank on SR 525 turn west on Ledgewood Beach Drive, which in 1/2 mile ends at a T intersection with Fircrest Avenue. Turn north on Fircrest, and in 1/2 mile head west on Seward Way, which winds downhill to the south. Midway down the hillside, in 1/4 mile, turn northwest on Driftwood Lane. In 200 yards, where the road drops to water level, a parking area sits just above the beach on the west side of the road. Stairs lead down to the beach facing on Admiralty Inlet.

LAGOON POINT. Two public beach accesses break the barricade of private homes at Lagoon Point on Admiralty Inlet, north of South Whidbey Island State Park. To reach the first, just south of the intersection of Smugglers Cove and Lagoon Roads, turn west off Smugglers Cove Road on West Cliff Drive. The road descends steep bluffs; at the beach, it forks into Seashore Road and Shell Avenue. Just west of this intersection is a 50-foot-wide public access sandwiched between private residences. Public beach below mean high tide level extends 114 feet south and 231 feet north of this access.

A second public access on the south side of the lagoon can be reached by turning south off West Cliff Drive on Lagoon View Drive. This road drops sharply downhill to the beach level and becomes Salmon Street as it turns west. A 30-foot-wide public access can be found at the end of Salmon Street near its intersection with Oceanside Drive.

BUSH POINT. This narrow road-end access on the southwest side of the island, near the end of Bush Point offers, at best, a boat hand-carry to the water. To reach the access from the Clinton ferry landing, take SR 525 northwest for 9 miles. Turn west on Bush Point Road, which in about 3 miles becomes Smugglers Cove Road. At 1 1/4 miles north of the point where Bush Point Road becomes Smugglers Cove Road, turn west on Scurlock Road, which intersects Spyglass Drive a few blocks uphill from the beach. From the south end of Spyglass Drive, turn west on Sandpiper Drive, and in a hundred yards arrive at the public access (Island County). Parking in the vicinity is limited.

Boats put in here can reach DNR Beach 101, a public beach 1 mile to the south. This 1650-foot section of beach lies beneath bluffs just north of Mutiny Bay. ❄Use care in small boats because the tide can be very strong in this area.

BORGMAN ROAD. This slender access on the east side of Whidbey Island overlooks Skagit Bay, the south entrance to the Swinomish Channel, and Goat Island. Take SE Regatta Drive north out of Oak Harbor, and turn east

The Beachcombers Road access is one of several on Whidbey Island that offer put-ins for hand-carried boats.

on Crescent Harbor Road. In 2 miles, turn north on Taylor Road, and in another ¼ mile, go east on Silver Lake Road. Continue east for 3½ miles to an intersection where Silver Lake, Strawberry Point, and Green Roads meet. Head northwest on Green Road for ¼ mile, and then northeast on Borgman Road for ¼ mile to a road end at the beach, an old launch ramp site. Parking is limited.

LONG POINT. Long Point is at the entrance to Penn Cove, on the east side of the island. At a sharp bend in SR 20, 2½ miles east of Coupeville, turn north on Parker Road. In 1¼ miles head northeast on Portal Place, which ends at a T intersection with Marine Drive in 200 yards. Follow Marine Drive northwest for ½ mile to a road end above the beach at Long Point. The broad gravel beach, tapering down to sand at low tide, overlooks Penn Cove and the high bank of Blowers Bluff across the bay.

BEACHCOMBERS ROAD. Another access on the east side of Whidbey Island is just north of Greenbank. At Greenbank, head northeast from SR 20 on North Bluff Road. In 2¼ miles, turn east on Neon Drive, which ends at a T intersection with Crane Landing Drive in a little over a block. Here, head north, and then twist downhill for ¼ mile, where Crane Landing Drive becomes Hidden Beach Drive as it continues down to the beach on Saratoga Passage. To the south is the Beachcombers Community Club (private); to the north is a public road end above a deteriorating pile bulkhead.

GLENDALE. At the top of the hill above the ferry landing at Columbia Beach in Clinton, turn south on Humphrey Road. In 3 miles, reach Glendale on Possession Sound. Just north of the intersection with Glendale Road, a short gravel spur between two residences gives access to a cobble beach. Parking is limited.

chapter seven

Possession Sound and Port Gardner

BOATING SPOTS ARE USUALLY THOUGHT OF in two categories—places you go to and places you leave from. In Washington, the wonderful change-of-pace destinations such as the San Juans, Port Townsend, or Poulsbo fall in the first group. In the latter category are spots boaters do not usually think of stopping at unless the motor suddenly develops palsy or (worse yet) it is discovered that all the food for the weekend is still sitting at home on the kitchen table.

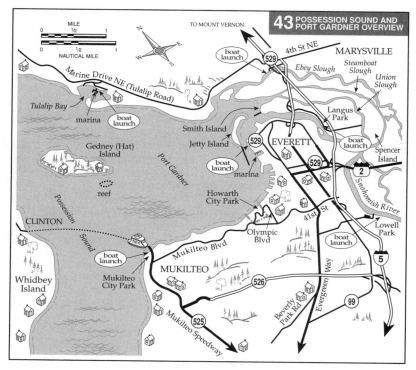

Opposite: *The Port of Everett marina has more than 2000 slips for resident and visiting boaters.*

To Puget Sound boaters, marinas and bays along Possession Sound usually fall in this second group—they are too close to home to offer a convenient first night's stop or too much like home to provide a real change of pace. A stop along Possession Sound can, however, be a real bonus. Boaters can add one more pleasurable day to the weekend by leaving the home slip in Seattle or points south on Friday afternoon and pausing somewhere along Possession Sound for the night before continuing north. Or they can use this as a last stop on a vacation trip before making the final leap for the locks.

For those not in transit to vacation getaways, Possession Sound offers beaches aplenty for a day's enjoyment wading in the waves, sculpting sand castles, lolling against sun-splashed driftwood, or casting a fishing line. For small craft, Possession Sound beaches and marinas offer ideal launch points for local exploration or fishing. Scuba divers also relish the opportunity to probe the underwater world within a short jaunt from home.

Captain George Vancouver, who was the first European explorer to venture into these waters, anchored off Gedney Island in June of 1792, after exploring the southern reaches of Puget Sound. In taking possession of all the inland waters in the name of King George III of England, he gave this arm of Admiralty Inlet its name. Possession "Sound" is a somewhat pretentious name for this body of water, which is, in truth, just one more wandering arm of Puget Sound itself. It bulges into Port Gardner, a broad basin south of the confluence of Saratoga Passage and Port Susan.

A long subterranean shelf reaches south from Camano Head to Gedney Island, in the middle of Possession Sound. This is a popular year-round salmon fishing area. To provide more habitat for fish, and thus improve fishing and scuba diving in the area, an artificial reef of massive chunks of

The Tulalip Bay Marina has a launch ramp and a few guest moorages.

broken concrete has been placed just off Gedney Island. The reef, marked by buoys, lies ½ mile south of the island.

All of the island is private; the small marina lying behind a breakwater on the northeast side is for the use of island residents. ✵ Avoid cruising too close to the south or east side of the island, as shoal water extends some distance from shore. In calm weather, the north side of the island offers some anchorages.

Tulalip Bay Marina Map 44
Boating • Fishing • Hiking

Facilities: 1-lane launch ramp with boarding float, guest moorage (limited), picnic tables, restrooms. *Nearby:* Hiking trail

🚙 From I-5, take Exit 199 (SR 528E, Marysville, Tulalip). Head west on Marine Drive, which soon bends northwest, for 4¾ miles. Turn west on 64th Street NW, and in another 1¼ mile, head north on Totem Beach Road to reach the marina in ¾ mile.

🚤 Tulalip Bay is 6 n.m. northwest of the mouth of the Snohomish River, and 8 n.m. northwest of Everett's Port Gardner. The bay ranges just 1 to 2 fathoms deep at mean lower low water.

The Tulalip Indian Reservation spreads along the shore between Kayak Point and Everett. The center of the reservation shoreline is marked by the small, shallow indentation of Tulalip Bay. The slender finger of Skayu Point frames the south side of the entrance to the bay. ✵ The north side of the bay is dotted with submerging rocks; the hull of the *Hicira*, a gas scow that burned and sank in 1919, lies in these rocks. When entering Tulalip Bay, favor the north side once past the entrance rocks to avoid drying shoals found near the center of the bay.

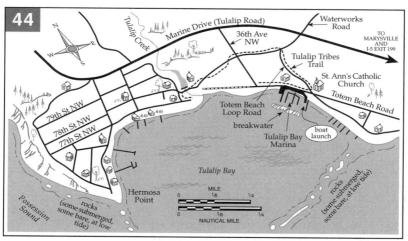

The small marina lies behind a short rock jetty at the center of the eastern shore of the bay. The 100 slips primarily provide full-time moorage for tribal fishing boats; however, a few slips might be available for day-by-day rental for visiting boaters. Check with the marina office for available moorage. A steep, 1-lane paved launch ramp is at the south end of the marina area; there is ample parking in the vicinity.

Tulalip Tribes Trail • Historic St. Ann's Catholic Church, built in 1904, sits prominently on the hillside above the marina. A ³/₄-mile-long walking loop along roads above the Tulalip Bay Marina offers insights into the history and way of life of the Tulalip Tribe. Each of eight stations has a large informational display with historical photos. Short posts nearby identify plants and shrubs and describe the uses made of the plants. The stations on the trail are found just above the marina along Totem Beach Road, and on the hillside above on Totem Beach Loop Road and Waterworks Road. The path between the stations is marked with rather obscure, rust-colored painted pipes.

THE SNOHOMISH RIVER ESTUARY
Maps 43, 45, and 46
Boating • Paddling • Fishing • Wildlife watching • Hiking

The main channel of the river is navigable by large boats for about ³/₄ n.m. east of the I-5 overpass. A railroad swing bridge and several highway bridges, some fixed, some opening, cross the waterway. The least vertical clearance of the fixed bridges is 56 feet. The three public launch sites in the estuary are at Ebey Slough, Langus Riverfront Park, and Rotary Park. A fourth launch site is at the mouth of the river at 10th Street Marine Park.

Between Marysville and Everett, the Snohomish River meanders soundward, dividing into a braided network of sloughs, backwaters, and channels. Several marinas are near the mouth of the river, at Ebey Slough, at Union Slough, and on the main channel. All have haulouts and marine repair, but none offer guest facilities. Small boats put in along the channel can explore the maze of quiet sloughs or cruise out to the bustling activity of Port Gardner. The tidal influence on the lower Snohomish estuary is significant, so paddle-powered trips should be planned with the tidal current in mind.

Snohomish River Estuary Watertrail • More than 40 miles of river channels and sloughs are accessible by paddlecraft in the Snohomish River Estuary. The best way to explore the shores of the half-dozen islands making up the estuary is by canoe or kayak, with consideration for the tide level and direction of the tidal currents; paddling against tidal currents can be exhausting. Some of the smaller sloughs are little more than mudflats at minus tides.

These waters at the river's mouth are a mix of freshwater from the river and Puget Sound saltwater introduced twice daily by the tide. Many of the islands in the estuary hold wetlands that are partially flooded at times of high tide or high river flow. Deer, beavers, coyotes, muskrats, raccoons, otters, harbor seals, and sea lions might be seen in the unique habitat.

Several species of salmon and trout are found here, and some of the more than thirty-five species of birds might be spotted. Snohomish County Parks and Recreation has an excellent recreation guide to the 19½-square-mile estuary. See their website, *www.co.snohomish .wa.us/parks*, for details.

Ebey Slough Launch Ramp • A

public launch ramp on the most northerly of the Snohomish River sloughs provides access to the many channels of the estuary. To reach it, leave I-5 at Exit 199 (SR 528E, Marysville, Tulalip). In Marysville, turn south on Beach Avenue, the first intersection after leaving the freeway. Follow Beach Avenue south to a T intersection with 1st Street, and then head west.

Canada geese on Ebey Slough are un-impressed by the scenery.

Just after the street ducks under I-5, a 2-lane launch ramp is on the left, facing on Ebey Slough.

A dirt parking area beside the road under the freeway has space for three or four cars with trailers. Park well off the road, as logging machinery and trucks make heavy use of the road during working days. Cars parked inside the concrete barriers on logging company property will be towed.

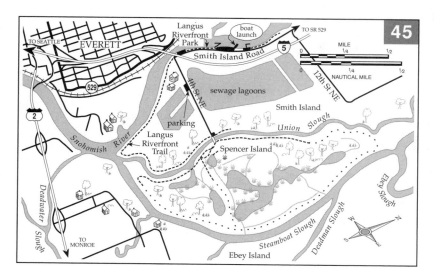

Langus Riverfront Park and Trail (City of Everett) Map 45

Boating • Paddling • Fishing • Hiking • Bicycling • Birdwatching • Picnicking • Views

Facilities: 2-lane launch ramp with boarding floats, fishing pier, restrooms, picnic tables, racing shell launch float, picnic shelter, riverside trail

Area: 96 acres; 5700 feet of shoreline

🚗 *From I-5 northbound:* Take Exit 195 (Port of Everett, Marine View Drive) and follow Marine View Drive north for 1¾ miles to SR 529N (Marysville). Head north on SR 529, and in 1 mile, turn east on 28th Place NE, and then in a block, south on 35th Avenue NE, which Ts into Ross Avenue in ¼ mile. Ross Avenue continues southeast near the bank of the Snohomish River and passes the dry storage area at Dagmar's Landing. At a Y intersection at 12th Street NE, a little over ¼ mile south of Dagmar's, bear south on Smith Island Road, and in another ½ mile reach the park. *To reach Ross Avenue from I-5 southbound:* At Exit 198 (SR 529, Marine View Drive), take SR 529 south for 1 mile. Turn west on Frontage Road and follow it south for ¾ mile to where it becomes Ross Avenue as it ducks east beneath SR 529.

🛥 From the Port of Everett Marina area, take Port Gardner north along the east side of Jetty Island and head east into the Snohomish River, Go under the SR 529 bridges and reach the park in 3½ miles.

This Everett city park on the main channel of the Snohomish River, tucked between the river and the freeway, offers picnic sites and an excellent 2-lane paved launch ramp. The south end of the park also has a concrete float for

The small float at the south end of Langus Riverfront Park is for launching racing shells. It is also good for fishing or putting in other hand-carried boats.

fishing or for launching racing shells and other hand-carried boats. Picnic tables lining this short stretch of open shoreline provide a place to munch a sandwich and watch birds or boats, whichever is your fancy. At the north end of the park, a short fishing pier offers another opportunity to drop a line into the river. Northeast, above the downstream channel, Mount Baker rises, and to the west loom the sharp summits of Whitehorse, Three Fingers, and Mount Pilchuck.

Along the top of the dike, a narrow, rough dirt path leads north down-river along the water's edge for nearly a mile. A few small pocket beaches along the dike provide more spots to relax and watch the river creatures and activities.

Langus Riverfront Trail • A flat, 1½-mile-long paved path that follows atop the dike along the east bank of the Snohomish River and the west bank of Union Slough is a favorite with birdwatchers. A parking lot at the south end of Langus Riverfront Park marks its start. Listen and look for myriad birds and waterfowl that use the riverside as their home or hotel.

In spring, clumps of skunk cabbage flash golden blossoms through marsh mud, and trailside shrubs wear a delicate mantle of pink and red blossoms. At 1½ miles, the bridge to Spencer Island is reached, and in another 100 yards, the trail peters out. Return to your car the way you came, or take a ¾-mile shortcut via 4th Street SE.

Spencer Island (Snohomish County and Department of Fish and Wildlife) Map 45

Hiking • Birdwatching • Nature study • Views • Hunting

Facilities: Trails, viewing platforms, interpretive signs, toilets
Area: 1117 acres; 13,000 feet of shoreline

See directions to Langus Riverfront Park, described previously. Park at the Langus Riverfront Trail parking area or at a roadside concrete slab on 4th Street SE, about ½ mile from the road end at the park. Parking is not permitted at road end.

Don't plan for a quick hike through Spencer Island. Although the paths are easy and the distance is not far, you'll soon discover that a leisurely pace is needed to see, hear, and absorb all the wonders that are here. Birdwatchers report spotting more than thirty different species in a single outing.

The island, sandwiched between Union and Steamboat Sloughs, was once an industrial dumping ground from nearby lumber mill operations. Dikes were built here to protect local farms from flooding. The marshy island now stands as a premier example of habitat restoration. Beginning in 1990, local agencies working with volunteers excavated debris from the north end of the island, creating a freshwater wetland pond and a cross-island levee. The north end of the island is preserved as a freshwater marsh environment for small mammals, migrating waterfowl, and other bird species.

South of the levee, the former dikes were breached to restore the flow of tidal saltwater to the remainder of the island. The hope is that the tidal flush-ing will create a transition zone for juvenile salmon headed from spawning

A dilapidated barn on Spencer Island speaks of the area's early use as farmland. Snowy Mount Pilchuck is in the distance.

grounds to the sea. Although habitat preservation was the primary objective in restoring the island, hiking, wildlife viewing, and seasonal hunting of migratory waterfowl are permitted. Paths threading across the island are occasionally bothered by washouts and erosion problems. The high costs of maintenance might change the use of the island in the future.

Rotary Park Boat Launch and Lowell Riverfront Trail (City of Everett)   Map 46

Birdwatching • Boating • Paddling • Fishing • Picnicking • Bicycling • Views

Facilities: *At Rotary Park:* 2-lane paved launch ramp with boarding pier, disabled-accessible toilets. *At Lowell Riverfront Trail:* Trail, park benches, picnic tables, fire braziers, toilet

Area: 14 acres; 7000 feet of shoreline

From I-5 Exit 193 (Pacific Avenue, City Center), head west on Pacific for about eight blocks to Broadway. Turn south on Broadway, and in ten blocks take the ramp labeled I-5 N, Lowell Road. Head east over I-5 on 41st Street SE. On the east side of the freeway, turn south on S 3rd Avenue, which progressively becomes Junction Avenue and S 2nd Avenue. In ½ mile, turn east on Lenora Street (Lowell River Road). Reach Riverfront Park in ¼ mile, and the Rotary Park Boat Launch in another 200 yards. The north end of the trail is a at a dirt parking lot at 38th

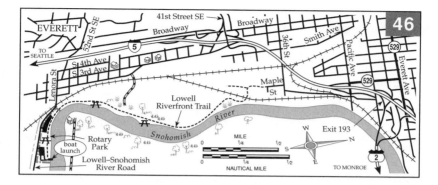

Street and Maple Street; there are no facilities, however, and no road identification at this point.

The south end of the Rotary Park Boat Launch is anchored by a large parking lot. A 2-lane paved launch ramp with boarding pier drops into the Snohomish River. Boaters launching here should remember the river level at this point is still very much affected by tide levels.

The Lowell Riverfront Trail goes north from the ramp area; the level paved path follows the west bank of the Snohomish River for 2½ miles along the route of an old railroad track. Plans are to continue the riverside trail all the way to the town of Snohomish.

Walk slowly, watch, and listen for river and marshland inhabitants. Frogs croak from ponds, dozens of tiny birds flit and chatter among the brush, cormorants sit on midriver logs drying their wings, and leggy blue herons flap away as you approach. Picnic tables and benches along the trail invite you to stop and enjoy it all leisurely. Across the river, the ghostly buildings of an abandoned farm invoke spooky thoughts or artistic opportunities. At about 1 mile, the path bends away from the river, separated from it by a cattail marsh, and continues north to a dirt parking area.

PORT GARDNER AND EVERETT
Map 47

One of the most striking features of Everett is its harbor. Back in 1895, town founder Henry Hewitt got the bright idea to divert the Snohomish River south along the waterfront to give the city a freshwater harbor. He planned to build a dike and a series of locks that would force the Snohomish River into a new channel. (Obviously, this was before the days of environmental impact statements.) The rock dike was built, but the mighty river was not to be domesticated; it retaliated by dumping silt in its new channel, making it unusable for navigation. These engineering problems, coupled with financial difficulties, caused the project to be abandoned. A cut, called Steamboat Gap, was made through the dike at its north end, permitting the silt to collect in two settling basins. With locks now out of the question, the city was left with a rock breakwater serving nicely to shelter its (still saltwater) harbor.

�֎ Except for the dredged river channel, the mudflat at the mouth of the Snohomish River, which fills a large part of the east side of Port Gardner, bares at low tide. The dredged cut of Steamboat Gap leads to the Everett waterfront.

Naval Station Everett has been a more recent major change to the Everett waterfront. After construction of the 200-acre site along Port Gardner, the first vessel arrived in the 1990s. It is home base for the carrier Abraham Lincoln, as well as the cruisers, destroyers, and frigates of a seven-ship battle group.

North and South Marine View Parks (City of Everett)   Map 47

Viewpoint • Walking • Birdwatching

Facilities: Park benches, information panel
Area: 4.5 acres; 1200 feet of waterfront

🚙 From I-5 at the north end of Everett, take Exit 195 (Port of Everett, Marine View Drive) and head west on Marine View Drive. In 3¼ miles, as Marine View Drive bends south along Port Gardner, reach the parks.

The city of Everett has turned a ½-mile stretch of shorefront along Port Gardner into a pretty little viewing and strolling area. Although they are considered two separate parks, North and South Marine View Parks are

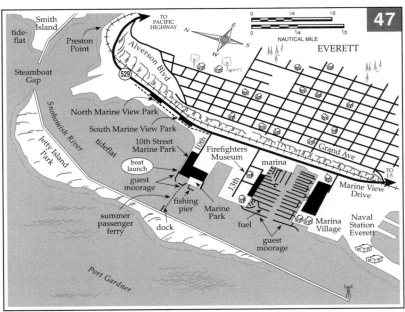

really two parking areas joined by a blacktop path, with several benches along the route. Up-close views are of an old log-booming area and lots of ducks, gulls, terns, hawks, herons, and cormorants. The more distant scene is of Possession Sound and blue-collar boats going about their daily work or pleasure cruisers headed for a day's leisure. An informational display at South Marine View Park tells some of the history of the area and describes local wildlife. From here, walks can continue south to the boat launch area of Marine Park or on to the Port of Everett Marina.

10th Street Marine Park (Port of Everett)   Map 47
Boating • Paddling • Picnicking • Fishing • No kite flying

Facilities: 13-lane paved launch ramp with boarding floats, guest moorage *(no power or water)*, marine pumpout station, fishing pier and float, paddlecraft launch ramp, picnic tables, benches, information displays, restrooms, deli, passenger ferry to Jetty Island Park (summers only)

Area: 21 acres; 710 feet of shoreline

See directions to North and South Marine View Park, described previously. The entrance to Marine Park is about three blocks to the south.

From the south end of Port Gardner Channel, head north between Jetty Island and the docks of Naval Station Everett. Pass the Everett Marina and in a few hundred yards, look for floats and the launch ramp on the east side of the channel.

Tenth Street Marine Park in Everett is ideal for launching either trailered or car-topped vessels.

This is, hands-down, the best boat launch facility on Puget Sound. In a region that hypes itself as a boating capital, there ought to be more like it. Located at the end of 10th Street, the paved launching area is thirteen lanes wide, with a short boarding float between each pair of ramps. The adjacent parking lot has space for 300 vehicles and trailers. The ramps are well maintained, have a good slope, and have protection from weather. To facilitate use of the ramps, separate sections are designated for launching or retrieving boats. Concrete floats on the west side of the launch area serve both as a breakwater and a guest moorage.

A pretty little grassy park on the bank south of the launch ramps offers picnic tables, benches, and nice views of Jetty Island Park and boating activities in the channel. A fishing pier and float in the river channel off the end of the park let the boatless share in the fun of angling. On the south edge of the park, a 1-lane paved ramp drops to water level for launching paddlecraft. A large modern metal sculpture adds to the "first class" ambiance.

The first weekend in June, the park is the site of "Salty Sea Days," a nautical festival featuring pirates, parades, log-rolling contests, a barbecue, kayak races, fireworks, and numerous other fun events.

Jetty Island Park (City of Everett) Map 47

Picnicking • Birdwatching • Beach walking • Nature walks • Kite flying

Facilities: Picnic tables, toilets, dock, interpretive hut, free passenger ferry (summer only)
Area: 160 acres; 13,200 feet of shoreline

Passenger ferry service runs from the Marina Park floats in summer.

From the south end of Port Gardiner Channel, head north between Jetty Island and the docks of Naval Station Everett. Pass the Everett Marina and in a few hundred yards look for floats on the west side of the channel opposite Marina Park.

For years, people took for granted the rock jetty that created the Everett harbor—it served nicely to shelter the moorages, it was a handy final resting place for old barges (which also served to stabilize the sand and silt), and it was an ideal seagull parking lot. Eventually, the secret got out about what a great spot the jetty is, and now it is the darling of the Everett waterfront—and if you don't have your own boat to get there, the city will transport you!

The Jetty Island Park dock is across from the boat launch area at Marine Park, making it convenient for small boats to cross the ¼-mile-wide channel; if traveling in paddle-powered craft, be aware that the current can be strong at times. Kayakers will enjoy a circumnavigation of 2-mile-long Jetty Island, exploring hulks of beached barges and passageways around old piles and logs. From July 1 through Labor Day, a city park–operated passenger ferry leaves from the Marine Park dock every half hour from 10:00 A.M. (11:00 A.M. on Sunday) to 5:30 P.M., Wednesday through Sunday, to carry visitors on the ten-minute jaunt to the jetty. The trip is a bargain—it's free! Just pick up a boarding pass at the kiosk in Marine Park. Group tours can be arranged through Everett Parks and Recreation.

Summer tides flowing over the long sandy shoals on the west side of Jetty Island are warmed to near-bathtub temperatures on sunny days; the sand is the best around for castle construction. A hands-on interpretive hut above the dock gives visitors the feel of the habitat, and free ranger-led activities are provided. Picnic tables are scattered in the beach grass at the top of the dike.

Ospreys nest atop pilings, and in winter and spring a large colony of sea lions frequents the island before heading to breeding grounds in Southern California. The sea lions can often be seen hauled out on the beached barges at the southern end of the dike. Observe them from a distance, as they have little fear of humans and can be dangerous.

Port of Everett Marina   Map 47

Boating • Paddling

Facilities: Guest moorage with power and water (some disabled accessible), wireless broadband, restrooms, showers, laundry, marine pumpout stations, dump for portable toilets, gas and diesel, haulouts (Travelifts, marine ways, hoist), groceries, restaurants, shopping, marine supply and repairs, boat charters and rental, whale-watch tours, hotel, farmers' market (Sundays in summer)

🚐 *From the north:* See directions to North and South Marine View Park, described previously. The entrance to the North Marina area is 1/4 mile to the south. The entrance to the South Marina area, Marina Village, and Naval Station Everett are 1/4 mile farther south. *From the south:* From I-5 Exit 193 (Pacific Avenue, City Center), head west on Pacific Avenue for 3/4 mile to Marine View Drive. Turn north on Marine View and reach the South Marina area in 11/4 miles.

🚤 *From the south end of Port Gardner:* Head north between Jetty Island and the docks of Naval Station Everett. The marina is on the east side of the channel; the entrance is in the center of the breakwater floats. *From the north:* The marina can be reached by going through Steamboat Gap.

Over the years, the Everett waterfront has seen a dramatic shift from a purely commercial status to a recreational one. Today, the 2000-plus slips in the Port of Everett boat harbor qualify it as the second-largest marina on the West Coast, surpassed only by Marina del Rey in California. The facility, lying behind the rock jetty, north of the commercial wharfs, is easily spotted from either water or land—just watch for a forest of aluminum spars.

❀ Two lighted markers are at the entrance to the dredged Port Gardner, at the south opening of the jetty breakwater. Boats should enter well from the south to avoid a huge, buoy-marked shoal lying off the end of the Snohomish River and extending from Tulalip Bay to the southern end of the jetty. The main channel of the Snohomish River flows behind the dike, and the current can be quite strong, especially when it is combined with an outgoing tidal flow.

The marina basin lies between two 2000-foot-long earth-filled piers. A network of floats extends from each of the piers, and a marine repair area with haulout slings is at the head of the basin. On the south pier is Marina Village, a collection of nice shops and restaurants done up in modern

Cyclists pause to check out the docks at the Everett Marina.

"olde-timey" decor; the marina administration office is on the east side of this complex.

Primary guest moorages are at the entrance to the basin on the two concrete floats that serve as a breakwater. When the river current is strong, docking at these outer floats can be difficult, and boats tied there will be buffeted by the currents and boat wakes. The finger piers on the inside of the floats are fairly stable. Some permanent moorage slips are also sublet for short term. For boaters moored on the north section, it is more than a mile-long walk around the basin to facilities on the south, although it is just a short row—if you brought your dinghy. Visitors on the north side can pay for moorage at the west side of the Yacht Club Building or the fuel dock to save a trip to the marina offices on the south side. At the east end of the marina, a 100-foot-long disabled-accessible guest float can also be found. Regular bus service connects Marina Village with downtown Everett, where there are stores and services to meet every need. Merchants can provide information on schedules.

On the north side of the marina, on 13th Street, a firefighters museum is housed in an old fire station adjacent to a more modern one. The building is filled with memorabilia such as vintage hoses, nozzles, switchboards, fire helmets, and a few old fire engines. The museum is not staffed, so its historic treasures are viewed from outside through large windows, or by appointment.

Howarth City Park (City of Everett) Map 43

Beachcombing • Hiking • Fishing • Picnicking

Facilities: Picnic tables, restrooms, hiking trails, tennis courts, horseshoe pits, children's play equipment
Area: 28 acres; 3960 feet of shoreline
🚗 From I-5 at the south end of Everett, take Exit 192 (Broadway, Naval Station,

Port of Everett). Head west on 41st Street SE, which becomes Mukilteo Boulevard in ½ mile. In another 1½ miles, turn northwest on Seahurst Avenue, which in a block becomes Olympic Boulevard at the upper entrance to Howarth Park. To drive to the lower section, go north on Olympic Boulevard and follow it as it twists downhill, passes a viewpoint, and reaches the lower entrance.

🛥 The park is 2½ n.m. south of the Everett Marina. Small boats or paddlecraft can be landed on the beach in calm weather.

In the late 1800s, when railroads first made their way to welcoming pioneer settlements on Puget Sound, the logical route for tracks was the path of least resistance. Inland were ravines, hills, and dense forests, and so the tracks were laid along the shoreline—between Seattle and Everett some 30 miles of beachfront is consumed by railroad beds. As it traveled along the shore, the railroad cut across numerous small spits, isolating them from the rest of the land. Several of these truncated spits eventually became community parks, with pedestrian viaducts crossing the tracks.

One of these parks, Howarth City Park, on the south side of Everett, spans not only the shoreline, but also an adjoining gully and bluff tops. Upper Howarth Park is the more "civilized" section, with grassy expanses, picnic tables, restrooms, tennis courts, horseshoe pits, and play equipment for kids. A trail and stairs descend the gulch to a viewpoint and the lower portion of the park.

From the lower parking lot, a trail follows the bank of Pigeon Creek No. 2 through thick brush and past some tiny waterfalls to reach the lower entrance. Another trail crosses the creek and climbs a tier of stairs to a railroad overpass. At the far end of the overpass, a spiral staircase winds around a remarkable castlelike, three-level view tower to the beach.

MUKILTEO
Map 48

Boating • Fishing • Beach walking • Scuba diving • Kite flying

Facilities: *In Mukilteo:* Ferry terminal, fishing piers, shoreline promenade, groceries, restaurants, stores. *At Mukilteo Lighthouse Park:* 3-lane paved launch ramp with boarding float, picnic tables, fireplaces, restrooms

Area: *Mukilteo Lighthouse Park:* 17.6 acres; 1495 feet of shoreline

🚗 From I-5 Exit 189 (SR 526W, Paine Field, Whidbey Island Ferry), head west on SR 526 and then 84th Street SW, to the Mukilteo Speedway (SR 525). Follow this road north to arrive at the ferry landing 7 miles from I-5.

🛥 Mukilteo is located at Elliott Point on the east side of Possession Sound near its north end.

After an early stint as a pioneer boomtown, today Mukilteo leads a quiet life as a suburb of Everett and a terminal for the ferry to Clinton on Whidbey Island. An L-shaped public fishing pier, operated by the Port of Everett, is on the east side of the ferry landing. In addition to fishing, it is a good place to watch the comings and goings of the nautical busses. The pier can be

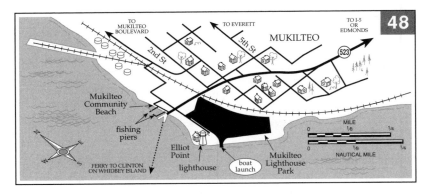

reached via a walkway angling off the east side of the ferry pier.

A second, newer fishing pier a block to the east of the ferry landing ties into a block-long boardwalk atop the concrete bulkhead. At the east end of the boardwalk, the bulkhead is interrupted at a street end, offering access to the sandy beach and scuba exploration of offshore piles.

The Mukilteo lighthouse, first staffed in 1906, is west of the ferry terminal, next to the city park. The lighthouse, with its handmade lens dating from 1858, is open to public tours weekdays and holidays from noon to 5:00 P.M. April through September. Special tours can be arranged by calling (425) 513-0962.

Mukilteo Lighthouse Park (City of Mukilteo) •

This day-use park consists primarily of a 3-lane launch ramp and a large parking lot. Be aware that a fee is charged for parking in the first four lanes of parking inside the park entrance. These slots, often used by commuters, are marked by painted stripes and numbers.

Although the boat ramp is heavily used, it is unfortunately considered one of the worst on Puget Sound. Launching is difficult because the point is exposed to westerly and southwesterly winds. The ramp is also difficult to use at low tide because of the very gradual slope at its upper level. About 15 feet beyond the last pile of the boarding float, the ramp drops off sharply. When winds are strong or the tide is low, boaters are wise to drive north to Everett to use the excellent ramps there.

The nicest part of the park is the picnic area stretching along the shore south from the launch ramp. Here are tables, fire stands, and a wide gravel beach for sunbathing. The chilly water is only for the brave or for those rare hot days when even Puget Sound water is inviting. Because the point picks up winds sweeping down Possession Sound, it is a grand spot for flying kites.

chapter eight

Picnic Point to Seattle

SOUTH SNOHOMISH COUNTY
Map 49

Picnic Point County Park (Snohomish County)
Picnicking • Scuba diving

Facilities: Picnic tables, fireplaces, toilets
Area: 15 acres; 1200 feet of shoreline

🚗 From I-5 Exit 186 (128th St. SW), head west on 128th Street SW (which becomes Airport Road) for 1¾ miles to Evergreen Way (SR 99). Turn south and in 2 miles, head west on Shelby Road. In ¾ mile, at Beverly Park Road, continue west on Picnic Point Road and follow it for 1 mile to the park.

🛶 The park is accessible only by paddlecraft. Nearby launch ramps are at Mukilteo, 4 n.m. north, and Edmonds, 4¾ n.m. south.

PICNICKING IS NOT REQUIRED, but if you forget your lunch you'll regret it because you'll want to stay here all day. Picnic tables are on a grassy, maple-shaded flat, complete with a trickling stream. The sand and gravel beach below fans ever outward, offering endless possibilities for sunbathing,

A pretty trail leads to the beach at Picnic Point Park.

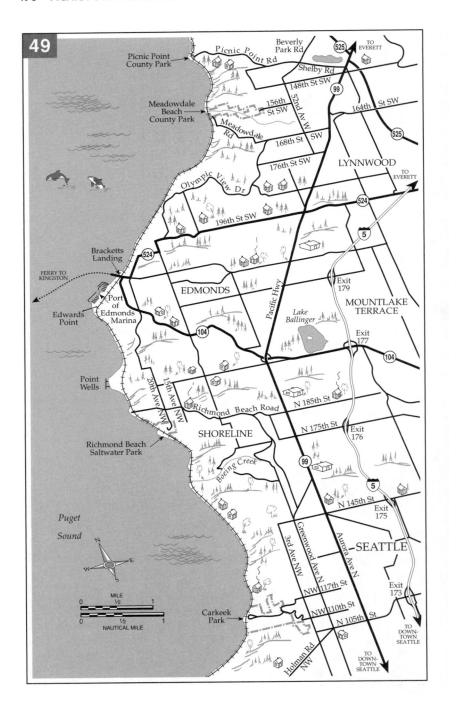

castle building, or Frisbee throwing. Scuba divers who explore the seabed, which slopes gently down to 70 feet, find crabs, flounders, skates, sea pens, moon snails, and other sand-loving critters. Pollution, however, has made the beach unsafe for swimming, fishing, or taking of shellfish. A disabled-accessible pedestrian bridge crosses the railroad tracks, giving safe access to the beach.

Meadowdale Beach County Park (Snohomish County) Map 50
Picnicking • Paddling • Beach walking • Hiking • Nature study

Facilities: Picnic sites, picnic shelter, toilets, hiking trail, volleyball court, CMT campsite

Area: 95 acres; 1000 feet of shoreline

🚗 From I-5 Exit 183 (164th St. SW), head west on 164th Street SW for 1¾ miles to Evergreen Way (SR 99) Here, turn north and in a little over a mile go west on 148th Street SW. In 1 mile, turn south on 52nd Avenue W, and in another ¼ mile turn west on 156th Street SW and reach the park in ¼ mile.

Disabled access: Leave SR 99 at 168th Street SW, and follow it west to 66th Avenue W. Turn north on 66th, then west on Meadowdale Road to 75th Place W. Follow 75th north to the gated access. Disabled persons can obtain a key card prior to going to the park by telephoning the Snohomish County Parks and Recreation Division.

🚣 The park, on the north side of Browns Bay, 3 n.m. north of Edmonds, is accessible only by paddlecraft.

This jewellike park lies between Norma Beach and Meadowdale. The beach and its adjacent picnic area are reached via a 1¼-mile-long hike down wooded Lunds Gulch, although a lower access is available for disabled persons. Check the park map at the kiosk at the upper parking lot before you head out. Just below the parking lot is the upper picnic area—a grassy bowl with a few trees and a pair of picnic tables along its edge. The trail descends through second-growth alder, then switchbacks steeply down to the floor of the gully where the creek and side streamlets nurture cedar, ferns, and salal.

On the floor of the gulch, several old cedar stumps, some up to 8 feet in diameter, show deep grooves that were cut for springboards on which loggers stood when cutting the trees. Most of these huge stumps now boast new trees growing from their tops. Interpretive signs identify tree species.

The trail continues through a cathedral arch of red alder and then breaks into the open a few hundred yards above

The trailhead at Meadowdale Beach County Park has a kiosk with a map.

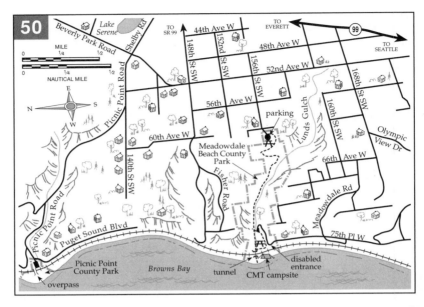

the beach. Picnic tables, a picnic shelter, and a volleyball court are scattered around the lawn. Wooden planks bridge the stream flowing under the railroad tracks, permitting access to the beach through an underpass.

At the shore, look out to the south end of Whidbey Island, across the sound to the Olympics, and up and down the shore to the abandoned boathouses at Norma Beach and Meadowdale. The gently tapering sand and gravel beach is ideal for wading, although swimmers should be cautious, as there are sudden drop-offs. The park can be reached only by very shallow-draft boats because of shoal waters. A CMT campsite is on the beach south of the underpass.

EDMONDS
Map 51

Boating • Paddling • Fishing • Shopping

Facilities: *Edmonds:* Restaurants, lodging, shopping, marine supplies, museum. *Port of Edmonds Marina:* Guest moorage with power and water, diesel, gas, boat launch sling, restrooms, showers, laundry, ice, bait, tackle, groceries (limited), boat charters and rentals, marine pumpout station, marine supplies and repair, picnic tables, restaurants

Leave I-5 at Exit 177 (Edmonds, Lake Forest Park, SR 104). SR 104 (Edmonds Way) goes directly into town. Stay left to avoid ending up in the waiting lanes of the ferry terminal.

The Edmonds harbor is 9 n.m. north of Seattle's Shilshole Bay, or 13 n.m. south of Everett.

From its elaborate underwater scuba diving park to its flowerbeds of blazing color, Edmonds has put a lot of effort into making its waterfront inviting and functional. The waterfront complex begins and ends with parks—and even has parks in between. In the center of everything is the ferry terminal, with its giant boats sailing hourly to Kingston on the Kitsap Peninsula.

The Edmonds business district, with its wide range of stores and services, is within walking distance of the waterfront, and a small complex on the waterfront has several stores, including one selling fresh seafood. Harbor Square, at the foot of Dayton Street, includes a hotel and shops that sell everything from marine supplies to lingerie. Old Mill Town, a shopping center with an 1800s atmosphere, is at Dayton Street and 5th Avenue S. Because of the area's popularity with scuba divers, air fills and other needed supplies are available in the town.

Walk two blocks north of Mill Town, past a prettily spurting fountain, to find the Chamber of Commerce and Edmonds Museum (open Tuesdays, Thursdays, Saturdays, and Sundays, 1:00 P.M. to 4:00 P.M.), just north of the corner of 5th Avenue N and Main Street. The Chamber of Commerce is in an interesting historic log cabin.

In 1870, a severe storm chanced to force the canoe of logger George Brackett onto the beach here. Brackett was so impressed with the spot that he purchased land north of Edwards Point, where he built a wharf and general store. The town's main claim to historic fame came in 1890 when, falling two short of the seventy-two signatures necessary for filing the petition to incorporate the town, Brackett added the names of two of his oxen, Bolivar

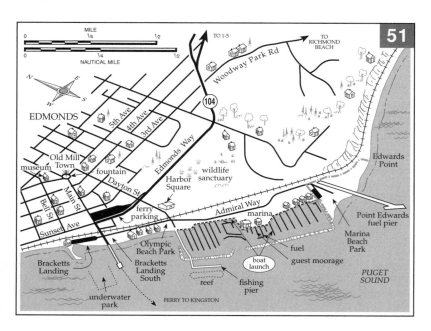

and Isaac, to the document. Thanks to his oxen, the town was incorporated and he became its first mayor.

Port of Edmonds Marina • The 900-slip Port of Edmonds Marina offers exceptionally nice moorages; some 50 to 100 slips are available for guest moorage. The entrance to the marina is in the center of the rock breakwater, marked with day marks and lights. A second breakwater inside the entrance channels traffic north and south. Guest slips are immediately south of the inner breakwater, along the bulkhead north of the fuel dock; power and water are available. Noise from the hoist just south of the fuel dock might jolt boaters out of their slumber when anglers begin to launch their boats just after daybreak. The Travelift and the launching facilities at the south end of the basin are for boats kept in the dry storage areas.

The Port of Edmonds office, on the shore by the fuel dock, has restrooms with showers. A nice little promenade, with picnic tables, benches, and flower boxes, lies above the moorage, offering balcony views of the activity below or out across the jetty to the frosty peaks of the Olympics. From here, sunset views can be exquisite.

Bracketts Landing (City of Edmonds) Map 51

Swimming • Scuba diving • Beach walking • Picnicking

Facilities: *Edmonds Underwater Park:* Restrooms, changing rooms, outdoor shower, picnic tables, underwater reef, submarine diver trails, tidepools, informational displays. *Bracketts Landing South:* Picnic tables
Area: 27 acres; 1800 feet of shoreline
🚗 Bracketts Landing is in Edmonds, flanking the ferry landing.
🛥 *Edmonds Underwater Park:* Directly north of the ferry landing. *Bracketts Landing South:* Immediately south of the ferry landing.

Edmonds Underwater Park • This park is unquestionably the most popular dive site on Puget Sound. It began accidentally when a 500-foot-long dry dock was sunk here in 1935, long before anyone (except perhaps Jules Verne) had even dreamed of scuba diving. The wreck, with its thickly encrusted marine life, became a focal point for divers, and in 1971 the area was declared a marine preserve. Since that time, eight major structures have been added, including two large tugboats, concrete culvert stars, and a reef of earthmover tires. Sea lions that have discovered this marine preserve move into the area in winter and spring. They are a fascinating sight, but they deplete the fish life and pose a threat to divers. By midspring most have departed for breeding grounds in California and Mexico. If they are present, give them a wide berth.

Floats mark the harbor line and the locations of the various underwater features, and submarine trails are marked by tethered ropes along the bottom of the cove. Boats, including canoes, kayaks, and dinghies, are not permitted within the boundaries of the park. Divers arriving by boat can anchor offshore in 30 to 35 feet of water. Because the area is protected, fish are quite tame, and divers might see huge rockfish, wolf eels, lingcod, cabezon, and a wide variety of other fish, as well as octopuses. The Edmonds Parks and Recreation Department offers a brochure showing a map of the underwater area and listing regulations and safety precautions.

For nondivers, the park is an interesting spot to watch the activity or, at low tide, to explore tidepools and marine life on the rock jetty; don't forget that this is a marine refuge and all plants, animals, and habitat are protected. Parks Department Beach Rangers are at the park during most summer afternoons on which minus tides occur. They will provide information about the marine and beach environment. Groups can schedule lectures by calling the Edmonds Parks Department. The beach can be walked north for some distance, but it soon narrows to a strip below the rocks of the railroad bed and disappears altogether at high tide.

Bracketts Landing South • This second park is on a 2-acre flat immediately south of the ferry landing. The grass-covered mounds on the uplands lead to a pleasant, driftwood-rimmed sandy beach. A path along the beach passes benches and picnic tables and outdoor art works, one a bronze sculpture of three youngsters playing in a rowboat, another a totem pole with images linking Edmonds and its sister city in Japan. The underwater area offshore is also a marine preserve, where taking of marine life is prohibited.

Bracketts Landing offers good views of the ferry's comings and goings.

Sailboarding on Puget Sound off Edmonds can be brisk.

Public Fishing Pier and Olympic Beach (City of Edmonds) Map 51

Fishing • Picnicking • Nature interpretation

Facilities: Fishing pier, restrooms, bait, tackle, snack bar, informational displays, picnic tables
Area: 4 acres; 300 feet of shoreline

🚐 In Edmonds, at Edmonds Way (SR 104) and Main Street, turn west on Main. In one block, cross the railroad tracks and head left on Railroad Avenue S. The park is reached in two blocks.

The Edmonds fishing pier was the first such facility on Puget Sound to be built exclusively for fishing, and it has served as a model for numerous other piers constructed since then. The L-shaped concrete pier begins on the northeast side of the Edmonds Marina yacht basin, inside the rock jetty, then crosses the breakwater and follows its outside edge. The pier, which is open twenty-four hours a day, has several bait- and fish-cleaning areas, along with informational displays telling of fishing gear and methods.

A reef of tires, placed 50 feet offshore from the pier, provides habitat for fish as well as for the marine life they feed on. The pilings of the pier and the rock jetty are placed to divert fish along the length of the pier to waiting anglers' hooks. Scuba diving is not permitted in the vicinity.

The pier is worth a visit for its art alone: on the rock breakwater, a school of fanciful salmon glitter and leap in the wind—they are a work of art created from recycled metal scraps such as can lids, forks, and fishing lures. A life-size bronze sculpture of a group of sea lions, watched by a man and two children, sits at one end of the park. Nearby, another whimsical sculpture features a group of adults and children watching for whales; two of the adults have seagulls perched on their heads.

Olympic Park, named for the town's athletes, is a stretch of manicured grass with picnic tables north of the fishing pier. The soft grass, or sandy beach below the bulkhead, is ideal for sunbathing or watching the ferries and feeding the city's official bird—the seagull.

Marina Beach Park (City of Edmonds) Map 51

Paddling • Fishing • Picnicking • Swimming • Scuba diving • Kite flying

Facilities: Picnic tables, fireplaces, children's play equipment, volleyball net, toilets, drinking fountain, dog off-leash area, hand-carry boat lunch
Area: 7 acres; 978 feet of waterfront

🚍 From Edmonds Way and Main Street, adjacent the ferry landing, take Main, then Railroad Ave S west to the marina, where it becomes Admiral Way. The park is at the southwest end of Admiral Way.

🛥 Only beachable boats can land at the park. It is between the south edge of Edmonds Marina and the old Union Oil tanker pier.

A gem of a little park is wedged into the beach between the Edmonds Marina and an abandoned oil tanker pier. Although the water might be chilly here, the sandy beach is so inviting one cannot help but want to wade into the waves. Above the beach is a nice assortment of driftwood to provide seats and backrests for an afternoon of lazing. Grassy mounds next to the parking lot are favorite spots for flying kites. A bridge over the south end of the marina connects the park to a waterfront promenade along the marina bulkhead.

Scuba divers frequently enter the water here and swim out to explore the old pilings of the pier. The bottom drops off rapidly to a depth of 100 feet, offering experienced divers deep dives a short distance from shore. Exercise extreme care and stay under the dock and away from any boats in the area; jagged scraps of metal on the bottom also pose a hazard. The dock itself is off limits. The beach south of the dock is park property that is maintained in a natural condition and is used for a dog off-leash area. The city of Edmonds hopes to eventually move the ferry landing to this area and create a regional transportation hub here.

NORTH KING COUNTY
Map 52

Richmond Beach Saltwater Park (City of Shoreline)

Beachcombing • Picnicking • Walking • Bicycling • Scuba diving • Tidepools • Views

Facilities: Picnic tables, picnic shelters, fireplaces, restrooms, children's play area, changing rooms, viewpoint, water
Area: 40 acres; 900 feet of shoreline

From Aurora Avenue N (SR 99), turn west on N 185th, which in ¼ mile becomes N Richmond Beach Road, NW Richmond Beach Road, and then NW 196th Street as it winds downhill to the community of Richmond Beach. Two miles from Aurora Ave, turn south on 20th Avenue NW to arrive at the park entrance in ¼ mile.

For a sunny afternoon getaway from the metropolitan areas along the east shore of Puget Sound, Richmond Beach is the ideal destination—however, if it is a weekend, you might find that hundreds of others had the same idea. This is the nicest beach north of Golden Gardens, and it is heavily used. However, the beach has space for a good-size throng, and picnic tables on the uplands provide ample spots to spread out a lunch and enjoy a broad view of the sound.

The park is divided by railroad tracks. Upland from the tracks near the large parking lot are children's play equipment and several picnic areas, one with a picnic shelter and lattice-shaded tables. A line of benches offer lazy viewing of the goings on in the sound south toward Meadow and West Points. On the opposite side of the entrance road, a level gravel path winds along the top of the bank for ¼ mile to arrive at a broad grass flat shaded by two stately madronas. This is one of the most magnificent view spots in Richmond Beach, overlooking the heart of Middle Sound and the entire span of the Olympic Mountains.

To reach the lower beach section of the park, follow an asphalt path from the parking lot that wanders through a wooded glen with some picnic tables and the requisite babbling brook. Beyond, the trail reaches an overpass above the railroad tracks, and then descends to the beach. Restrooms, a picnic

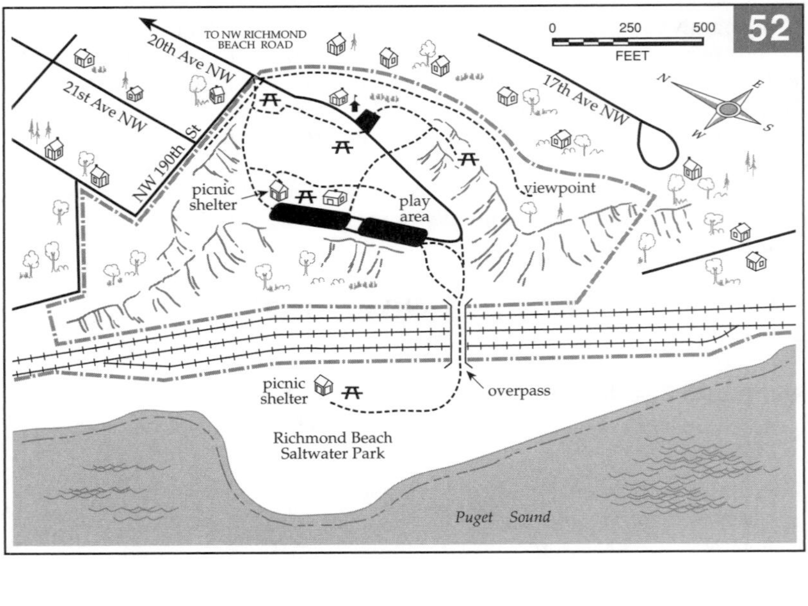

Richmond Beach Saltwater Park has a wide, sandy beach.

shelter, and nearby picnic tables perch on a bench above the steep sandy slope to the shore. The sand and gravel beach below is backed by grassy dunes and a string of driftwood. Shoal areas on either side of the point are exposed at moderate tides, extending the beach far to the north and south; at extreme low water, tidepools and the scattered remains of an old wreck lying just offshore are exposed. The most inviting beachcombing is south, below a wild 100-foot bluff.

During the 1930s, many old sailing ships reaching the end of their days were towed to Richmond Beach and burned so that copper and brass could be salvaged from the ashes. Corroded iron fittings frequently uncovered on the beach might be from these old vessels. The gradually sloping bottom at the beach is excellent for beginning scuba divers, who can see sea pens, starfish, hermit crabs, and snails.

Boeing Creek Fishing Reef (DFW) • About 1 mile south of Richmond Beach is the deep wooded ravine of Boeing Creek. An artificial reef, marked by buoys, has been placed offshore to improve fishing in the area. The reef is 3½ n.m. from the launch facilities at either Edmonds to the north or Seattle's Golden Gardens to the south. There is no upland access.

Carkeek Park (City of Seattle) Map 53

Hiking • Nature trail • Picnicking • Views • Beachcombing • Kite flying

Facilities: Picnic tables, shelters, fireplaces, restrooms, toilets, playfield, trails, model airplane field, Environmental Education Center, children's playground
Area: 186 acres; 2000 feet of shoreline

🚗 *Main entrance:* From Aurora Avenue (SR 99), turn west on N 105th Street and follow it to 3rd Avenue NW. Turn north on 3rd, and in seven blocks, head west on NW 110th Street, which becomes NW Carkeek Park Road as it twists steeply downhill to the park entrance in ½ mile. *Upper (Eddie McAbee) entrance:* At N 105th Street and Holman Road NW, go southwest two blocks to NW 103rd Street, west for a block to NW 100th Place, and southwest for two blocks to 6th Avenue NW and the Pipers Creek trailhead parking.

The park is 2 n.m. north of Seattle's Shilshole Bay Marina. Only beachable boats can land on the shore.

Carkeek, the most northerly of Seattle's parks fronting on Puget Sound, combines two worlds: the saltwater and the forested. The saltwater offerings are nice enough—even though approach by boat is difficult, and the gently sloping sandy beach is ample to hold several hundred sunbathing, wading, sand-castle building, or beachcombing people.

Ah, but the forest! The park plunges deeply inland along the canyon of Pipers Creek and the side ravines of Venema and Mohlendorph Creeks and several smaller freshets. Miles of trails wander along the ravine bottoms and up hillsides in a semiwilderness with a dense cover of wild rose, berry

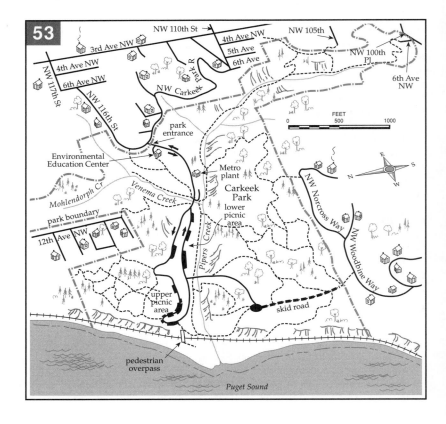

The pedestrian overpass at Carkeek Park crosses the railroad tracks and provides high views of the Olympic Mountains and Puget Sound.

bushes, nettles, devil's club, alder, maple, birch, and ferns. A maze of trails loop about, joining each other or the park roads; some are wide and well trod, others are scarcely more than boot paths. The ravines of Venema and Mohlendorph Creeks contain the few cedar and hemlock that survived the logging that stripped the area, and here is the park's closest approximation of an old-growth forest environment. A botanical trail in the ravines has been developed where introduced plants have been cleared out and native ones replanted in an attempt to return the area to its natural state.

At one time, great numbers of salmon swam up Pipers Creek and spawned in the gravel beds of Pipers and Venema Creeks, but as erosion from civilization's activities covered the gravelly spawning grounds and pollution fouled the water, the salmon runs ceased. A recent effort has been made to restore the creek and surrounding habitat to its original state and reestablish the salmon runs. Adult salmon are now seen in ever-increasing numbers as they return to spawn. The Environmental Education Center is just above the main entrance to the park.

chapter nine

Admiralty Inlet

AT ADMIRALTY INLET, the waters of Puget Sound and Hood Canal flow together for the final 20-mile leg of the journey to the Strait of Juan de Fuca. It was here, on May 10, 1792, that George Vancouver paused, contemplating whether either of these two channels led to the hoped-for Northwest Passage across the top of the continent. It was here also, at Foulweather Bluff, that Vancouver discovered the "joys" of Northwest weather, and named the site accordingly.

❀ Admiralty Inlet flows between the north tip of the Kitsap Peninsula, Whidbey Island, and the northeast edge of the Olympic Peninsula. The 3½-mile-wide channel is unobstructed throughout; the only hazards are severe tide rips off Foulweather Bluff that occur when the merging ebbs from Hood Canal and Puget Sound meet with a strong north or northwest wind. In calm weather, boats cutting close to the bluff should watch for rocks that lie 100 yards north of the highest part of the promontory.

NORTH KITSAP PENINSULA
Map 54a

Kingston (Port of Kingston) Map 55
Boating • Paddling • Picnicking • Fishing

Facilities: Guest moorage with power and water, diesel, gas, 2-lane paved launch ramp with boarding float, restrooms, showers, laundromat, portable toilet dump, marine pumpout station, picnic tables, fishing pier. *Nearby:* Marine supplies and repairs, groceries, tackle, bait, stores, restaurants, beach access trail

🚗 Kingston is the western terminal of the Edmonds ferry and is at the east end of SR 104 on the Kitsap Peninsula

⛴ The marina is behind a rock breakwater on the south side of the Kingston ferry landing at Appletree Cove. Edmonds is 6 n.m. east, and Seattle's Shilshole Bay is 10½ n.m. southeast.

As the Kitsap Peninsula sweeps north to its climax at Foulweather Bluff, gone are the sheltered beaches and forest-edged channels of the lower sound and Hood Canal. Beaches here are wild and wind torn, with mounds of ragged beach grass and a strand of silvered driftwood deposited by the waves of Puget Sound. The one bit of shelter offered along the northeast side of the

Opposite: *What could be better than the Fort Worden State Park beach on a warm day?*

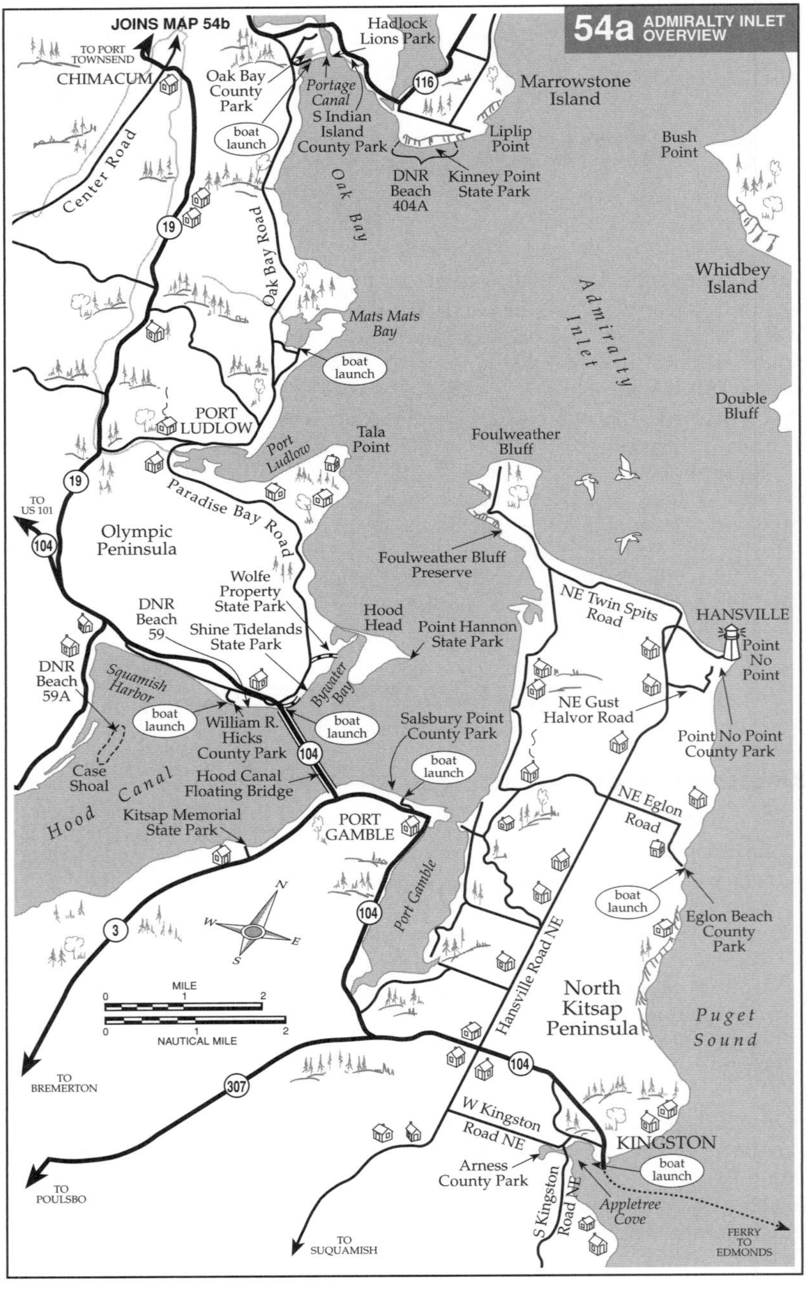

JOINS MAP 54b

54a ADMIRALTY INLET OVERVIEW

TO PORT TOWNSEND

CHIMACUM

Oak Bay County Park

Portage Canal

Hadlock Lions Park

116

Marrowstone Island

S Indian Island County Park

boat launch

Liplip Point

Bush Point

DNR Beach 404A

Kinney Point State Park

Center Road

Oak Bay

19

Oak Bay Road

Whidbey Island

Admiralty Inlet

Mats Mats Bay

boat launch

Double Bluff

PORT LUDLOW

Port Ludlow

Tala Point

Foulweather Bluff

19

Paradise Bay Road

TO US 101

104

Olympic Peninsula

Foulweather Bluff Preserve

Wolfe Property State Park

NE Twin Spits Road

HANSVILLE

DNR Beach 59

Hood Head

Point No Point

Shine Tidelands State Park

Point Hannon State Park

DNR Beach 59A

Squamish Harbor

Brown Bay

NE Gust Halvor Road

boat launch

William R. Hicks County Park

boat launch

Salsbury Point County Park

Case Shoal

104

boat launch

NE Eglon Road

Hood Canal Floating Bridge

PORT GAMBLE

boat launch

Kitsap Memorial State Park

Hood Canal

boat launch

Point No Point County Park

3

N

104

Port Gamble

Eglon Beach County Park

W E

S

North Kitsap Peninsula

Puget Sound

MILE
1   2

Hansville Road NE

0   1   2
NAUTICAL MILE

TO BREMERTON

307

104

TO POULSBO

W Kingston Road NE

KINGSTON

boat launch

Arness County Park

S Kingston Road NE

Appletree Cove

TO SUQUAMISH

FERRY TO EDMONDS

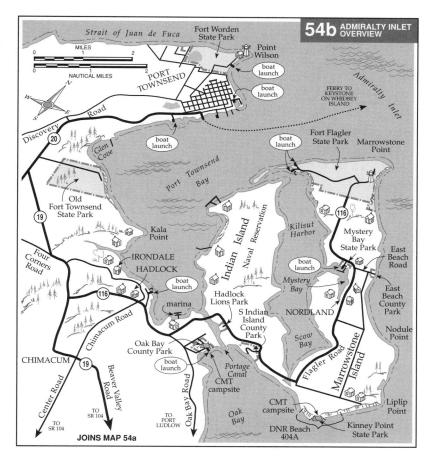

54b ADMIRALTY INLET OVERVIEW

peninsula is at Kingston on Appletree Cove. A dredged yacht basin behind a rock breakwater has full facilities for boaters. The forty-nine-slip visitor float is just behind the rock breakwater. The cove itself is an extremely shallow tideflat; do not stray out of the dredged channel. Self-register at the head of the dock above the fuel float or at the marina office.

The building with the marina office has restrooms, a laundromat, and a portable toilet dump. All but the latter are key coded for use by marina guests. Picnic tables in a little park above the marina provide a nice overlook of boating activities. The marine pumpout station is on a wing of the fuel float. A paved boat launch ramp at the southwest corner of the marina becomes only marginally usable at low tide.

Immediately to the north of the marina is the Washington State ferry terminal. Ferries from here zip across the sound to Edmonds, carrying commuters to and vacationers fro. Most visitors' only view of Kingston is from the holding lot. Some wander far enough to buy an ice-cream cone, but all

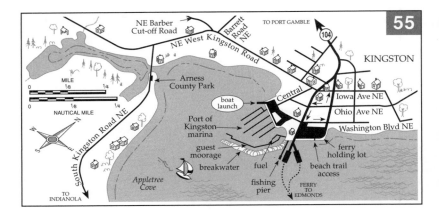

stay within dashing distance of their cars, in case their boat approaches. In addition to the businesses clustered around the ferry landing, a small shopping area is two blocks up the highway, at the top of the hill.

A long, covered pedestrian ramp at the ferry landing leads to a small glassed-in waiting room. Between the pedestrian ramp and the marina breakwater is a 350-foot-long public fishing pier, with rails drilled for holding poles and lower rail sections for junior anglers. On a clear day, the entire span of Cascade summits, from Mount Rainier to Mount Baker, is vividly displayed. North of the ferry ramps, a boardwalk along the bank has a view platform and informational display; stairs drop down to the sand beach and a short trail.

A Washington State ferry runs between Kingston and Edmonds.

Arness County Park (Kitsap County) Map 55

Picnicking • Paddling

Facilities: Picnic tables, fireplace, toilet, boat launch (hand-carry)
Area: 1 acre; 400 feet of shoreline

🚗 Four blocks uphill from the Kingston ferry landing, turn south on NE W Kingston Road. At a Y intersection, stay left on W Kingston Road, and in ¼ mile head east on S Kingston Road NE. The park is on the north side of the road in about 500 feet.

Bring out the picnic lunch—here's the place to enjoy it! This little park at the head of Appletree Cove is a pleasant surprise. Small boats can be hand-launched here for paddling about the bay (when there's water in it), and the beach is nice for sunning and sand castles. Unfortunately, pollution makes swimming and shellfish gathering risky business. If lunch is all you had in mind, just soak in the salty atmosphere.

Eglon Beach Park (Port of Eglon) Map 56

Picnicking • Boating • Paddling • Beachcombing • Wading

Facilities: Picnic tables, picnic shelter, fireplace, toilet, changing rooms, 1-lane paved launch ramp

🚗 From Kingston, take SR 104 west for 3 miles to a stoplight, and turn north on Hansville Road NE. In 7¼ miles, turn east on NE Eglon Road. In a mile, Eglon Road makes a sharp turn to the south and then in another ½ mile turns east to reach the park in ¼ mile.

🚢 The park is on the east side of the Kitsap Peninsula, midway between Apple Cove Point and Point No Point.

Eglon Beach Park is small, but it is the only public beach for quite a stretch. Aside from the 1-lane paved launch ramp and a parking lot that can accommodate a dozen or so cars, the park consists of a small grass picnic area with a picnic shelter and tables. A pair of tiny changing rooms were converted from old toilets.

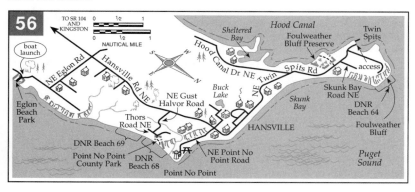

The beach itself is quite nice, with sand, beach grass, and views. Watch freighter and barge traffic in Admiralty Inlet and fishing boats skimming along the shoreline en route to their favorite "hot spot." The horizon is sprinkled with Cascade summits from Snoqualmie Pass to the Canadian border and capped by the glaciated cones of Glacier Peak and Mount Baker.

Hansville and Point No Point   Map 56

Hiking • Fishing • Picnicking • Beach walking • Birdwatching • Shellfish • Historic lighthouse

Facilities: *County park:* Hiking trail. *Hansville:* RV park, fishing tackle, bait, groceries

🚗 *County park:* From Kingston, take SR 104 west for 3 miles to a stoplight, and turn north on Hansville Road NE. In 9 1/4 miles, turn east on NE Gust Halvor Road, and at a T intersection in 1/2 mile head north on Thors Road NE to arrive at the park in another 1/4 mile. *Hansville:* Bypass NE Gust Halvor Road and continue on Hansville Road NE. Reach Hansville 10 1/4 miles from SR 104. To get to the lighthouse, at the south side of Hansville, turn southeast on NE Point No Point Road, and reach the lighthouse in 1 mile.

🛥 The point is 12 n.m. north of Kingston and 13 n.m. northwest of Edmonds.

Any local saltwater angler can tell you where Point No Point is—the area is legendary for its great salmon fishing, either by mooching from boats drifting just offshore or by casting from the beach near the point, where the bottom plummets to a depth of 90 feet. Don't expect posh resorts—the weathered little town is for dedicated anglers and vacationers who prefer the sting of salt air to the swank of tennis courts.

The first settlers here were Anton Husby and Hans Zachariasen. Locals insist (with a straight face) that Husby was a teetotaler, but the other man enjoyed his spirits, and when local Norwegian loggers came to town, they soon learned that "Husby von't drink with you, but Hans vill!"—and thus the town got its name.

Point No Point County Park (Kitsap County) • A small park a little over a mile southeast of Hansville provides a brief woodsy walk and a route to a terrific beach. There is parking for about four cars outside the gate. Beyond the gate, an overgrown road continues north through second-growth cedar and alder. A pleasant 1/4-mile hike leads to the top of the bluff and a brushy overlook of Puget Sound. Here a picturesque dirt and log staircase leads steeply down the bluff to the shore. Use care on the staircase—it might be slippery, especially in wet weather. Near the base of the stair is a huge rock erratic that was plunked down here by a long-ago glacier. The beach continues north to join county property surrounding the Point No Point Light.

Point No Point Lighthouse • Point No Point is well named, as it is only a minor sandy protuberance on an outward bulge on the west side of the Kitsap Peninsula; however, it serves admirably as a site for a navigational marker.

The lighthouse began service in 1880, when a lantern was first hung in the tower and a bell used as a warning signal. The building was constructed the previous year, and orders had been given for it to begin its work on New Year's Day. Unfortunately, although the lighthouse was completed, window glass for the lantern house had not yet been delivered. Orders were to be followed, however, and the lighthouse keeper and his assistant spent a hectic month struggling to keep the kerosene lantern lit through gales of the dead of winter until the glass finally was installed.

The U.S. Coast Guard Auxiliary opens the lighthouse to the public between noon and 4:00 P.M. on weekends from mid-April to mid-September or at other times by appointment by calling (360) 337-5362. The large radar tower north of the lighthouse is part of the Vessel Tracking System that controls all the commercial marine traffic on Puget Sound and the Strait of Juan de Fuca. Parking is a problem at the lighthouse at the end of the road, so overflow parking has been created in the roadside grass outside the fence of the RV park.

Point No Point Beaches • Nearly 1½ miles of beaches wrapping the point are public. To reach the shore, drive to the lighthouse and walk down the road. Two DNR beaches lie just around the point to the south. Beach 68 is 3036 feet long, and Beach 69, to the south of it, is an additional 2420 feet.

A huge rock erratic, left behind long ago by a glacier, sits on the beach south of Point No Point.

The public lands on both of these beaches are below mean high water level, and some of the upland property is private. Thirty acres of beach and undeveloped wetlands surrounding the lighthouse are county owned, extending 600 feet west and 900 feet south from the lighthouse. Shellfishing is not good here because of heavy wave action from the sound, but shore fishing can be excellent. Piles of driftwood in the soft sand provide convenient nooks for watching the scenery, reading, or snoozing.

Foulweather Bluff Map 56

Paddling • Birdwatching • Beachcombing

Facilities: Hand-carry boat launch. *Preserve:* Hiking trail
Area: *Preserve:* 100 acres

🚗 *Twin Spits access:* Hansville Road NE becomes NE Twin Spits Road in Hansville as it continues north to the tip of Foulweather Bluff. In 3½ miles, the road ends at a narrow road-end public access. There is daytime roadside parking for a few cars nearby. *Preserve:* On NE Twin Spits Road, 3 miles north of Hansville (¼ mile south of Skunk Bay Road), look for an unmarked roadside pulloff on the west side of the road with space for several cars. The trailhead is near the center of the parking area.

🛶 The bluff is 3½ n.m. southeast of Port Ludlow and 12 n.m. northwest of Edmonds. ❋ The only hazards are severe tide rips off Foulweather Bluff that occur

A redwing blackbird takes flight at Foulweather Bluff Preserve.

when the merging ebbs from Hood Canal and Puget Sound meet with a strong north or northwest wind. In calm weather, boats cutting close to the bluff should watch for rocks that lie 100 yards north of the highest part of the promontory. *Preserve:* Boats launched at Twin Spits can easily be paddled south to the preserve, 1 n.m. away—the marsh is easily spotted from the water.

The Kitsap Peninsula ends in the dramatic headland of Foulweather Bluff. Here waves and wind batter the shore, sculpting the bluffs and depositing sand and silvered driftwood on the beaches. The beach on the north, below the 200-foot-high bluff, is designated as DNR Beach 64. This 3364-foot strip of public tideland ends at the northeast corner as the shore turns toward Skunk Bay. The beach drops off quite steeply, with no shellfish in evidence; its main attraction is the opportunity for a front row seat on the ever-changing maritime scene of Admiralty Inlet. To access the beach, hand-carried boats can be put in at the NE Twin Spits road end.

Foulweather Bluff Preserve (The Nature Conservancy) • Since you are in the area, slip around to the west side of the Kitsap Peninsula for a nice little nature walk in a 100-acre marshland south of the bluff. A short hike through forest leads to the rock and gravel beach. Waterfowl and shorebirds abound. Because this is a sanctuary, camping, fires, clam digging, and pets are not permitted; the park closes at dusk.

At high tide, the beach is not exposed, but low water reveals a wide rock and gravel shelf with marvelous tidepools to explore. The thick clay of the bank north of the marsh is studded with cobbles and small boulders, a clear giveaway to its origin: these are deposits left behind by the continental glaciers that covered the region some 15,000 years ago. The view is south to Port Gamble, Hood Head, misty Olympic peaks, and the inviting corridor of Hood Canal—but that's another book.

THE HOOD CANAL ENTRANCE
Map 54a

The mouth of Hood Canal opens into Puget Sound at Admiralty Inlet. Two bays along the Olympic shore, Mats Mats and Ludlow (the first snug, the second generous) are interesting to boaters or shore visitors.

❋On the west side of the entrance to the canal, a series of hull-claiming rocks lie just off the entrance to Mats Mats Bay and extend south for a mile to the entrance of Port Ludlow. These rocks are especially hazardous because they lie in the path of boats running between Port Townsend Canal and Hood Canal. Klas Rock, at the northern end, is covered at extreme high water. It lies 1/4 mile from shore and is marked by a lighted buoy on the north side and an unlighted one on the south. Colvos Rocks, 3/4 mile farther south, are also marked by a light; a second light shows the end of a shoal running southeast from it. Snake Rock, which is unmarked, is 300 yards offshore, southwest of Colvos Rocks.

Port Gamble   Map 57

Sightseeing • Picnicking

Facilities: Groceries, deli, historic buildings, museums

🚗 From the Kingston ferry terminal, head east on SR 104 for 4 miles to its stop-light junction with SR 307. Here, continue north on SR 104 along the west side of Port Gamble Bay to arrive in Port Gamble in another 3½ miles.

It is hard not to stop at charming little Port Gamble, a town that played a vital role in this area's early history. A. J. Pope and William Talbot (whose names still linger hereabouts), along with Cyrus Walker, founded the town in 1853. Here they built a company town and a small sawmill. The mill was enlarged and modernized several times; many of the homes kept close ties to their Victorian pasts, however, and were historically preserved. After a long history of operation, the mill closed in 1995. Plans for the historic old company town are vague; however, it might have a marina and condominiums in the future.

The town's general store displays old-time memorabilia and offers picnic supplies, a deli, and gifts to visitors. The museum on the second floor of the building displays a fascinating collection of more than 14,000 shells and marine fossils from around the world. Sandwiches from the deli can be enjoyed just above the beach in a lawn that has several tables and provides a sweeping view of the bay and Hood Canal. Signs around the town give highlights of the town's history, while the historical museum in the basement of the general store traces in more detail the story of the mill and the people who shaped this country. The museum is open from 10:30 A.M. to 5:00

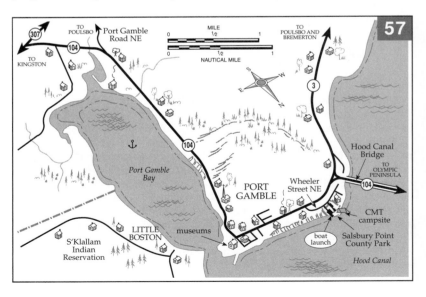

P.M. from May 1 to October 31, and by appointment; call (360) 297-8074.

There is no public shore access for pleasure boats on Port Gamble Bay. However, the bay does offer boaters a pleasant overnight stay, with excellent anchorages in 3 to 5 fathoms. ❀ Water immediately outside the entrance to the bay is quite shoal; boaters can locate the dredged channel entrance by heading for the outermost of two channel markers on pilings by the entrance. From there, a range located on a small point of land about a mile to the north can be used to line up on the channel. Be wary of numerous deadheads that might be in the bay. Favored anchorages are in the small bight on the east shore at the southern end of the bay.

On the east side of the bay, the sandy spit on the S'Klallam Indian Reservation was the site of Little Boston, an early village. These Native Americans called the bay *Teekalet*—"brightness of the noonday sun." The launch ramp on the spit is for tribal use.

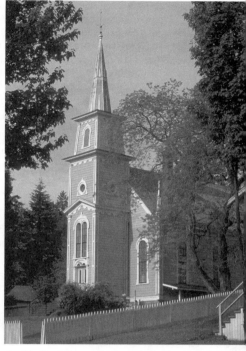

St. Paul's Episcopal Church, built in Port Gamble in 1870, is one of the town's many historic buildings.

Salsbury Point County Park (Kitsap County) Map 57

Boating • Paddling • Picnicking • Swimming • Hiking • Scuba diving

Facilities: 2-lane launch ramp with boarding float, picnic tables, picnic shelter, fireplaces, children's play equipment, nature trail, water, restrooms, shower, CMT campsite

Area: 6.5 acres; 520 feet of shoreline

🚗 From Port Gamble, take SR 104 west for ½ mile and turn northwest on Wheeler Street NE, which is signed to the park. In ¼ mile, at Whitford Road NE, arrive at the park.

🛥 The park is on the east side of Hood Canal, ¾ n.m. west of Port Gamble and ⅛ n.m. north of the Hood Canal Bridge.

A small park with a boat launch just off the northeast end of the Hood Canal Bridge provides easy access to the canal for fishing, boating, and scuba diving. There is a large parking lot but vehicles often overflow along the sides of Whitford Road.

The road into the day-use picnic area has three small parking areas. A path into the woods passes numerous examples of early logging techniques, such as cedar stumps with springboard notches. These are from the 1850s, when the area was logged to provide lumber for the mill at Port Gamble. The timber gives way to an open lawn with picnic tables and a picnic shelter. Below, the sand and gravel beach slopes gently enough to allow wading or swimming during warm temperatures. Trees rimming the south end of the beach hold a CMT campsite—the only camping permitted here.

The park is a favorite take-off point for scuba divers who explore bridge abutments and cables of the Hood Canal Bridge, just ⅛ mile to the southwest. The swift current brings nourishment to extraordinary numbers of feather duster worms, plumose anemones, sponges, and other filter-feeding invertebrates. The growth of this marine life is so heavy that it must be regularly cleaned from the bridge cables, or they would break from the weight. Due to the severity of the current, only experienced divers should dive here, and only at slack tide.

Kitsap Memorial State Park Map 58

Camping • Picnicking • Boating • Swimming • Scuba diving • Hiking • Shellfish

Facilities: 18 RV sites (EW), 28 standard campsites, 5 walk-in bicycle campsites, 32-person group camp, rental cabin, 2 mooring buoys, picnic shelter, picnic tables, fireplaces, restrooms, showers, community hall, volleyball court, children's play equipment, hiking trail

Area: 58 acres; 1797 feet of shoreline

🚐 See instructions for the Hood Canal Floating Bridge, to follow. The park is on NE Park Street, on the west side of SR 3, 3 miles south of the Hood Canal Bridge.

🛥 The park is on the east side of Hood Canal 2½ n.m. south of the bridge.

Summer afternoons find this waterfront state park jammed with local people. The park's location, close to Kitsap Peninsula towns, makes it the perfect spot to have a family outing or a scout troop campout. For boaters, the park is a nice place to stop and enjoy an onshore barbecue after a day's recreation on Hood Canal. The two mooring buoys offshore provide a handy spot for midsize boats to tie up.

The beach at Kitsap Memorial State Park is reached via a stairway.

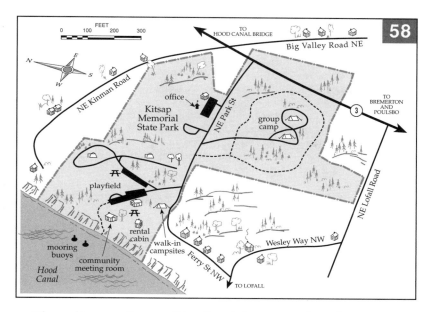

The park's campsites are all in a forested area away from the water; some are tightly packed along the edge of a large playfield, but most are strung along a more spacious loop to the north. A small group camp is in the woods in the inland portion of the park, and a trail leads from it to the other park areas above the beach.

The day-use picnic area sits on the embankment above the beach. The area's community hall, cabin, and adjoining shelter are a popular spot for weddings. A short trail, bordered by Scotch broom and madrona, drops down from the picnic area to a staircase that leads to the beach.

At high tide, the water covers the sandy upper portion of the beach and reaches to the base of the log bulkhead. Low tide exposes boulders and barnacles—difficult for walking in bare feet but holding some promise of shellfish. Geoduck clams were planted offshore, as part of an experimental program. It takes several years for them to mature to harvestable size, so in the future you might be able to gather this leviathan of shellfish!

Hood Canal Floating Bridge   Map 54a

🚗 The bridge is 10 miles west of the Kingston ferry landing via SR 104, 21 miles northwest of the Bainbridge ferry landing via SR 305 and SR 3, and 26 miles north of the Bremerton ferry terminal via SR 304, SR 310, and SR 3.

Most famous of the human-made features of Hood Canal is the 1¼-mile-long Hood Canal Floating Bridge, located (usually) at the northern entrance of the channel. Built over a four-year period and finally opened in 1961, the bridge is constructed of a series of twenty-three floating concrete pontoons linked together. Similar floating bridges had been built on Lake Washington in Seattle, but never before had one of such size been put on saltwater, where it would be affected by tidal changes of up to 18 vertical feet, as well as heavy currents and waves. In February of 1979, during a period of extreme tidal current, a violent gale smashed down from the north and destroyed the western half of the bridge.

The trusty state ferry, which had shuttled between Lofall and South Point prior to the building of the bridge, was pressed back into service for another four years while the bridge was reengineered and rebuilt. Reopened in 1982, the bridge now serves as an important transportation link between Puget Sound cities and the Olympic Peninsula.

William R. Hicks County Park (Jefferson County) Map 59

Shellfish • Boating • Paddling • Birdwatching

Facilities: 1-lane paved launch ramp, picnic table, fireplace, toilet
Area: 0.7 acre; 460 feet of shoreline

Either ¼ mile west or 2½ miles west of the west end of the Hood Canal Bridge, turn south on Shine Road. The park road is ¼ mile west or 1 mile east of these exits, respectively.

The park is on the north side of Squamish Harbor, 1 n.m. west of the Hood Canal Bridge.

Hood Canal offers very few boating detours along its narrow length; Squamish Harbor is a notable exception. The bay lies hard to the starboard immediately after passing under the bridge. Midway along the northern shore of the bay is William R. Hicks County Park, which has a 1-lane concrete launch ramp. Because the ramp runs down to a gradually sloping gravel beach, it is not usable at low tide. The Squamish Harbor tidelands are a popular forag-

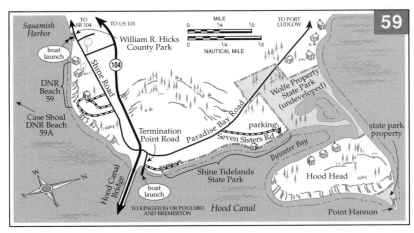

ing area for dozens of great blue herons that nest nearby. As gracefully as dancers, they wade in tidepools hunting for stranded fish.

❄A lighted beacon near the northern shore marks Sisters Rocks. Navigational caution within Squamish Harbor is imperative, as lying along the southeast side is Case Shoal, a large gravel bar filling nearly half the broad bay and drying at a minus tide. The shoal is marked by a nun buoy 2 at its southern end, a marker on a piling on the north, and a small floating buoy between. Water is adequately deep along the north shore and offers some good anchoring possibilities; the bay is quite open, however, and doesn't provide much shelter when strong winds kick up.

Squamish Harbor DNR Beaches Map 59

The major attraction of Squamish Harbor is a pair of DNR beaches offering some of the best opportunities for clam, crab, and oyster harvesting in the area. Take along a sturdy shovel and a lot of determination, and try to dig for the geoducks rumored to be plentiful here.

BEACH 59. On the north shore, DNR Beach 59 is a 2800-foot strip beginning directly below a steep, 100-foot cliff and running westward. It can be reached by boat or by walking the beach from the county park launch ramp area at low tide.

BEACH 59A. The second DNR beach, 59A, includes all the tidal area of Case Shoal, which at a minus tide offers several acres of prime shellfish gathering for butter, horse, and littleneck clams.

Shellfish at Shine Tidelands State Park keep two oyster shuckers busy.

Shine Tidelands State Park and Wolfe Property   Map 59

Beach walking • Birdwatching • Fishing • Clamming • Oysters • Crabbing

Facilities: *Shine Tidelands:* Picnic tables, toilets, no water. *Wolfe Property:* None. *Nearby:* Launch ramp

Area: 147.6 acres; 21,154 feet of saltwater shoreline on Hood Canal

🚙 At the west end of the Hood Canal Bridge, turn northeast on Paradise Bay Road, and then immediately southeast on Termination Point Road. At the bottom of the hill is a paved launch ramp; a dirt road heads northeast to the Shine Tidelands picnic area. The beach at the Wolfe Property can be reached by continuing northeast on Paradise Bay Road for ½ mile, and then turning north on Seven Sisters Road, a narrow paved road. In another ½ mile, reach a parking area and the Wolfe Property access.

🛥 The park is on Bywater Bay on the west shore of Hood Canal, immediately north of the Hood Canal Bridge.

The almost-island of Hood Head, lying close to the western shore of Hood Canal, encloses a mile-long tideflat appropriately named for what it is: a bywater bay. Such bays are formed by the action of waves building a sandspit and partially enclosing a small backwater.

On the northwest side of the Hood Canal Bridge, Termination Point

An eagle nest can be seen in a tree snag at Wolfe Property.

Road drops down to a 1-lane paved launch ramp, usable at all tide levels. A gravel road north from the launch ramp reaches Shine Tidelands in a short distance. The day-use-only park is little more than a parking area and a few picnic tables above a sandy, gently sloping beach, bare at low tide for some distance out.

The 130-acre Wolfe Property at the head of the bay is lushly forested waterfront land facing Bywater Bay and Hood Canal that is being held by state parks for possible future development as a park. The area is open to public use but has no amenities; usage is limited to beach areas.

Bywater Bay, which nearly dries at a minus tide, has been planted with shellfish for public harvest and provides a bounty of clams throughout the beach and oysters near its northern end. Explore the bay and adjacent lagoon by walking the beach. The long stretch of beach along the north shore of Hood Head and halfway down its east side is also public below mean high tide levels. Note the differences between the intertidal marine life found on the wave-washed north side and that seen in the protected bay and lagoon.

Point Hannon (Whiskey Spit) State Park Property Map 59

Paddling • Shellfish • Nature study

Facilities: None

Area: 7 acres; 1800 feet of saltwater shoreline on Hood Canal

🛶 The property is at the northeast end of Hood Head, at the head of Hood Canal. The nearest launch ramps are at Termination Point Road at the west end of the Hood Canal Floating Bridge, 1½ n.m. south, or at Salisbury County Park, north of the bridge, 1½ n.m. east.

Point Hannon is also known by the more colorful name of Whiskey Spit. The long finger of sand extending into the throat of Hood Canal has a navigation marker on its tip and a shallow marsh at its heart. Mud along the edge of the marsh might reveal visits by raccoons or deer. The beach on the south side of the spit is gently sloping sand and gravel, but the north side is a rougher cobble. The only legal land access is from the Wolfe Property via the beach along the north shore of Hood Head at low tide. The beach is barnacle-encrusted cobble and boulders, so it is slow, rough walking. High tide covers the beach, making land approach impossible.

Port Ludlow Map 60

Boating • Paddling • Fishing • Bicycling • Golf • Picnicking

Facilities: Guest moorage with power and water, restrooms, showers, laundry, groceries (limited), fishing tackle, bait, marine supplies, diesel, gas, marine pumpout station, boat and kayak rental, bicycle rental, restaurant, lodging, golf course, tennis and squash courts, children's play area

🚗 From SR 104 at the west end of the Hood Canal Bridge, turn north on Paradise Bay Road and continue north for 7 miles to Oak Bay Road. The resort is ½ mile to the east. *Alternatively:* Continue west from the Hood Canal Bridge on SR 104 for 4¼ miles. Turn north on SR 19. In 3 miles, head east on Oak Bay Road to its intersection with Paradise Bay Road in another 2 miles.

The bay is 22 n.m. northwest of Edmonds, and 19 n.m. south of Port Townsend.

For many boaters, the Port Ludlow marina, with more than one hundred guest slips, is not just a stopover on the way to somewhere else but is a destination in itself, with great things to do onshore for both adults and children. Visitors can maneuver paddleboats on the resort lagoon, rent bicycles to tour the quiet byroads, rent kayaks to tour the bay, play a round of golf on the resort's eighteen-hole course (one of the best in the Northwest), or just lie in the sun and enjoy the ambiance. Shuttle service is provided to the golf and tennis courts. The swimming pool is for resort guests only, not marina visitors.

The marina, restaurant, and resort facilities are at the northeast corner of the inner harbor. Even without the handsome resort and marina, Port Ludlow would make a dandy overnight stop, offering boaters dozens of good spots to drop a hook all along the shore. The broad outer harbor takes a 45-degree dogleg to the west and becomes the inner harbor, on which the resort marina fronts. ✵Channel markers guide the way into the inner harbor. From red nun buoy 2 off the north end of Foulweather Bluff, head southwest between Tala Point and red nun buoy 2 south of Colvos Rocks. Follow the middle of the channel south, and then west into the outer bay.

For boaters, the special delight of Port Ludlow, however, is the miniature bay at its extreme southwest end, tucked behind two tiny wooded islets named The Twins. ✵Enter this hidden cove through the small channel between the two islands—the eastern channel between the shore and the smaller of the islands has many snags and rocks. Be wary also of a rock lying off the south end of the smaller island.

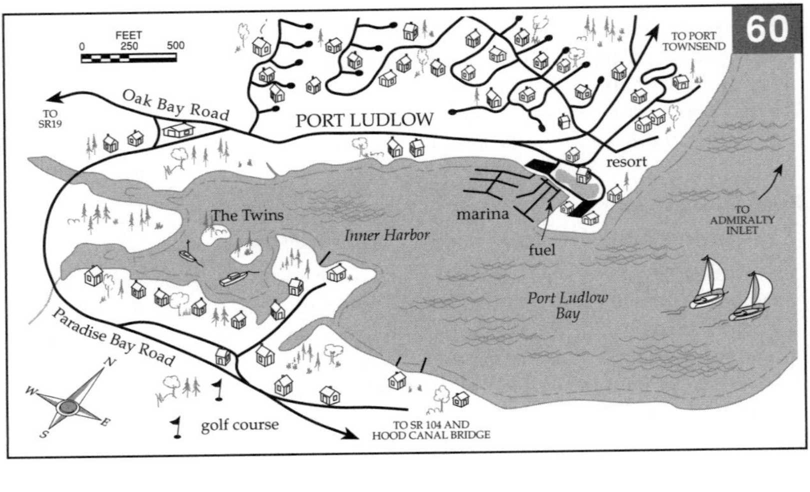

The resort and marina at Port Ludlow offer fine facilities for visiting boaters.

Once inside, you will find bombproof anchorages for even the worst of weather, or tranquility for calm summer nights. Don't plan on solitude though, for the spot is well known. The once densely wooded shoreline above the tiny cove has been transformed into a Port Ludlow subdivision, with homes and condos blanketing hillsides overlooking the anchorage.

Mats Mats Bay Map 61

Boating • Paddling • Fishing

Facilities: Launch ramp with boarding float, picnic tables

🚗 From Oak Bay Road 2 miles north of Port Ludlow, turn east on Verner Boulevard (marked for boat launch) to reach the launch ramp in ½ mile.

🚤 The entrance to the channel lies ¼ n.m. west of Klas Rock on the southwest shore of Admiralty Inlet. ✳ Upon entering the narrow, dredged channel, align with the range located at the west end of the first leg of the channel. The shallowest portion, 5 feet at mean low tide, extends from the dogleg where the channel

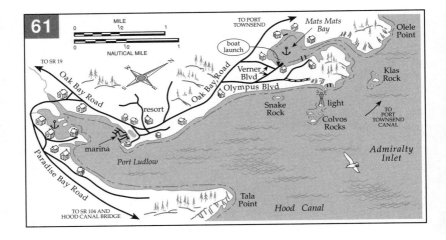

turns southward to where it opens into the bay itself. Proceed cautiously, staying midchannel in this section! Once inside, good anchorages can be found in the bay in 5 to 12 feet of water.

Boaters know that "gunkholing" means exploring out-of-the-way spots. Whoever invented the term surely had Mats Mats Bay in mind. It is the ideal little cranny for the adventuresome, with a twisting, timber-shrouded channel opening up into a round little lagoon. At the south end of the bay are a very nice little park and launch ramp operated by the Port of Port Townsend. Although the ramp and float extend about 150 feet out into the bay, at low tide the water recedes well beyond their end, leaving a long mudflat that makes the ramp unusable. Relax at a couple of picnic tables onshore and enjoy the scenery while waiting for the incoming tide.

INDIAN AND MARROWSTONE ISLANDS
Map 54b

These islands are reached by land from the Hood Canal Bridge and SR 104 by turning north on any of several roads that stretch the length of the Quimper Peninsula. Signs direct you to Marrowstone Island and Fort Flagler State Park. Flagler Road crosses the bridge that joins the islands to the mainland.

The islands are edged by Admiralty Inlet on the east, Port Townsend Bay on the northwest, and Oak Bay on the southwest

To drive to an island might seem to be a contradiction in terms, but people around Puget Sound are used to such a paradox. Here are not one, but two, nice little islands that are easily reached by road. Most of Indian Island is an off-limits, chain-link fence enclosed, Naval ammunition storage depot. Two public parks on its south end front on Oak Bay and Port Townsend Canal.

Replacing the small ferry that once operated here, a bridge over Port Townsend Canal joins Indian Island to the Olympic Peninsula.

Marrowstone Island is primarily devoted to residences, small farms, and the large state park that encompasses its northern end. Some beach homes are along Kilisut Harbor. The main concentration of homes is mid-island at the community of Nordland, where the only businesses are a combination gas station and grocery store and a few seasonal shellfish sellers.

❀ The western shore of Marrowstone Island is well protected by its neighboring island and the Olympic Peninsula. The windward shore is frequently buffeted by heavy weather from Admiralty Inlet. Severe tide rips can occur off Marrowstone Point and at Kinney Point at the south end of the island, especially when the wind and tide are moving in opposite directions. Boats heading out of Port Townsend Bay can run into trouble when they round Marrowstone Point and are suddenly confronted by southerly winds howling down the sound.

In early days, the two islands were joined to the Quimper Peninsula by a low neck of land known as the Chimacum Portage. Pressure from commercial shippers in Port Townsend for a protected shortcut up the sound resulted in the dredging of Port Townsend Canal between the Quimper Peninsula and Indian Island in 1913. Island residents were forced to use private boats, and later a small ferry, to reach the mainland. It wasn't until 1952 that a bridge finally linked the islands to the mainland.

For Puget Sound boaters accustomed to expansive channels, the narrow, ¾-mile-long canal is an interesting diversion, as well as a quick route between Hood Canal and Port Townsend Bay. The passageway is shown on some nautical charts as Port Townsend Canal, but is known locally as Portage Canal. Public parks lie along both sides of the south end, which opens into Oak Bay.

✺The dredged canal has a controlling depth of 14 feet, and the fixed bridge that crosses to Indian Island has a vertical clearance of 58 feet. Both ends are marked with lights. Tides can run up to 3 knots in the channel; tide rips that form at either end, depending on the direction of the current, can cause small boats some concern. Liplip Point, at the southeast end of Marrowstone Island, is a Chinook word meaning "boiling water"—take warning!

Oak Bay County Park (Jefferson County)   Map 54b

Camping • Picnicking • Fishing • Clamming • Crabbing • Boating • Swimming • Scuba diving • Beachcombing • Paddling

Facilities: 5 RV sites with power, 40 campsites, CMT campsite, picnic tables, fireplaces, water, toilets, children's play equipment, 1-lane paved launch ramp
Area: 31 acres; 1840 feet of shoreline on Oak Bay

🚙 From the south, drive north from Port Ludlow on Oak Bay Road for 8 miles to the junction with two roads from the east, Portage Way Avenue and Cleveland Street. From the north, reach the same junction by following Oak Bay Road south 1¼ miles from Hadlock. From this junction, Portage Way Avenue drops east to the beach and the lower campground in ¼ mile, and Cleveland Street heads north for ¼ mile to the entrance to the upper campground.

🛥 The park is on the northwest side of Oak Bay just south of the breakwater at the southern entrance to the Port Townsend Canal.

Jetty fishing on Oak Bay

Oak Bay County Park, on the northwest shore of Oak Bay, is divided into two sections: the upper campground sits on the bluff above a lagoon, the lower campground lies on a strip of land between the lagoon and the south entrance to Port Townsend Canal. The lower portion of the park encompasses a rock jetty and a gravel and sand beach that extends north to the bridge. Campsites are stretched along the southern arm of the beach between Oak Bay and a saltwater lagoon. This section of the campground is best suited for self-contained RVs as there is only one water faucet and one toilet at the entrance to the camping area. CMT campsites are at the north end of the lower campground. The launch ramp at the end of the campground road is usable but is not in the best condition. The area is excellent for fishing and clamming. Geoducks can be dug here at extreme low tide. Check current regulations regarding season and limit, and always fill in your holes after digging

The upper section of the park has two campground loops on the bluff overlooking the lagoon and the lower campground. One loop has some power hookups for RVs. Children's play equipment is in the center of the outer loop. There is no direct beach access from this part of the park.

Hadlock Lions Park (Lloyd L. Good Memorial Park) Map 54b

Picnicking • Fishing • Clamming • Beach walking • Hiking

Facilities: Picnic tables, picnic shelter, fireplace, toilet, hiking trail, no water
Area: 2.5 acres; on Port Townsend Canal

From Oak Bay Road ½ mile south of Hadlock, drive east on Flagler Road (SR 116) for ¾ mile and cross the Port Townsend Canal bridge. The park is on Indian Island on the southwest side of Flagler Road (SR 116) less than ¼ mile from the bridge.

This park on a grassy hillside on Indian Island is a convenient spot for watching activity in Port Townsend Canal and Oak Bay. Facilities are few, but the view is grand. At the top of the slope, 50 feet above the water, is a picnic shelter next to an old orchard. After polishing off the fried chicken and potato salad, wander downhill to the beach, where Hadlock Lions Park joins South Indian Island County Park property. From here, enjoy beach walks south to the jetty at the end of the canal or continue east around the corner to the picnic area at the county park, ½ mile away. South Indian Island Trail runs along the wooded bluff between the two parks. The trailhead is on the east side of the picnic area.

South Indian Island County Park (Jefferson County) Map 54b

Picnicking • Fishing • Paddling • Clamming • Crabbing • Swimming • Scuba diving • Beachcombing

Facilities: Picnic table, toilet, no water
Area: 54 acres; 11,350 feet of shoreline on Oak Bay

From Oak Bay Road ½ mile south of Hadlock, drive east on Flagler Road (SR 116) for ¾ mile and cross the Port Townsend Canal bridge. The park is on Indian Island on the south side of Flagler Road (SR 116) ¾ mile east of the bridge. The narrow dirt road into the park is not recommended for large vehicles or trailers.

The park is on the east side of the jetty at the southeast end of the Port Townsend Canal. The beach is quite shoal, so the shore can only be reached by beachable boats. The nearest launch ramp is at Oak Bay County Park, less than ½ n.m. to the west.

This park is a companion to lower Oak Bay County Park, which it faces across the bay. It has minimum facilities; its great attractions lie in its beautiful saltwater lagoon and its 2-mile-long stretch of smooth, gravelly beach.

Near the entrance to the park, a marked trail heads southeast to the lagoon at the east side of the park. Midway down the bluff is the east end of the South Indian Island Trail running from Hadlock Lions Park.

A picnic table and a bench are found in a grassy area near the lagoon. Beach walks go north all the way to the bridge, with an interesting side trip out onto the rock jetty; beyond the bridge, Navy property begins. South, the shore can be walked to the sandspit that joins Indian and Marrowstone Islands. At low tide, dig for geoducks and other clams in the beaches facing on Oak Bay.

Kinney Point State Park Property and DNR Beach 404A Map 54b

Paddling • Camping

Facilities: Kayak rack, CMT campsites, composting toilet
Area: *State Park:* 76 acres; 3500 feet of saltwater shoreline on Admiralty Inlet and Oak Bay. *DNR Beach:* 3900 feet of saltwater shoreline

Kinney Point is at the south end of Marrowstone Island, accessible only by beachable boats. The nearest launch ramps are at Oak Bay County Park, 3/4 n.m. to the northwest, or Bush Point on Whidbey Island, 3 1/2 n.m. northeast.

At Kinney Point, on the extreme south end of Marrowstone Island, DNR Beach 404A includes a 3900-foot section of beach that wraps around the point. This handy addition to the Cascade Marine Trail provides a break point for paddlers on extended trips through Admiralty Inlet. ❋ If approaching the point by boat, be wary of tide rips.

In the trees above the shore are ten primitive CMT campsites; the beach itself disappears at high tide. Adjacent uplands are part of the park property,

Paddlers on the Cascadia Marine Trail can make use of designated campsites such as those at Kinney Point.

but there is no access from above. The beach can be reached only by boat or by walking (politely) across private beaches east of the park, if landowners will tolerate it and tide levels permit.

East Beach County Park (Jefferson County)   Map 54b
Picnicking • Paddling • Fishing • Clamming

Facilities: Picnic shelter with tables, fireplace, toilets
Area: 1 acre; 100 feet of shoreline on Admiralty Inlet
From Oak Bay Road ½ mile south of Hadlock, drive east, and then north on Flagler Road (SR 116) for 6 miles to Nordland on Marrowstone Island. Just north of Nordland, turn east on East Beach Road to reach the park in ¼ mile.
The nearest launch ramps are at Bush Point on Whidbey Island, 3½ n.m. east, or Fort Flagler State Park, 5 n.m. north, then west around Marrowstone Point.

A small county park mid-Marrowstone Island provides a nice access to the Admiralty Inlet shores. Because most of the mobs head north to Fort Flagler, there is a good chance of finding privacy here, along with gorgeous views across to Whidbey Island, Mount Baker, and the Cascades.

A pretty stone and log shelter holding picnic tables and a fireplace provides protection from winds off Admiralty Inlet. The park is on the only stretch of low-bank waterfront on the east side of the island. The wide, tapering beach, cobble above mid-tide levels and sand below, holds some promise of clams at low tide, or at least a good time romping in the waves.

Kilisut Harbor   Map 54b and 62

Indian and Marrowstone Islands are separated by a long waterway that is almost a channel rather than a harbor. Before the digging of Port Townsend Canal, boats sometimes avoided heavy weather in Admiralty Inlet by traveling up Kilisut Harbor and crossing the high-tide-covered sandspit that ran between the two islands. Today, the islands are joined together at the south by a man-made dirt causeway over which Flagler Road runs. A ¾-mile-long sandspit reaches out from Marrowstone Island at the northern end of the harbor.

⚓ Entrance to the winding channel is at the far west end of the spit by Indian Island. Follow navigational markers carefully; the S-curve channel is dredged to a depth of 5 feet at mean low water, and in some places shoal water lurks immediately outside the marked channel. Use care approaching the

Small boy, large clam

harbor entrance from the north and consult navigational charts because a submerged pile lies north of the west end of the sandspit. Once the channel is cleared inside Kilisut Harbor, good anchorages can be found in 4 to 6 fathoms of water. Stay well away from the Navy-owned shore of Indian Island.

The 5-mile-long inlet was originally known as Scow Bay, and the pair of islands were the Scow Peninsula. Today, it has its more lyrical Klallam Indian name of Kilisut, meaning "protected waters"; only the far southern end of the harbor is now called Scow Bay.

Kilisut Harbor and the waters surrounding Indian and Marrowstone Islands are ideal for small-boat exploration, with numerous put-ins for dinghies, kayaks, and canoes. A circumnavigation of Indian Island is about a 12-mile trip, with a variety of adventures ranging from the quiet water of the harbor to the busy highway of Port Townsend Canal. Boats can easily be carried across the causeway and sandbar at the south end of Kilisut Harbor. ❀ Plan the trip so the direction of the tidal current is favorable in the canal, and watch for tide rips. Do not go onshore at Indian Island except at the parks on its south end.

Mystery Bay State Park Map 54b

Picnicking • Boating • Paddling • Fishing • Crabbing • Clamming

Facilities: Picnic tables, picnic shelter, fire braziers, toilets, dump for portable toilets, marine sewage pumpout station, dock with float, 7 mooring buoys, 1-lane paved launch ramp

Area: 10 acres; 685 feet of shoreline on Kilisut Harbor

🚐 From Oak Bay Road ½ mile south of Hadlock, drive east and then north on Flagler Road (SR 116) for 6 miles to Nordland on Marrowstone Island. The park is on the west side of the road ½ mile north of Nordland.

🚤 Follow the boating directions (and cautions) in the description of Kilisut Harbor, described previously. The park is on the east shore of Kilisut Harbor, 2 miles south of the last channel markers at the harbor entrance.

Halfway down the north shore of Kilisut Harbor, past a scattering of beach homes, is Mystery Bay. The small recreation area near the entrance to the curving bay is an outpost of Fort Flagler State Park. The onshore portion of the park is day-use only, but the boating facilities allow overnight moorage. The pier has a 550-foot float at its end; additional tie-ups are on seven mooring buoys, and there is plenty of space for dropping a hook. ❀ The only hazards in the bay are two submerged concrete blocks that lie 20 to 30 feet off the east end of the float.

Picnic tables and a picnic shelter onshore have a nice view of the Olympic Mountains rising behind Indian Island and of bird life in the bay. The Navy manages Indian Island as a wildlife refuge, and herons, cormorants, and a wide variety of ducks and shorebirds are commonly seen along the beaches.

If nautical legs are aching to be stretched, take a ¾-mile stroll across the narrow island to East Beach County Park. Walk south from the park on

The excellent docks are the main attraction at Mystery Bay State Park.

Flagler Road and then east on East Beach Road. Quiet walkers might be rewarded by seeing deer—if not, cows and other local wild and not-so-wildlife are assured. The windswept beach of East Beach County Park is a marked contrast to the calm shores of Kilisut Harbor.

Fort Flagler State Park   Map 62

Camping • Picnicking • Boating • Paddling • Bicycling • Fishing • Clamming • Crabbing • Beachcombing • Windsurfing • Hiking • Swimming • Scuba diving • Historical displays

Facilities: 101 standard campsites, 14 RV sites (EW), 2 bicycle campsites, 2 group camps, 3 ELCs, 4 units of rental housing, group day-use area, picnic tables, fire grates, picnic shelter, restrooms, showers, RV pumpout station, dump for portable toilets, fish-cleaning station, hiking trails, nature trail, interpretive display, groceries and snack bar (limited, summer), 2 1-lane paved launch ramps, dock with float, 7 mooring buoys, (campgrounds and boat launches closed November 1 through February 28), youth hostel, historic gun emplacements, underwater park, interpretive museum

Area: 783 acres; 19,100 feet of shoreline on Kilisut Harbor, Port Townsend Bay, and Admiralty Inlet

🚐 From Oak Bay Road ½ mile south of Hadlock, drive east, and then north on Flagler Road (SR 116) for 8 miles to reach the park on the north end of Marrowstone Island.

🛥 The state park is 2 n.m. from Port Townsend and 11 n.m. from Port Ludlow, via the Port Townsend Canal. For navigation comments on entering the channel leading into the harbor, see the section on Kilisut Harbor, previously described.

Scow Bay Spit, a ¾-mile-long curving sandbar, nearly blocks the entrance to the harbor. At high tide, water covers a low spot midway along the spit—do not attempt to shortcut through this gap in a boat as it is very shallow. One of the park's launch ramps is on Kilisut Harbor, the other on Port Townsend Bay.

Mile upon mile of goodies—so much that one can hardly appreciate it all in a weekend. Here are beaches, bluffs, woodlands, and the most spectacular sandspit to be found on the inland waters, all flavored with the intrigue of a historic old fort. At moderate to low tides, the full length of the sandbar is exposed for beach roaming or clam digging. Old piles offshore to the north were used during World War II for holding four antisubmarine nets that reached across to Port Townsend.

Park facilities are on the edges of the park, with a network of roads and hiking trails connecting them. The park office and buildings of the old fort are on the east, inside the park entrance. Building 9, across from the head-quarters, houses an interesting interpretive museum that is open from 11:00

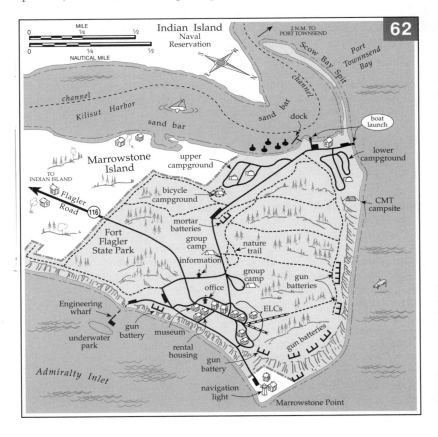

Battery Downes guarded Admiralty Inlet during World War I.

A.M. to 4:00 P.M., daily in summer, and weekends only in winter. Standing at the park headquarters is a 3-inch antiaircraft gun, similar to those deployed here during World War II. The ELCs and vacation rental houses are nearby, edging the fort's old parade field.

Camping and boating areas are on the west. The upper campground is on a wooded bluff above the water; the lower one is situated on an open, windswept flat near the beach. The docking float on a T-shaped pier has space for about ten boats. Seven mooring buoys stretched along the shore to the south provide tie-ups for additional boats, with some anchoring space nearby.

From the fort residence campus, a hard turn to the right leads downhill past a gun emplacement to a parking lot. A trail continues down to a badly deteriorated wharf originally used by the Army Corps of Engineers during construction of the fort. The underwater park lying on both sides of the wharf is marked by buoys. A forest of pastel sea anemones coats the old piles. Because this is a sanctuary, spear fishing is prohibited.

Battery Wansboro, the gun emplacements on the hillside above the wharf, is the only one of the Fort Flagler batteries to have guns in place. The original guns were removed long ago; the two 3-inch guns that are here now were placed after the fort became a park. Battery Gratten, at the northeast corner of the park, is down a short trail behind the buildings of the ELCs, former World War II barracks.

The Triangle of Fire

Flagler was one of the forts that, along with Casey and Worden, guarded the entrance to Puget Sound from foreign invasion. The three forts, facing each other across Admiralty Inlet, formed what was known during World War I as the "Triangle of Fire." Construction began on Marrowstone Island in 1897, and by 1905 all ten batteries were completed and armed. At full strength, the fort bristled with eighteen guns, ranging from 3-inch to 12-inch, and eight 12-inch mortars, aiming death at any enemy ship that dared to poke its prow into view. It soon became apparent that the fort was poorly situated because of its limited sector of fire—Point Wilson obstructed the view of the Strait of Juan de Fuca, and the guns could not engage targets much south of Marrowstone Point.

Initially, Fort Flagler was to be headquarters for the Harbor Defense, but pressure by Port Townsend bigwigs, who felt their fair city should host the headquarters, caused it to be relocated at Fort Worden. The only noticeable change was the transfer of the Artillery Band.

With the onset of World War I, the fort served as a training center for troops, but because there was no threat of naval attack on Puget Sound, many of the guns were removed and sent to the European front. At the end of the war, the fort languished in a caretaker status until a new global war revitalized it. Antiaircraft guns were installed in World War II to combat the new threat from the skies, and new buildings were constructed to house another generation of trainees. The final military use of the post was as a base for training an engineering amphibious brigade after World War II. In 1953, the fort was deactivated, and two years later it was acquired by Washington State for use as a park.

The Marrowstone Point lighthouse is reached via a steep, narrow road that goes north from the east side of the residential campus. The automated lighthouse is not open to the public, but at moderate to low tides the shore here opens the way to beachcombing and fishing—west for 1½ miles to the park campground, or south for ¾ mile to the old engineering pier. Buildings near the lighthouse are occupied by a U.S. Fish and Wildlife Service research laboratory.

Walks can be extended beyond the beaches to include bluff-top routes or forested trails. A complete circuit of the park's perimeter, following beach, road, and trail, is about 5 miles; exploring inviting side paths can occupy an entire afternoon. Watch for deer, squirrels, raccoons, and bald eagles. Foxes and coyotes also live here but are shyer and harder to spot. The trail that heads south along the east edge of the park was initially beaten out in the early 1900s by the boots of thirsty soldiers heading for a saloon on the bluff just outside the fort boundary. The saloon, known as "The Stump,"

Bluffs of glacial till edge the moorage at Fort Flagler State Park.

hauled its supplies up the steep bluff by means of a winch wrapped around a tree stump.

Along the park road to the west, well inland, are the mortar emplacements of Battery Bankhead. Batteries Downes and Caldwell, situated on the north side of the bluff, can be reached by trail from the park campus or the lower campground. These are quite overgrown, and brush hides the view of the water that the guns once commanded. The main batteries are farther east.

PORT TOWNSEND BAY

Map 54b

It is hard to understand why geographers or town founders name cities after waterways, thus causing an endless amount of confusion. The large inlet here is correctly named Port Townsend, but in order to avoid confusion with the better-known town, we end up referring to it as Port Townsend Bay. ☸The bay is well protected and without obstructions along its 6-mile length. Some good anchorages can be found at its south end, along the west shore near Hadlock and Irondale. The huge piers and cranes on Indian Island along the east shoreline of the bay are where the Navy loads and unloads ammunition from ships headed to the Puget Sound Naval Shipyard in Bremerton.

Lower Hadlock and Hadlock Inn Marina Map 63

Boating

Facilities: *Lower Hadlock:* 2-lane paved launch ramp, dock and float, toilet, no water. *Marina:* Limited guest moorage, boat pumpout station, restaurant, lodge, gift shop

🚙 *Lower Hadlock:* Turn off Oak Bay Road ¼ mile south of Hadlock on Lower Hadlock Road, which angles off to the northeast and drops steeply downhill to the shore. *Marina:* From Oak Bay Road ½ mile south of Hadlock, head east on Flagler Road (SR 116). In a few hundred feet, Hadlock Bay Road branches northwest and drops down to the marina and lodge.

🛥 The marina is at the southeast end of Port Townsend Bay.

The small town of Hadlock lies on the bluff above the water at the southwest corner of Port Townsend Bay. Beneath the bluff is a small portion of the community called Lower Hadlock, where there is a public launch ramp (Port of Port Townsend). The launch area has an excellent dock and boarding float. Short-term moorage on the float is limited to twelve hours.

Although one would never guess it from today's quiet demeanor, Hadlock, along with Irondale to the north, was once a hotbed of industry. When the sawmill at Seabeck burned in 1886, it was relocated at Hadlock. In addition to shipping lumber throughout the Pacific, the mill provided lumber for the construction of Forts Worden, Flagler, and Casey.

As its name suggests, Irondale was a major smelting center, turning out 300 tons of steel daily in its prime. When the local ore proved to be of a poor quality, better ore was imported from Texada Island in British Columbia. Eventually, bringing ore from Canada or even farther afield proved too costly and the mill closed. The last fling at industrialism was a wood

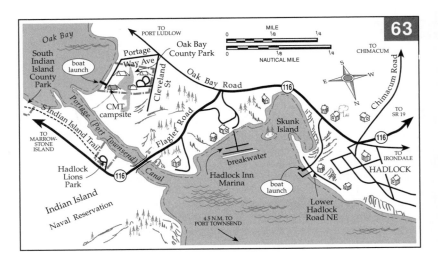

alcohol plant at Hadlock, but this was short-lived and the area settled back to a quiet residential existence.

The Hadlock Inn Marina, near the north entrance to Port Townsend Canal, makes a nice layover alternative to bustling Port Townsend. The floats, behind a substantial breakwater, offer guest moorage with power and water on a space-available basis; call to check on the status of guest space. The building onshore, which sat vacant for many years, was initially used to make wood alcohol from lumber scrap—a far cry from the elegant inn that holds forth today.

Old Fort Townsend State Park   Map 64

Camping • Picnicking • Boating • Historical displays • Hiking • Fishing • Clamming • Crabbing

Facilities: 40 standard campsites, 3 primitive campsites, group camp, picnic tables, fireplaces, kitchen shelters, restrooms, showers, RV pumpout station, 4 mooring buoys, hiking trails, nature trail, interpretive trail, children's play equipment, horseshoe pits, softball field, amphitheater

Area: 367 acres; 3960 feet of shoreline on Port Townsend Bay

From SR 20 2¼ miles south of Port Townsend, turn east on Old Fort Townsend Road and reach the park in ½ mile.

Buoys lie 1 mile south of Glenn Cove on the west side of Port Townsend Bay. The nearest launch ramps are at Port Townsend, Fort Flagler, and Hadlock.

After you have tramped through numerous World War I and II forts throughout Puget Sound, Old Fort Townsend comes as a surprise—this one is a relic from the time of the Indian Wars. The fort was established in 1856 when settlers in the Port Townsend area became uneasy about the growing hostility of Natives after the government's efforts to move them on to reservations. The uprisings had largely been settled by the time the fort was garrisoned, and troops were left with little to do.

As the Civil War was proving a more serious problem, all the troops at Fort Townsend were withdrawn in 1861 and the post was manned by local volunteers. After the end of the Civil War, the fort was active for another twenty years, even though there was no particular threat from either Natives or foreign nations. There were few residents in the area who needed protecting, and the military commanders thought the fort should be abandoned because it was poorly located as a defensive position. In 1895, a kerosene lamp caught the barracks on fire and, perhaps fortuitously, it burned to the ground. This proved a good excuse for the Army to decommission the fort and ship out the troops.

In 1958, Fort Townsend gave up all claim to a military existence when the land was purchased for a state park. The only military building remaining is the tall, brick, World War II–era Navy Explosives Laboratory at the group camp near the park entrance. A self-guided historical walk begins near the old parade grounds and passes the sites of the buildings and facilities of the early fort.

The building that housed the Navy Explosives Laboratory is the only remaining structure of the former fort.

The park sits on a bluff 200 feet above the water, with a commanding view though the trees of Port Townsend Bay and Indian and Marrowstone Islands. Beautiful old-growth Douglas-fir and cedar surround the upper campgrounds; in spring, rhododendrons in the camp area and along the entrance road bring a splash of blazing pink to the somber green forest. A smaller, lower campground is on an open level area above the parade ground.

The road twists downhill, ending in a loop near the edge of the bluff. From here, a trail along the old service road continues steeply down to the water. Piles in the water along the north edge of the park are from the fort's old wharf. Four mooring buoys are for the use of visiting boaters. A nature trail that climbs a forested gully provides a nice alternative return route to the upper parking area.

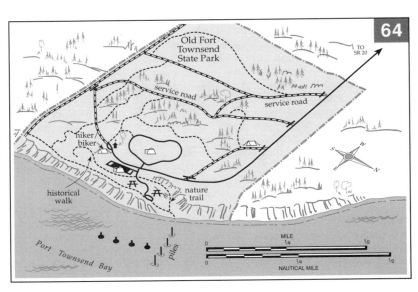

Other trails follow the top of the bluff or wander into the hinterland, back to the group camp.

PORT TOWNSEND

Map 65

Informational displays • Boating • Paddling • Picnicking • Boardwalk • Shopping

Facilities: *Jefferson County Historical Museum:* Restrooms. *Downtown Waterfront Parks:* Picnic tables, children's play equipment, pier with float. *Northwest Maritime Center (when completed in 2007):* Marine chandlery, gift shop, paddlecraft rentals, meeting rooms, classic boat construction labs, viewing decks, boardwalk, dock and floats, interpretive displays

🚐 Port Townsend lies at the north end of the Quimper Peninsula. It can be reached by driving west 5¼ miles from the Hood Canal Bridge and turning north on SR 19, which is signed to Port Townsend. The Keystone ferry, which docks at the ferry terminal on the south side of town, reaches the town from Whidbey Island.

🛥 Port Townsend Bay sits at the confluence of the Strait of Juan de Fuca and Admiralty Inlet.

Port Townsend has made a graceful transition into a tourist-oriented town without sacrificing its integrity. This is no Victorian Disneyland, but a real city with genuine old antique-filled buildings. The antique ambiance is complemented by a cultural one, with shops selling work by the finest Northwest artists, photographers, and craftspeople. Whatever your interest, there is something to lure you here.

Annual events include a Victorian Days festival, a low tide festival, a classic car show, a sea kayaking symposium, a wooden boat show, a salmon fishing derby, a county fair, a quilt show, dance festivals, a boating regatta, plays, music festivals ranging from Bach to bluegrass to Count Basie, and prose and poetry readings by nationally known writers. Many of the events are sponsored by Centrum, a performing arts foundation on the grounds of Fort Worden. Check the website, *www.ptguide.com*, for a schedule.

Even if you do not go to Port Townsend to take in an event, there is still plenty to fascinate you. The town, the best example of a Victorian seacoast town to be found north of San Francisco, has been designated as a National Historical District. Stores in beautifully restored old commercial buildings along Water Street offer hours of wonderful browsing and buying—heavy on the nautical and Victorian. Food purveyors have everything from homemade ice-cream cones to gourmet dinners.

The town's real jewels are its beautiful old Victorian homes, built when Port Townsend seemed destined to be a major center of commerce on Puget Sound. The Chamber of Commerce provides a map describing some seventy points of historical interest that include nearly three dozen private homes built before the turn of the last century. Two weekends a year, in May and September, many of these residences are open for viewing during the city's Historic Homes Tours. Some of the homes operate as bed-and-breakfast inns.

Jefferson County Historical Museum • The numerous antiques stores provide a history lesson in themselves, but for an added dash of nostalgia, drop in at the Jefferson County Historical Museum, in City Hall at the corner of Water and Madison Streets. The museum is open Monday through Saturday from 11:00 A.M. to 4:00 P.M., and on Sunday from 1:00 P.M. to 4:00 P.M. Exhibits include a history of early explorers and settlers, artifacts from local Native tribes, Port Townsend's role in the filming of several movies, the role of the Chinese in the city history, the county maritime heritage, and a grim basement jail.

Downtown Waterfront Parks • On the waterfront across the street from the museum is John Pope Marine Park. This grassy nook above the beach

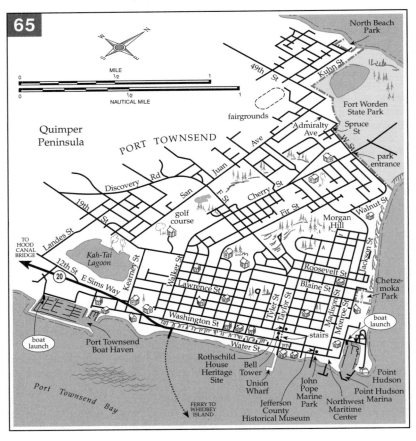

Much of the Port Townsend waterfront is built on piles.

has a few picnic tables and a huge driftwood log with seats carved into both sides and a group of frolicking seals carved at one end. A pier boasts a 60-foot-long float on its north side that, in calm weather, can be used for temporary moorage for downtown visits.

A second public pier, Union Wharf, three blocks to the south at the end of Taylor Street has a float alongside for visitor use. A series of plaques on the rail describes the marine life below and tells the history of the waterfront.

The Northwest Maritime Center • A shoreline boardwalk links to the jetty walkway at Point Hudson, where a terrific facility, designed to celebrate Port Townsend's rich maritime history and culture, is scheduled to open in 2007. The buildings, sitting at the north end of Water Street, immediately south of the Port Hudson Marina, will include a maritime heritage and resource building and a maritime education building. Plans for outdoor public areas include view decks that will wrap around both buildings and a beachfront commons area that will host outdoor community events. A dock with floats will serve the center's moorage requirements.

Port Townsend Marinas (Port of Port Townsend) Map 65

Boating • Paddling • Camping

Facilities: *Point Hudson Resort and Marina:* Guest moorage with power and water, 1-lane paved launch ramp with boarding float, restrooms, showers, laundry, boat pumpout, RV park, bed-and-breakfast inn, motel, restaurants, banquet and meeting rooms, sling hoist, marine chandlery, marine repair. *Boat Haven:* Guest moorage with power and water, 2-lane paved launch ramp with boarding float, gas and diesel, restrooms, showers, laundry, boat pumpout, dump for portable toilets, Travelift hoist, chandlery, marine repairs, U.S. Customs. *Nearby:* Groceries, shopping

Two marinas operated by the Port of Port Townsend bracket the town's waterfront. On the south side is the larger and more modern of the two facilities, Port Townsend Boat Haven; at the north end is Point Hudson Marina, in Point Hudson Harbor. A rock jetty protects the 375 moorages at Boat Haven. The entrance, on the northeast, is clearly marked. Just inside the breakwater are a small basin for commercial boats, the U.S. Coast Guard installation (where the Point Bennett is tied up), and a fuel dock. Once past these, the harbormaster's office and registration dock are immediately on the right.

Here, sling launching is available for trailered boats. A launch ramp at the southwest corner of the harbor is only usable at higher tide levels. The highway between the marina and downtown Port Townsend is filled with a continuous row of new stores—groceries, gas stations, restaurants, and all types of services. The older section of town is about a ¼-mile walk from the marina; bus service is available.

Point Hudson Harbor is closer to downtown attractions, although the facilities are not as large or as nice as those at Boat Haven. The dredged basin lies behind pile jetties immediately south of the point. The jetty on the south side of the entrance has a viewing boardwalk along the top that links with the boardwalk at the Northwest Marine Center.

A float with numerous finger piers is on the northeast side; a long dock on the southwest has additional tie-ups. If the harbor is full, rafting is permitted on this long float. At the southwest corner of the basin, a 1-lane ramp provides launching for trailered boats. The ramp is not usable at low tide levels.

Behind the harbormaster's office on the northeast shore is a commercially operated RV campground with some tent-camping space, a restaurant, a café, and a small

The Hastings Building, the most beautiful of Port Townsend's commercial buildings, dates from 1889.

motel. From here, except at high tide, the beach can be walked all the way north to Point Wilson.

Port Townsend Parks   Map 65

Picnicking • Beachcombing • Paddling • Clamming • Swimming

Facilities: *Chetzemoka Park:* Picnic tables, shelter with fireplace, restrooms, bandstand, children's play equipment. *North Beach Park:* Picnic tables, kitchen shelter, fireplaces, toilets, no water

Area: *Chetzemoka Park:* 5.1 acres; 750 feet of shoreline on the Strait of Juan de Fuca. *North Beach Park:* 1 acre; 310 feet of shoreline on the Strait of Juan de Fuca

🚐 *Chetzemoka Park:* From the north end of Water Street in Port Townsend, drive northwest on Monroe Street for six blocks. Take Blaine Street northeast for a block to Jackson Street and the park. *North Beach Park:* From E Sims Way (SR 20) at the south end of the town, turn northwest on Kearney Street, which Ts into 19th Street in seven blocks. Head west on 19th, and in two blocks, turn north on San Juan Avenue. In 1 1/2 miles, turn west on 49th Street, and in 1/4 mile, go north on Kuhn Street to reach the park in just under 1/2 mile.

🚤 *Chetzemoka Park:* Paddlecraft can be beached at the park 1/4 mile northwest of Point Hudson. The nearest launch areas are at Point Hudson and Fort Worden. *North Beach Park:* Paddlecraft can be beached at the park, which is on the north shore of the Quimper Peninsula, 1 mile west of Point Wilson.

Chetzemoka Park (City of Port Townsend) • This small city park pays tribute to the Klallam Indian chief who proved to be a good friend to early Port Townsend settlers. During the Indian Wars, he was instrumental in discouraging an attack on the whites, an action that surely would have resulted in the loss of far more Indian lives than white.

The city park is on a slight bluff facing Admiralty Inlet, within walking distance of downtown Port Townsend. It can be reached by walking the beach north from Point Hudson for about 1/4 mile at all but extreme high tide. The shore is narrow at high tide, but low tide exposes an expanse of sandy beach.

The park was opened in 1904 when prominent Port Townsend socialites decided that any civilized city should have a public park. With its covered bandstand and formal rose garden, the area is still reminiscent of an old-fashioned park, and one expects to see straw-hatted dandies strolling with their ladies under the blossom-covered arches. During early times, it also held a "zoo" consisting of a deer, a peacock, and a bear.

North Beach Park (Jefferson County) • At North Beach, the steep bluffs on this side of the Quimper Peninsula briefly dip down to the shore. Early Native Americans landed their canoes here and portaged south across the swampy flat to Kah-Tai Lagoon by Port Townsend Bay to avoid tide rips off Point Wilson. Park facilities are rather meager—a few picnic tables and two toilets—but the beach is glorious. The sand slopes gradually into the waters of the strait. Swim if you like, build sand castles, or just let the nearly constant

wind off the channel fill your nostrils with brine-scented air.

The small county park, which abuts the west side of Fort Worden State Park, provides a handy starting point for beach walks east beneath the 200-foot-high bluffs of Fort Worden all the way to Point Wilson, 1½ miles away, or even to Port Townsend another 2 miles distant. The way is passable at all times except high tide, so check the tide table.

Fort Worden State Park and Conference Center   Map 66

Camping • Picnicking • Kite flying • Bicycling • Boating • Paddling • Fishing • Scuba diving • Conferences • Cultural arts • Educational and historical displays • Hiking • Beach walking

Facilities: 80 RV sites (30 EW, 50 EWS), 5 primitive campsites, 3 CMT campsites, picnic tables, water, kitchen shelters, fireplaces, restrooms, showers, bathhouse, toilets, RV pumpout station, laundromat, vacation housing, dormitories, youth hostel, dining hall, snack bar/grocery, 2-lane paved launch ramp with boarding float, fishing pier, moorage floats, 8 mooring buoys, visitor center, Commanding Officer's House, Coast Artillery Museum, Marine Science Center, natural history exhibit, History Center, underwater marine park, hiking trails, tennis courts, gymnasium, outdoor basketball court, volleyball court, chapel, performance theater, conference center, playfields, children's play equipment

Area: 434 acres; 11,020 feet of shoreline on Admiralty Inlet and the Strait of Juan de Fuca

🚐 From Sims Way (SR 20) at the south end of town, turn northwest on Kearney Street. In seven blocks turn northeast on 19th Street, which Ts into Cherry Street in three blocks. Head north on Cherry to arrive at the park in 1½ miles. *Alternatively:* From Water Street at the north end of town, head northwest on Monroe Street, jog a block northeast at Roosevelt Street. Continue northwest on Jackson Street, which becomes Walnut Street in ½ mile. At the park boundary, head west on W Street to Cherry and the park entrance.

🛥 The park launch ramp, moorage floats, and mooring buoys are at the large pier on Admiralty Inlet ½ mile south of Point Wilson and 1 mile northwest of Point Hudson.

Among the state's many outstanding parks, Fort Worden ranks as one of the grandest. Although it lacks the primeval forest environment (there are plenty of parks elsewhere to provide that), it packs a wealth of activities. Since 1972, when the fort became a state park, the facilities at Fort Worden have seen ever-increasing use, not only for traditional state park purposes, but also as a site for conferences, retreats, workshops, sport and music camps, and festivals. It ranks as the most heavily used of the state parks, with more than 1.25 million visitors passing through its gates annually.

The fort's campus exudes the atmosphere of what it once was as a military installation. Although the grounds are nicely kept, they are not quite as carefully manicured as when a crew of up to 300 enlisted men mowed lawns, swept walks, and groomed flowerbeds. Twenty-five of the housing units and historic buildings are available at reasonable rates to groups or families for overnight stays. Many have been refurbished with reproductions of Victorian-era furniture.

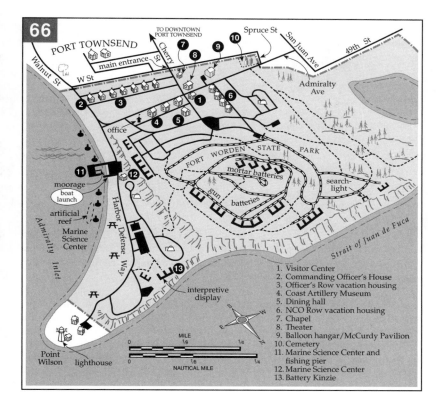

66

PORT TOWNSEND

TO DOWNTOWN PORT TOWNSEND

Spruce St

San Juan Ave

49th St

main entrance

Walnut St

W St

Cherry St

Admiralty Ave

office

FORT WORDEN STATE PARK

mortar batteries

gun batteries

search-light

moorage
boat launch

artificial reef

Marine Science Center

Harbor Defense Way

Admiralty Inlet

Strait of Juan de Fuca

interpretive display

MILE
0   1/8   1/4

NAUTICAL MILE
0   1/8   1/4

Point Wilson   lighthouse

1. Visitor Center
2. Commanding Officer's House
3. Officer's Row vacation housing
4. Coast Artillery Museum
5. Dining hall
6. NCO Row vacation housing
7. Chapel
8. Theater
9. Balloon hangar/McCurdy Pavilion
10. Cemetery
11. Marine Science Center and fishing pier
12. Marine Science Center
13. Battery Kinzie

Barracks now serve as dormitories for use by larger groups. Meal service in the park dining hall is also available. Meeting rooms can be reserved by the day, week, or month, and the post chapel is a favorite spot for weddings. Two fully equipped theaters rent performance space.

A stop at the state park office or the visitor center near the entrance will arm the visitor with maps and a list of current activities. In summer, Centrum, a nonprofit arts foundation, might be sponsoring a music festival or a play. A park leaflet guides the way on a historical walk around the fort's many buildings. Several miles' worth of strolls are available: to the fort cemetery, to the gun emplacements, to the beach, to the lighthouse—to wherever impulse leads.

Next to the park office is the Coast Artillery Museum (open daily, 10:00 A.M. to 4:00 P.M. year-round, 10:00 A.M. to 5:00 P.M. Saturdays in July and August). It displays memorabilia from the fort and has historical information about the coastal fortifications. A video program depicts life at the fort in the early 1900s. The park road leads past the row of officer's quarters to the Commanding Officer's House, which is open to self-guided tours daily from April through October.

Harbor Defense Way drops down to the east beach where a large wharf

Most of the buildings of the old fort remain, making it a fine example of military posts of the early twentieth century.

and a float are the center of marine activity. The float has space for about four boats; overnight moorage is permitted. A 2-lane boat launch ramp on the north side of the pier is protected by its L-shaped bend and a concrete bulkhead. Eight mooring buoys are spaced along the shore north and south of the wharf, although wind and wave action might make an overnight tie-up uncomfortable. Three CMT campsites are on the beach south of the wharf.

On the wharf is the Port Townsend Marine Science Center, which has hands-on exhibits of marine life and conducts summer weekend beach walks, classes, and other marine-oriented activities. Fishing is permitted from the pier; a fish-cleaning station is next to the building. A natural history exhibit across the road from the pier is a collaborative effort with the Burke Museum at the University of Washington; it has exhibits on the geology, ecology, and fossils of the area.

The offshore waters are designated as an underwater park. Scuba divers explore the piles of the old wharf and the sandy bottom along the east shore. North of Point Wilson, a reef attracts divers expert enough to handle the swift current on this side of the point. The white rock of the reef makes a dramatic contrast with brightly colored sea anemones and fish. Spear fishing is not permitted in the waters of the park.

Two types of beaches are found at Point Wilson: on the east, facing on Admiralty Inlet, is a gradually sloping sandy beach, partially protected by the point's curving arm; on the north, the Strait of Juan de Fuca shoreline is a narrower strip, enclosed by rising bluffs and dropping off quickly into the sea. Winds off the strait frequently batter the shore, making walking difficult but exhilarating. The beaches can be followed south or west of Point

Fort Worden: A Changing Scene

The bristling guns of Fort Worden were intended, along with those at Forts Casey and Flagler, to guard the entrance to Puget Sound. Construction on the fort began in 1898 and the first soldiers were assigned in 1902. On the day scheduled for their arrival, the citizens of Port Townsend turned out en masse, complete with a brass band, to welcome them. With dismay and drooping pennants the gentry watched the troop-laden steamer *Majestic* chug by, unaware of the planned celebration, headed for the pier at the fort instead of landing at the town's Union Wharf.

Some small parcels of land within the designated area of the fort had previously been claimed by Port Townsend settlers. The land was needed for fort buildings, and there was also concern that nonmilitary residents so close to the fort might pose a security risk. When negotiations for the property began, there was considerable disagreement between the government and the property owners as to its value. However, when practice firings of the mortar batteries commenced, plaster walls cracked from the concussion, pictures and bric-a-brac came crashing down, and homeowners rushed to sell.

With sixteen 12-inch mortars and twenty-five guns ranging from 3 inches to 12 inches, at full strength Fort Casey was the most heavily fortified of the Puget Sound posts. By 1904 underwater cable communications linked Fort Worden to Forts Casey and Flagler, and the following year it was fully garrisoned with four companies of Coast Artillery troops. With the completion of fire-control stations and five 60-inch searchlight emplacements, the stronghold stood completed by 1912.

In just five years, with the beginning of World War I, the entire character of the fort changed. As additional troops were sent there to be trained for battle on the European front, more barracks were built, and eighteen of the guns were removed for shipment to Europe. At the end of the war, the number of troops stationed at Fort Worden decreased drastically. The only new activity was the construction, in 1920, of a huge balloon hangar and the addition of two companies of men who experimented, unsuccessfully, with using large balloons for gunfire control and observation stations.

The fort saw some activity during World War II as a Harbor Entrance Control Post to monitor radar sites and new underwater sonar and sensing devices; it also served to coordinate all defensive activities on the inland waters. With the end of World War II, all the remaining guns were removed and scrapped. The last military use was during the Korean conflict when units of an Army engineering regiment were stationed here prior to being shipped to the Far East. After the deactivation of the post in 1953 the state of Washington used it as a juvenile diagnostic treatment center, and finally in 1972 it was transferred to the State Parks Commission.

Battery Ash at Fort Worden State Park is one of several batteries that can be explored.

Wilson for some distance, depending on the stamina of the walker. Use care on the north shore not to get trapped by incoming tide.

One of the two camping areas, with fifty campsites, is in an open grassy field west of Harbor Defense Way. None of these campsites are protected from the wind, which can get quite brisk in this exposed location. The road continues on to a parking lot near Battery Kinzie. At the battery, wander through the gun emplacements and rooms where munitions were stored. Still in evidence are the overhead metal tracks that were used for transporting munitions. From the top of the battery is a sweeping 300-degree view of the Strait and Admiralty Inlet, blocked only by the hill behind. Battery Kinzie is the best maintained of the fort's twelve batteries; the others, which are on the hill to the southwest, can be reached by trails from the campground or the residential area.

The park's second campground is upland on the west side, west of the rental houses. Here are two loops with thirty campsites in a wooded section. Five primitive bicycle sites are nearby.

Point Wilson Light Station   Map 66

Views • Historical information • Beach walking

Facilities: Toilets

🚗 Continue through Fort Casey State Park on Harbor Defense Way to the light station gate

🛥 Paddlecraft can be landed on the Point Wilson Beach. The south side is the most protected.

The lighthouse at Admiralty Head on Whidbey Island, which began operation in 1879, was one of the earliest to guide boaters on Washington's inland waters. In order to avoid shoals at Point Wilson, shippers navigating in the dark or fog kept the light well in sight and stayed to the east side of Admiralty Inlet, following the Whidbey Island shoreline. It was not until almost twenty years later that two more lighthouses, at Point No Point and here at Point Wilson, enabled ships to safely follow the shorter route along the western shoreline.

The original lighthouse at Point Wilson was equipped with the most modern Fresnel lens, consisting of an aggregation of seventy-two glass prisms and bull's-eye lenses. The light source, a wick-type lamp that nightly burned three gallons of whale oil, kerosene, or lard, was eventually replaced by a 1000-watt electric bulb. A 12-inch steam whistle signaled a warning to boats in the fog.

A Coast Guard Auxiliary volunteer explains the working of the light at Point Wilson.

Until 1939, when the Coast Guard took over lighthouse administration, the U.S. Lighthouse Service operated most stations with civil service personnel. In addition to keeping the light clean, winding the clockworks that rotated it, polishing the brass, trimming the lamp wicks (which prompted the nickname "wickie"), and other maintenance tasks, the keeper was expected to keep a garden and livestock to feed himself and his family. Life at Point Wilson, within a short distance of Port Townsend, was far better than at many of the more remote light stations along the coast.

The beacon is now automated; public tours of the lighthouse are conducted by the Coast Guard Auxiliary on Wednesday from 1:00 to 4:00 P.M., April through September. A short, very interesting film introduces visitors to the workings of a lighthouse.

chapter ten

The Eastern Strait of Juan de Fuca

NEARING THE END OF THEIR NORTHWARD JOURNEY, the waters of Puget Sound pour into the long tongue of the Strait of Juan de Fuca before making the final transition to the open sea. The 100-mile-long waterway is a commercial superhighway down which freighters and tankers stream, linking Puget Sound ports with markets throughout the world.

❊ Many pleasure boaters avoid the open stretches of the strait, favoring inland waters or hugging the comforting western shore of Whidbey Island. Stomach-churning swells can be built up by winds sweeping the length of the channel. Fog banks creeping in off the ocean linger in the strait long after they have cleared from inland waters. At such times, when you cannot rely on line of sight, good navigational skills are essential to make the 25-mile crossing from Admiralty Inlet to Victoria or the San Juan Islands.

On clear days and when seas are calm, this long arm of the sea offers sailors steady winds and joyously endless tacks, while cruisers find numerous bays and beaches to explore. Waters here are legendary for salmon, enormous halibut, and bottomfish; many of the small boats seen in the strait are those of anglers intent on landing their limit.

The eastern half of the strait, from Port Townsend to Port Angeles, provides boaters somewhat of a transition from the shelter and civilization of the inland waters to the more rigorous demands of the outer reaches of the passage. Two deep inlets, Sequim Bay and Discovery Bay, offer the only well-protected harbors with good anchorages along this south shore. The only town with marine facilities is Port Angeles, which is somewhat sheltered by Ediz Hook and man-made breakwaters.

PROTECTION ISLAND
Map 67a

Not many boaters take note of the rhinoceros auklet, a black, stubby little bird that has been described as flying with the grace of a "winged brick." It is under water that it moves like a ballet dancer, using its wings for propulsion as it pursues herring or smelt and scoops them into its blunt beak. The auklet hunts open waters during the day, and not until twilight does it return to cliff-edge burrows, with fish for its chicks dangling from its heavy, bony

Opposite: Hikers disappear into fog rolling in off the Strait of Juan de Fuca at Dungeness Wildlife Recreation Area.

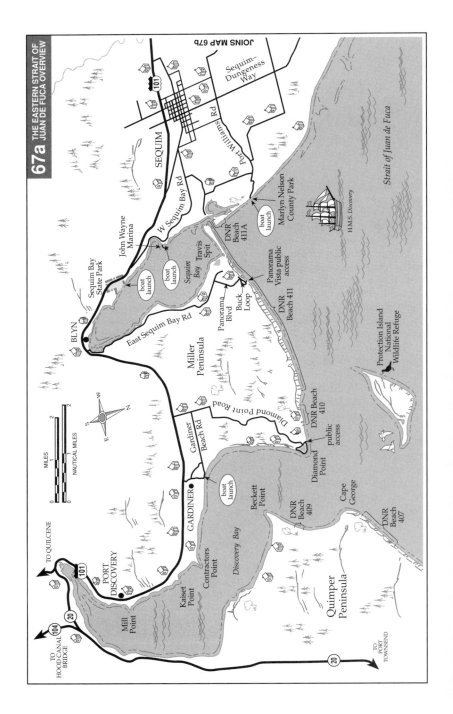

JOINS MAP 67b

SEQUIM

Sequim-Dungeness Way

Port Williams Rd

Strait of Juan de Fuca

Marlyn Nelson County Park

boat launch

H.M.S. Discovery

DNR Beach 411A

Panorama Vista public access

Protection Island National Wildlife Refuge

John Wayne Marina

W Sequim Bay Rd

Sequim Bay State Park

boat launch

boat launch

Sequim Bay

Travis Spit

Panorama Blvd

Buck Loop

DNR Beach 411

BLYN

East Sequim Bay Rd

Miller Peninsula

DNR Beach 410

Gardiner Beach Rd

Diamond Point Road

public access

Diamond Point

MILES

NAUTICAL MILES

N W S E

GARDINER

boat launch

Beckett Point

DNR Beach 409

Cape George

DNR Beach 407

Quimper Peninsula

TO QUILCENE

PORT DISCOVERY

Discovery Bay

Contractors Point

Kaiset Point

Mill Point

HOOD CANAL BRIDGE

104

20

101

TO PORT TOWNSEND

20

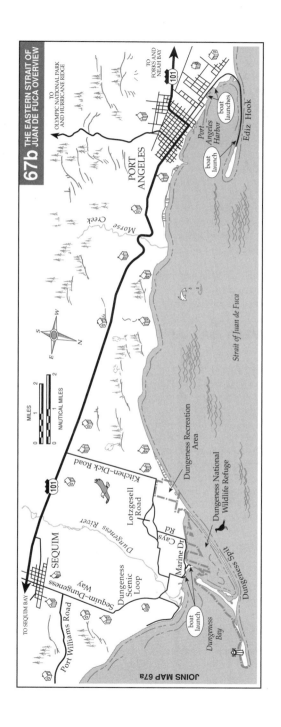

67b THE EASTERN STRAIT OF JUAN DE FUCA OVERVIEW

TO
OLYMPIC NATIONAL PARK
AND HURRICANE RIDGE

TO
FORKS AND
NEAH BAY

101

PORT
ANGELES

Port
Angeles Harbor

boat
launches

boat launch

Ediz Hook

boat
launch

Morse Creek

Strait of Juan de Fuca

MILES
0   1   2

NAUTICAL MILES
0   1   2

N
W   E
S

Dungeness Recreation
Area

Dungeness National
Wildlife Refuge

Kitchen–Dick Road

Lotzgesell
Road

Dungeness River

Cays
Rd

Marine Dr

Dungeness Spit

SEQUIM

Dungeness Scenic Loop

Sequim–Dungeness Way

101

TO SEQUIM BAY

Port Williams Road

boat
launch

Dungeness
Bay

JOINS MAP 67a

bill. Studies revealed that an estimated 17,000 pairs, or about 96 percent of the rhinoceros auklets in the Lower 48 states, along with pelagic cormorants, glaucous-winged gulls, pigeon guillemots, black oystercatchers, and other seabirds nest and raise their young in the sandy cliffs of the 400-acre island. The few remaining pairs of tufted puffins still remaining on Puget Sound are believed to nest on Protection Island.

Although the island was briefly farmed, and then scheduled for a gargantuan real estate development, environmentalists, including the Audubon Society and The Nature Conservancy, rallied to protect it. In 1980 Congressman Don Bonker introduced a bill to appropriate $4 million for purchase of land on the island, and in 1988 Protection Island was officially established as a National Wildlife Refuge. The U.S. Fish and Wildlife Service currently owns 316 acres; the remaining 48 acres of land are owned and managed by the Washington State DFW.

The federally owned portion of Protection Island is closed to all public use year-around. Visits to the state-managed lands at the west end are strongly discouraged from March through September when birds are nesting. These intrusions might also disturb harbor seals, which in spring deliver their pups on sun-warmed sandspits. A 200-yard buffer zone has been established around the island; boaters should stay at least this distance offshore.

DISCOVERY BAY AND THE MILLER PENINSULA
Map 67a

Boating • Paddling • Birdwatching • Beach walking

Facilities: *Gardiner:* 1-lane paved launch ramp, toilet

🚗 *Gardiner:* From US 101 6³/₄ miles north of the intersection with SR 20 at the south end of Discovery Bay, turn east on Gardiner Beach Road. Follow it for a little over ¹/₄ mile to the water and the launch ramp. *Diamond Point:* Turn north off US 101 8¹/₄ miles northwest of the SR 20 intersection at the south end of Discovery Bay, turn on Diamond Point Road, and follow it for 4³/₄ miles to the junction with Diamond Shore Lane North. In 200 yards this road intersects Beach Drive and Access Road. The latter extends about 300 feet to the north to an opening in the bulkheads and a signed public access. There is limited parking along the head of the road and on Beach Drive, south of the access point.

🛥 *Gardiner:* The ramp is on the west side of Discovery Bay, 2³/₄ miles south of Diamond Point. *DNR beaches:* From the Diamond Point access, Beach 409 is 1¹/₂ n.m. to the east, and Beach 407 is 2 n.m. to the northeast.

After his arduous voyage around Africa's Cape of Good Hope and across the Pacific, George Vancouver was pleased to find the sheltered arm of Discovery Bay for a nearly week-long layover to repair his ships and provide the crew some R and R. He wrote glowingly of the beauty of the bay; although the bay is lovely, perhaps his enthusiasm was affected by all those months at sea with only a scruffy crew to look at.

Discovery Bay hasn't changed a great deal since Vancouver dropped anchor here. Only a few communities and homes along the shore mark the arrival of civilization. The sinuous 8-mile-long inlet provides excellent anchorages at numerous spots along the shore, but there is nothing in the way of boating facilities except the launch ramp at Gardiner. ❋Explore the length the bay, but be wary of the mile-long mudflat and submerged piles at its head

The only public shorelands on the bay are two sections of DNR beach at Cape George. Beach 409, a 1475-foot strip of tidelands, is about a mile north of Beckett Point; Beach 407, which is just east of the tip of Cape George beneath a sheer 1500-foot cliff, is 5035 feet long. Neither beach has upland access, but both can be reached by boat from Gardiner; only the shorelands below mean high water are public.

Gardiner Launch Ramp (Port of Port Townsend) ● This boat launch site is more easily found than the one at Diamond Point, and is farther into Discovery Bay. It is suitable for launching trailered boats in addition to hand-carried craft. A gravel lot across the road has parking for a dozen cars.

Diamond Point ● Historically, Diamond Point is unique. Although this point on the Miller Peninsula originally was one of the many military reservation lands along the sound, in 1894 it became a quarantine station, with a hospital and detention area for ship passengers suspected of having been exposed to contagious diseases. It operated until 1935, when the facility was moved to Port Townsend. A deteriorated wharf on the south side of the point was once used by ships waiting out the quarantine period and undergoing fumigation for vermin and insects.

Unlike other military reservation lands that became parks, Diamond Point now sports row upon row of summer homes. From a small break in the

The shack and wharf that were used by the quarantine station at Diamond Point during the early twentieth century can still be seen today.

bulkheads along the north shore, you can launch a cartop boat or paddlecraft to explore the offshore perimeter of Protection Island or to visit two strips of DNR beach to the west.

West of Diamond Point, DNR Beach 410, a 2710-foot stretch of tidelands, begins just beyond the beach homes, below a wooded bluff. DNR Beach 411 begins 1/4 mile beyond the west end of Beach 410 in the middle of Thompson Spit and continues for nearly 5 glorious miles to the end of Travis Spit by Sequim Bay.

Panorama Vista Access (Clallam County)   Map 67a
Beach walking • Birdwatching

Facilities: None

🚐 Turn off US 101 on Blyn Crossing (at the south end of Sequim Bay, about 2 1/4 miles south of the state park). Follow Old Blyn Road east from Blyn Crossing for 1/2 mile to E Sequim Bay Road. Continue northeast on it for 4 miles to Panorama Boulevard. Turn right (east) here, and in 3/4 mile, at Buck Loop and Buck Court, turn right (east) again on Buck Loop. In another 1/4 mile, at the intersection of Buck Loop and Deer Court, is a gate at a small Clallam County park

🚤 The beach can be reached by boat from Diamond Point, Sequim Bay, or from Marlyn Nelson County Park at Port Williams, north of Gibson Spit. Small boats and paddlecraft can be landed easily.

DNR Beach 411, on the Miller Peninsula, can be reached on foot from a road on the east side of Sequim Bay and a Clallam County beach access point. Park at the gate to the access and walk down a wide grassy path 500 yards to the beach. Here a staircase below a small clearing drops down to Beach 411.

The public beach, which lies below mean high water and runs for 25,710 feet, extends west to the end of Travis Spit and east to the middle of Thompson Spit near Diamond Point. Protection Island can be seen to the east. Some walkable beach is exposed at all times except extreme high water. At high tide, the beach is about 6 feet wide or less, with high steep bluffs above in spots. Much of the beach is cobble, although Travis Spit is sandy; shellfish should not be taken from Travis Spit because they are hazardous to eat due to a domestic sewage outfall on nearby Gibson Spit. Leave dogs at home or keep them on a leash; use special care in walking to avoid disturbing shorebirds and waterfowl nesting in beach grass and driftwood.

SEQUIM BAY
Map 67a

The continuous action of wind and waves from the Strait of Juan de Fuca wears away the soft glacial-till bluffs and then deposits the material on several long curving sandspits along the north shore of the Olympic Peninsula. Travis Spit and Gibson Spit, at the entrance to Sequim Bay would join, if it were not for dredging of the channel. If they did, Sequim Bay would be merely an enormous lagoon.

❋ Boat access to the inlet is via a dredged channel that starts at the red entrance buoy, runs parallel along the north side of Travis Spit, and then threads along the western shore. Consult a good navigational chart and enter with care, favoring the west side and watching channel markers closely to avoid Middle Ground, a large shoal that lies just inside the entrance; some buoys tow under during strong tides and might not be visible. Once inside there are no navigational hazards, and excellent anchorages can be found throughout the bay in up to 20 fathoms.

Some early maps show the name of the bay as Washington Harbor, but local settlers preferred the more descriptive Indian name of Sequim, generally thought to mean "quiet water." Today, Washington Harbor refers only to the small community at the entrance.

Pitship Point and John Wayne Marina (Port of Port Angeles) Map 68
Boating • Paddling • Picnicking • Clamming • Fishing

Facilities: Guest moorage with power and water, 2-lane paved launch ramp with boarding float, gas and diesel, boat pumpout, dump for portable toilets, restrooms, showers, restaurant, marine supplies, laundromat, public meeting rooms, picnic tables, fireplaces, bait, tackle, kayak, bike, and crabbing gear rentals

🚗 From US 101 2 miles south of Sequim, turn north on Whitefeather Road to reach the marina in ¾ mile.

🚤 The marina is on the west side of the bay, south of Travis Spit.

On the west shore of Sequim Bay, where a meager little boat launch and a strip of public beach once existed, now stands a sparkling marina—and it's all due to movie actor John Wayne. Wayne brought his converted mine sweeper, the *Wild Goose*, into Sequim Bay on his frequent visits to Puget Sound and was so fond of the area that he acquired property at Pitship Point. The Port of Port Angeles asked him for land for a marina to serve the needs of Sequim and Port Angeles residents, and he generously donated 23 acres adjoining the port's existing public lands.

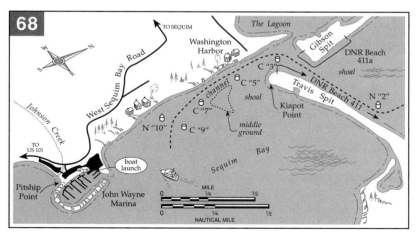

John Wayne Marina is named for the movie actor, who often visited the area.

The marina snuggles neatly behind a curving rock breakwater on the north side of the point. A walkway leads south across a scenic bridge where Johnson Creek empties into the bay. The beach south of the breakwater remains natural, with a long sandy tideflat for clam digging and puddle dabbling.

The first pier inside the marina breakwater is open for guest moorage on the inside. Next to it are the gas dock and a fine 2-lane paved launch ramp. Floats G and H, the first two piers in the moorage area, have guest slips at the inner end of the floats. Guest moorage is on a first-come, first-serve basis.

Sequim Bay State Park Map 69

Camping • Picnicking • Boating • Paddling • Fishing • Clamming • Crabbing • Hiking • Scuba diving • Field and group sports • Marine life study • Birdwatching

Facilities: 60 standard campsites, 16 RV campsites (EWS), 3 primitive campsites, group camp, picnic tables, fireplaces, picnic shelters, group picnic areas, restrooms, showers, amphitheater, dock and float (removed in winter), 7 mooring buoys, 2-lane paved launch ramp with boarding float, interpretive center, hiking trails, children's play equipment, tennis court, softball field, quarter basketball court, horseshoe pits, ELC

Area: 94.62 acres; 4909 feet of shoreline on Sequim Bay

The park is 4 miles south of Sequim on US 101.

The park is on the southwest side of Sequim Bay.

Here's a wonderful state park for either boaters or land-bound campers! Visitors arriving by water can tie up to the dock, send the kids ashore to work off energy on hiking trails and tennis courts (or even to camp for the night), and settle back to enjoy some peace and quiet. Or perhaps even the "old folks"

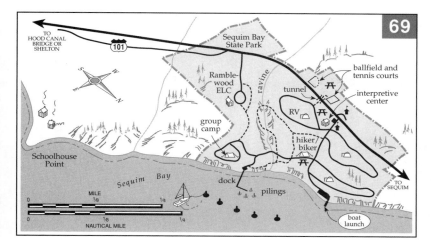

would enjoy a ramble through the woods and along the beach. One draw-back: US 101 runs along the west edge of the park, and in some campsites the drone of traffic is not obscured by the trees. At the park entrance, a one-room interpretive center explains the various habitats and characteristics of the marine invertebrates and bivalves found on the beach.

At the south edge of the park, a long pier has a 50-foot float on the end

Nature's Evening Fireworks

At times, boaters can see stunning displays of nighttime luminescence in Puget Sound. Sequim Bay is an especially good place to experience it. When this phenomenon occurs, any disturbance in the water, even the slightest dip of an oar, produces a burst of ghostly radiance. A churning motor leaves a milky white wake on the black water, and glittery streaks mark the trails of fish swimming just below the surface. Such luminescence is caused by certain dinoflagel-lates—minute single-celled marine organisms that are part of plankton. Small numbers of these organisms are nearly always present in the water, and many boaters have been startled by fireworks in their darkened toilets when they flushed with seawater.

Certain combinations of nutrients, water salinity, and temperature can cause a sudden "bloom," or rapid increase in organisms of a particular kind. Dinoflagellates such as *noctiluca* ("night light") or a species of *Gonyaulax* noted for its luminescence might be the ones affected, resulting in a remark-able nighttime display. Several kinds of jellyfish also have this quality, but their luminescence shows as specific points of light when they are disturbed, rather than an overall glow of the water.

Sequim Bay State Park provides a dock, float, and buoys for the convenience of visiting boaters.

where overnight tie-ups are permitted. ❄At mean low water, the float has 6 to 7 feet of water under it, but a pile directly north stands in only 3 feet at the same time; use care approaching or leaving the dock at low tide. Additional moorage is on seven state park buoys spread along the shore. A 2-lane launch ramp, farther north along the beach, is steep enough to be used even at minus tides.

The park flows down a series of wooded terraces on the hillside above the bay. A ravine with a cool trickling stream separates campsites on the north from picnic areas and a group camp on the south. Trees obscure the view of the bay from the campground, but there are water vistas, both high and low, from trails that thread along the embankment and shore.

A tunnel leads under the highway from the main park area to a few more picnic sites, tennis courts, and a baseball diamond on the west side of the highway. A separate entrance, a few hundred yards south of the main park entrance, leads to Ramblewood, the park's ELC, which can be reserved for group use.

Marlyn Nelson County Park (Clallam County) Map 67a

Boating • Paddling • Picnicking • Beach walking

Facilities: 1-lane launch ramp, picnic tables, fire grates, toilet, no water
Area: 1 acre; 500 feet of shoreline on the Strait of Juan de Fuca

🚐 From US 101 at Sequim, take the (Sequim Avenue, City Center, Dungeness Scenic Loop) exit and continue north on Sequim Avenue for 1½ miles to Port Williams Road. Turn east on Port Williams Road and follow it to its end at the park in 2¾ miles.

🚢 The park is on the south side of the Strait of Juan de Fuca, 1½ miles north of the entrance to Sequim Bay.

The influence of the little steamers of the early-day Mosquito Fleet extended clear out into the Strait of Juan de Fuca; Port Angeles was one stopover point, and Port Williams, near the entrance to Sequim Bay, was another. Cars followed a rough route from the villages of Sequim and Port Washington to reach the Port Williams dock, where passengers disembarked and freight was unloaded. Where once there was a post office, hotel, dance hall, and residences, there is now only a tiny county park with a launch ramp, some picnic tables, and two fire grates.

The park opens the way to beach walks below 80-foot-high bluffs of vertical glacial till. The beach walk north is halted in ½ mile by the boundaries of a private game farm. South is Gibson Spit, which encloses a salt-marsh lagoon. The ½-mile section of tidelands wrapping around the tip of the spit is designated as DNR Beach 411A. Shellfish taken from either Gibson Spit or Travis Spit might be hazardous to eat due to a nearby domestic sewage outfall.

DUNGENESS BAY
Map 70

🚐 To access the recreation areas on Dungeness Bay, from the town of Sequim, at the intersection of Washington Street and Sequim Avenue, head north on Sequim Avenue, which is signed as the Dungeness Scenic Loop (well worth the drive in itself); the western end of this loop drive rejoins US 101 at Kitchen–Dick Road, 4 miles west of Sequim.

🚢 The entrance to the bay is on the west shore of the Strait of Juan de Fuca, 17 n.m. west of Port Townsend and 16 n.m. east of Port Angeles

One of the most spectacular land features on Washington's inland waters is Dungeness Spit, the 5-mile-long ribbon of sand at the delta of the Dungeness River. This longest natural spit in the United States has been built up by action of the wind and water current, which causes silt from the river and eroded material from nearby glacial-till bluffs to be deposited in a long, curving sandbar. The spit encloses Dungeness Bay, a broad harbor open on the east. Graveyard Spit, a secondary finger of sand, extends from the north, nearly bisecting the bay.

✳ A shoal extending ¾ mile to the northeast from the lighthouse is marked by a lighted bell buoy; however the buoy might tow under during strong currents. Boaters with local knowledge enter the inner lagoon through a winding, unmarked channel, but much of this lagoon holds less than a fathom of water at mean lower low tide, so great care must be used. Anchorages can be found south of the tip of Dungeness Spit in 5 to 9 fathoms of water. The hook of land affords some protection from swells off the strait, but there is little shelter from strong winds.

George Vancouver gave the area its name. It reminded him of Dungeness in the British Channel, so he called this New Dungeness. Over time, local usage shortened it to Dungeness, a name that now applies to the spit, the harbor, the river, the community, and also the tasty crustacean that frequents the bay. Only the lighthouse retains the original name.

The New Dungeness Lighthouse was the first to guard Washington's inland waters. In 1857, when it was built, it stood 100 feet tall, but over the years the masonry weakened, caused perhaps by a structural flaw. When the Canadian army began practice firing cannons from fortifications on Vancouver Island in 1927, the reverberations caused serious cracks in the lighthouse mortar. It became necessary to remove the upper third of the tower, bringing it down to its present height of 63 feet. When this was done, the old oil-fired light was scrapped and a larger Fresnel lens was brought

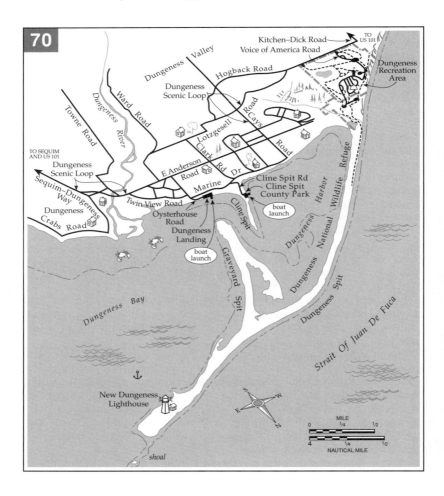

from the decommissioned lighthouse at Admiralty Head. That well-traveled lens is now in the Coast Guard Museum in Seattle. The current light is a prosaic rotating aero beacon.

Graveyard Spit did indeed once serve as a graveyard. A group of Tsimshian Indians from British Columbia who camped here in 1868 were descended upon in the night and massacred by a party of local Klallam Indians. One woman escaped, despite serious wounds, and sought refuge in the lighthouse. The bodies of her companions were buried on the spit. Graveyard Spit itself is now a National Wildlife Refuge.

Several public accesses are on the mainland shore, facing on Dungeness Bay. Clam digging and crabbing are permitted on any of the public lands; all oysters in Dungeness Bay are private property, however. Buy them from a local store.

Dungeness Bay Boat Launches (Clallam County) Map 70

Boating • Paddling • Clamming • Crabbing

Facilities: *Dungeness Landing:* 1-lane paved launch ramp with boarding float, restrooms, picnic tables, informational display. *Cline Spit County Park:* 1-lane launch ramp, parking, toilet

🚗 *Dungeness Landing:* Follow the Dungeness Scenic Loop, as described previously. At the junction with Twin View Road, Marine Drive, and Oysterhouse Road, 8 3/4 miles from Sequim, take the latter downhill 1/4 mile to the launch area. *Cline Spit County Park:* At the corner of Marine Drive and Oysterhouse Road, take Marine Drive west for 1/2 mile to Cline Spit Road, which drops downhill 1/4 mile to the park

⛴ *Dungeness Landing:* The ramp is on the south side of Dungeness Bay, and the east side of Cline Spit. ❀ The water offshore is quite shoal, and the narrow channel from the end of the ramp to deeper water is marked on both sides by white poles. *Cline Spit County Park:* The park is on the west side of Cline Spit. Approach the harbor from Dungeness Bay, winding through the shallow channel between Graveyard Spit and Cline Spit. ❀ The channel is unmarked, and it and the bay have about a fathom of water at low tide, so caution is advised when approaching.

Dungeness Landing Boat Launch • The 1-lane paved ramp faces on a long tideflat that extends outward toward the tip of Graveyard Spit; a dredged channel makes the ramp usable even at minus tides. At the beach are a few picnic tables and a pair of information panels describing the shellfish of Dungeness Bay and the bay environment.

Cline Spit County Park • Clallam County has developed a strip of state park property on Cline Spit, facing on the inner lagoon, as a launch ramp and small day-use public access area. The 1-lane ramp is quite long and is usable at lower tides; however, boats leaving the lagoon must negotiate the circuitous channel around the ends of Cline and Graveyard Spits. There is parking here for about a dozen cars and trailers. The ramp provides an ideal put-in for paddle exploration of Dungeness Bay.

Dungeness Recreation Area (Clallam County)   Map 70

Camping • Picnicking • Hiking • Birdwatching • Viewpoints • Horseback riding

Facilities: 67 campsites, picnic tables, fire pits, group camping/picnic area with shelter, restrooms, showers, RV pumpout station, hiking trails, horse trails, children's play equipment

Area: 216 acres; 2500 feet of shoreline on the Strait of Juan de Fuca

🚐 Follow the Dungeness Scenic Loop, described previously, or catch the west end of it on the west side of Sequim by taking Kitchen–Dick Road (signed to Dungeness Recreation Area and Dungeness National Wildlife Refuge) north for 3¼ miles to where it bends east as Lotzgesell Road. In another ¼ mile, turn north on Voice of America Road, signed to the park and refuge, and reach the park in ½ mile.

This fine Clallam County park serves as a companion to the Dungeness National Wildlife Refuge, providing camping and upland recreation for people visiting the spit. The park is on a 100-foot bluff above the water. No paths

lead directly to the shore; however, several cliff-edge picnic areas and a trail that threads between them provide stunning views of the strait and islands to the north. To the south is an equally breathtaking panorama of snow-draped Olympic peaks.

A large section of the park is open grassland with occasional thickets, providing a home for California quail, pheasant, bobwhites, mourning doves, and songbirds such as western meadowlark. A small pond hidden behind a low ridge attracts ducks and sometimes even whistling swans. The park's several horse trails are closed on weekends and holidays between April 15 and October 15.

Facilities here rival the best of the state parks. Spacious, level campsites are separated by a nice buffer of shrubbery, and restrooms are modern and clean. The northern boundary of the park abuts the wildlife refuge; trails through a wooded upland lead down to the spit.

A trail skirts the top of a bluff in the Dungeness Recreation Area.

Dungeness National Wildlife Refuge Map 70

Hiking • Beach walking • Birdwatching • Fishing • Clamming • Crabbing

Facilities: Hiking trails (entrance fee charged), restrooms, interpretive displays, no water

Area: 755 acres; 45,000 feet of shoreline on Dungeness Bay and the Strait of Juan de Fuca

Follow directions to the Dungeness Recreation Area, described previously. The National Wildlife Refuge trailhead is just beyond the camping areas of the recreation area.

Among birdwatchers, Dungeness Spit is legendary, although one doesn't need to be a dedicated ornithologist to appreciate the natural treasures of the refuge. Here is the beach walk to end all beach walks; only the most hardy could explore all the shores in one day—but dawdling is so enjoyable that it doesn't really matter if the end of the spit is reached. Leave your pets home—none are permitted in the refuge, and it can be a long, roasting wait in the car until you return.

Two view platforms (with disabled access) near the top of the bluff offer views east over the spit and the lighthouse at its end. Separate trails for horses and hikers leave the trailhead. An entry fee is paid at the trailhead ($3 per person in 2005). The grove that the trail passes through before descending to

Dungeness Spit extends for five miles along the Strait of Juan de Fuca.

the beach offers a chance to enjoy a contrasting environment. Here fir and spruce provide homes for owls, sparrows, chickadees, bald eagles, raccoons, squirrels, and other wildlife common to coniferous forests. Informational displays describe the variety of life that can be seen along the spit, in the lagoon, or in offshore waters.

The inner shore of Dungeness Spit peters out gradually into tideflats and eelgrass-filled shallows and a limited area where, in season, clams can be dug and crabs can be trapped. The outer, breaker-washed shore of the spit is smooth and slopes more steeply into the water, with silver piles of nature-sculpted driftwood lining the high tide level. For extended walks, pack a lunch, a canteen of water, and spare clothing. If the weather is severe, stay off the spit because wave-tossed drift logs can be hazardous. Beyond the first ½ mile, the inner beach of the spit, on Dungeness Harbor, is closed to public access year-round because of the significant nesting grounds found there.

The lighthouse near the end of the spit has been deactivated and is controlled remotely; however, volunteers keep the facilities open for tours during summer months. If you are determined to reach the end of the spit, be aware that it is a 5½-mile hike from the parking lot to the lighthouse.

Nearly every species of waterfowl known to Washington shores can be found here at some time of the year. A display at the refuge compares the spit to a large hotel—some of the residents are permanent, while others check in at various times for short stays. The kinds of birds vary somewhat from the inner shore to the outer shore and as one advances along the spit. Some, such as black brants, prefer brackish waters, while gulls and terns favor the outer shore where currents bring small fish to the surface. Shyer species, such as scoters, dunlins, cormorants, and plovers, stay at the outer end of the spit, where fewer hikers stray. Harbor seals might also be seen here, sunning on the shore or popping their heads from breakers to stare curiously.

Hunting is not permitted in the refuge, but in the fall birds might be shy because of nearby hunting and might stay out farther and be more difficult to spot. During the spring nesting season, use special care to not disturb the birds or their nests. Visitors might unwittingly distress wildlife with their activities. Windsurfing disturbs marine mammals, and kite flying frightens birds from their nests, as they mistake the hovering kites for predators.

PORT ANGELES

Map 71

Boating • Paddling • Fishing • Shopping • Views • Bicycling • Walking

Facilities: Stores and businesses offering a full range of services and shopping
🚐 On US 101, 17 miles west of Sequim.
🚤 ❄ The only obstructions in the bay are the log-booming sites at the north-west end. Small boats must watch for logs and deadheads that sometimes float in the bay, creating a hazard. Use care when large ships are moving about.

Port Angeles, with a population of 28,000, is the largest city on the Olympic Peninsula. It boasts a dramatically scenic setting—the Olympic Mountains rise abruptly at its backdoor, on the eastern skyline is the glacier-covered pyramid of Mount Baker, and the gently encircling arm of Ediz Hook guards its waterfront.

Although it has long been known as a portal to the high peaks of the Olympics, Port Angeles rarely had been considered as a marine cruising destination. That changed, however, with the opening of its fine waterfront facilities catering to tourists and pleasure boaters. The city remains distinctly blue collar, however, with smokestacks dominating the skyline, mountains of logs lining the waterfront, and boat basins filled with far more fishing boats than pleasure craft.

The 3½-mile-long sandspit of Ediz Hook encloses Port Angeles Harbor. The natural harbor enjoys a colorful flow of commercial boat traffic. Freighters stop here to load logs and lumber products, tankers as well as freighters sometimes anchor in the protected waters of the broad, deep bay, and the MV *Coho*, a 340-foot-long Black Ball ferry that runs from Port Angeles to Victoria, British Columbia, is berthed on the downtown waterfront. Victoria, on Vancouver Island, lies directly north across the Strait of Juan de Fuca. Canadian boaters entering American waters often stop at Port Angeles to check through U.S. Customs.

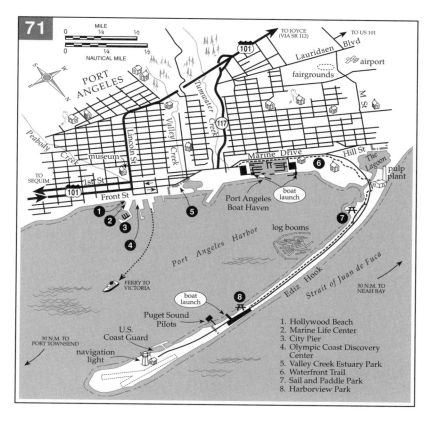

1. Hollywood Beach
2. Marine Life Center
3. City Pier
4. Olympic Coast Discovery Center
5. Valley Creek Estuary Park
6. Waterfront Trail
7. Sail and Paddle Park
8. Harborview Park

Waterfront Trail • This fine walking, jogging, and bicycling path circles Port Angeles Harbor for some 6 miles. Begin at City Pier, and then follow Marine Drive around the west end of the harbor. Along the way, the trail pauses briefly at Valley Creek Estuary Park at the west end of W Front Street. Here, a covered pavilion, view tower, and informational displays give trail users a nice rest. At the south entrance to the pulp mill, the trail switches to the other side of the road, and then crosses back to the inside of Ediz Hook at a pedestrian crosswalk in the heart of the mill. From here, it continues eastward along the inside of the hook to its end at Harborview Park, near the Coast Guard station gate.

The full extent of the trail, known as the Olympic Discovery Trail, currently goes east from Port Angeles to Sequim. Plans are for it to eventually run from Port Townsend to Forks, a total distance of some 150 miles.

Port Angeles Boat Haven Map 71

Boating • Paddling

Facilities: Guest moorage with power and water, diesel, gas, restrooms, pumpout station, dump for portable toilets, restrooms, showers, marine supplies and repair, 2 1-lane launch ramps with boarding floats, sling and marine rail haulout, U.S. Customs, groceries, ice, bait, deli, restaurants, tidal grid, boat rental and charter. *Nearby:* Shopping

🚗 The marina is on the west side of the city on W Marine Drive. The boat basin has two entrances, one on the east, with the port offices, and one on the west.

🛥 The boat basin is at the southwest side of Port Angeles Harbor behind a jetty and log-boom breakwater. Both east and west ends of the boat basin have launch ramps. Guest moorage is on the middle float on the east side of the marina.

Raising the Roof in Port Angeles

Four mountain streams drain from the Olympic foothills through Port Angeles. In early days the business district on the waterfront was subject to frequent flooding during high tides and heavy rains. In 1914, dirt was sluiced down from a hill to the east and the waterfront was filled in, elevating it 10 feet. Existing buildings were raised, or their first floors became basements. A number of these lifted structures, as well as hollow sidewalks built on pillars, can be seen in a walk through town. The basement level of Harbor Towne was once at street level. Raised buildings on piles can be seen from the alley between Front and 1st from Oak to Cherry, and an elevated sidewalk can be seen by looking south from Railroad Avenue to Front Street between Laurel and Oak. The Clallam County Historical Museum, housed in the old County Courthouse at 4th and Lincoln, has displays showing further town history.

Valley Creek Estuary Park, along the Waterfront Trail, is a nifty place to stop and explore.

The Port Angeles Boat Haven, operated by the Port of Port Angeles, lies in a breakwater-protected basin on the west end of the waterfront. Guest moorage is on Dock F, which is in the middle on the east side. Restrooms and most facilities are onshore at the east end; the marina office and gas float are at the end of the jetty, opposite this dock.

Two separate boat ramps are found at the marina. The primary launch facility is on the west side of the basin, where there is a 1-lane ramp that empties directly into the bay. Floats are placed here in the summer, but are removed at other times to protect them from weather. At the northeast corner of the basin, well protected by the landfill jetty, is a 1-lane ramp. Maneuvering space and parking on the east side are less generous than those to the west, so the ramp is generally used only when weather makes the other ramp difficult to use. The outboard side of the marina berm is lined with log booms.

City Pier   Map 71

Fishing • Viewpoint • Informational display • Marine laboratory • Boat tours

Facilities: Guest moorage *(no water or power)*, U.S. Customs, picnic tables, restrooms, performance stage, marine research laboratory, viewing tower, fishing pier, waterfront trail

Area: 0.1 acre; 300 feet of shoreline on Port Angeles Harbor

🚐 The pier is at the intersection of Lincoln and Front Streets in downtown Port Angeles.

🛥️ The pier is at the southeast side of Port Angeles Harbor. Guest floats are on the inland (southeast) side of the pier.

The focal point of the Port Angeles waterfront is City Pier, a multiuse facility that serves nicely to welcome visiting boaters to the city. Two floats, one with finger floats, are secured to the inside of the pier. Guest moorage here is limited to craft up to 40 feet, with a maximum stay of twenty-four hours. At the end of the pier, a two-story viewing tower provides a 360-degree view of harbor activity, the strait, Mount Baker, and Hurricane Ridge rising dramatically behind the city. Large ships such as military research vessels

The midsummer sand sculpture competition at Hollywood Beach is a highlight of a visit to Port Angeles. Dozens of sculptures, many as elaborate as this one, are displayed

and mine sweepers sometimes moor on the outer side of the pier. The U.S. Coast Guard cutter stationed here, when in port, is usually open on Sunday afternoons for curious visitors.

The center of the pier is occupied by the Arthur D. Feiro Marine Life Center run by Peninsula College. Visitors can check it out daily during summer. Open-topped aquarium tanks display local marine life, a touch tank is available for kids to experience marine life intimately, and displays feature marine mammal skeletons and pressed seaweed collections; personnel are on hand to answer questions.

The wooden causeway edging the waterfront leads to tiny Hollywood Beach, where there is driftwood and enough sand to keep any toddler happy, and provide for elaborate sand sculpture art at a midsummer competition. In the building just west of the pier is the Olympic Coast Discovery Center with interactive kiosks showing regional resources and an underwater relief model of the Olympic Coast.

Ediz Hook Map 71

Picnicking • Beach walking • Viewpoints

Facilities: *Sail and Paddle Park:* Picnic tables, fire braziers, toilet. *Harborview Park:* 5-lane paved launch ramp with boarding floats, restrooms, toilets, RV parking, picnic tables

From City Pier, take Front Street west to where it joins 1st Street and becomes W Marine Drive. Follow W Marine Drive around the west end of Port Angeles Harbor through the pulp mill property and then west along the spit to its end.

Hand-carry launch areas are at Sail and Paddle Park on the middle of the north side of the spit, and at the launch ramps near the end of the north side of the spit.

Ediz Hook, the 3½-mile-long spit that creates a natural breakwater for Port Angeles Harbor, is a startling contrast to Dungeness Spit, its sister to the east. While Dungeness Spit has remained largely untrammeled, Ediz Hook is a workingman's spit—and, boy, has it been trammeled! Despite the bustle of activity on the spit, the outer beach offers opportunities for long walks, exploration, and even some solitude among the scattered driftwood. Look north to Victoria and the San Juan Islands or west to Striped Peak. Or simply enjoy the play of gulls in wind and wave.

A road traverses the length of the hook, and logging interests, anglers, boaters, the Coast Guard, and Puget Sound Pilots all make use of this fragile strip. To ensure its continued stability, the outer beach has been built up with gravel and a revetment of enormous boulders to control erosion.

To reach the spit, follow Marine Drive north along the Port Angeles waterfront. A large pulp mill covers the base of the hook, spewing steam and noise. Logging trucks roar along the road, and the northwest end of the bay is a booming ground filled with logs awaiting the bite of the saw. Just beyond the pulp plant, a gravel pulloff strip, which is the Sail and Paddle Park, offers low-bank access to the harbor for kayaking and windsurfing;

In Port Angeles Harbor log booms and piles blend into drifting fog.

at its east end is a small grassy park that is dandy spot to enjoy the Cheez Doodles and Cokes you brought. Near the end of the spit is grassy Harborview Park—with a spacious launch ramp, picnic shelters, picnic tables, fire braziers, and restrooms.

The U.S. Coast Guard station and airstrip is beyond the gate at the tip of the spit. Helicopters stationed here are used in rescues and other Coast Guard work throughout the inland waters. From the time of earliest settlement, pioneers built bonfires on the end of the spit to guide ships. The lighthouse built here in 1865 was replaced by a new but still traditional structure in 1908. That light, too, gave way to progress when it was replaced in 1945 by the current mundane automated Coast Guard beacon that serves as a navigational light. The home station for the Puget Sound Pilots is also located here; all vessels traveling east from Port Angeles are required to have a licensed pilot aboard to ensure their safe passage to ports within Puget Sound.

chapter eleven

The Western Strait of Juan de Fuca

🚗 Land access to this western section of the Strait is from SR 112. Follow US 101 west out of Port Angeles for 4½ miles. At a major intersection, turn right (northwest) on SR 112. Once it reaches saltwater at Twin Rivers, the 2-lane road follows the shoreline much of the way to Neah Bay, heading inland in only a few spots. The twisting road is slow driving, especially if you are pulling a boat trailer or camper, but the scenery is spectacular. Logging trucks might be encountered on weekdays.

WEST OF PORT ANGELES the pulse of the strait quickens. The southern coastline becomes bold, with rock-strewn beaches soaring upward in places to rugged, 300-foot-high bluffs. Waves generated by wind sweeping in from the ocean pound against the shores, making approach by boat difficult and at times dangerous. The few boating facilities along the channel suffer from the severe environment: launch ramps are sometimes washed out or clogged by debris, and floats must be removed off-season to prevent damage by storms. The towns of Sekiu and Neah Bay, which have boat basins behind rock breakwaters, are the only harbors of refuge along this section of the strait.

The greatest attraction here is for anglers who come from great distances to find exciting action fishing for salmon, halibut, lingcod, or rockfish. Most fishing is done from boats as small as 15-foot kicker boats or from moderate-size trailered craft. Halibut caught here range from young 20-pounders called "chicks" up to an occasional 200-pound monster that must be towed to shore behind the boat.

Few pleasure boaters choose this area as a destination; most seen here are in transit to or from ocean voyages. In addition to Neah Bay and Sekiu, a few small bays offer some limited anchorages when seas are calm. ❋ When navigating near shore, watch for submerged rocks and reefs. The warmer summer months are often accompanied by dense fog, which usually clears off by midmorning. Many beaches are rocky and drop off steeply. ❋ When approaching by boat, use extreme care because a wave or surge can throw a boat against the rocks. Landings on these beaches should be attempted only in calm weather, and even then with caution. Experienced paddlers can get a taste of sea kayaking by putting in at any of several spots to explore along the rugged coast.

Some 40 miles of shorelands at twenty separate locations along this section of the Strait are public. Many of these sites are DNR beaches, where

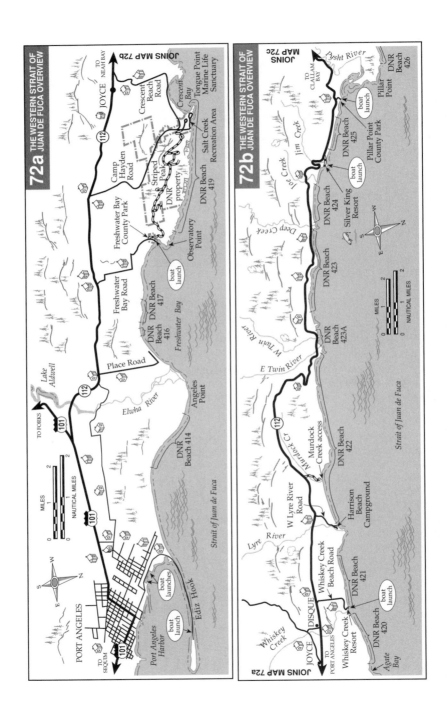

72a THE WESTERN STRAIT OF JUAN DE FUCA OVERVIEW

JOINS MAP 72b

TO NEAH BAY

JOYCE

112

Camp Hayden Road

Crescent Beach Road

Crescent Bay

Tongue Point Marine Life Sanctuary

Striped Peak

DNR property

Salt Creek Recreation Area

DNR Beach 419

Observatory Point

Freshwater Bay County Park

boat launch

Freshwater Bay Road

DNR Beach 417

DNR Beach 416

Freshwater Bay

Place Road

112

Lake Aldwell

TO FORKS

101

Elwha River

Angeles Point

DNR Beach 414

Strait of Juan de Fuca

101

101

MILES
0   1   2

NAUTICAL MILES
0   1   2

N
W   E
S

PORT ANGELES

TO SEQUIM

101

Port Angeles Harbor

boat launch

boat launches

Ediz Hook

72b THE WESTERN STRAIT OF JUAN DE FUCA OVERVIEW

JOINS MAP 72c

Pysht River

TO CLALLAM BAY

boat launch

Pillar Point

DNR Beach 426

Pillar Point County Park

DNR Beach 425

boat launch

Jim Creek

Silver King Resort

DNR Beach 424

DNR Beach 423

Joe Creek

Deep Creek

DNR Beach 423A

W Twin River

E Twin River

N
W   E
S

MILES
0   1   2

NAUTICAL MILES
0   1   2

Murdock Cr

Murdock Creek access

DNR Beach 422

112

W Lyre River Road

Harrison Beach Campground

Lyre River

Whiskey Creek Beach Road

DNR Beach 421

boat launch

DISQUE

JOYCE

TO PORT ANGELES

Whiskey Creek Resort

DNR Beach 420

Agate Bay

Whiskey Creek

Strait of Juan de Fuca

JOINS MAP 72a

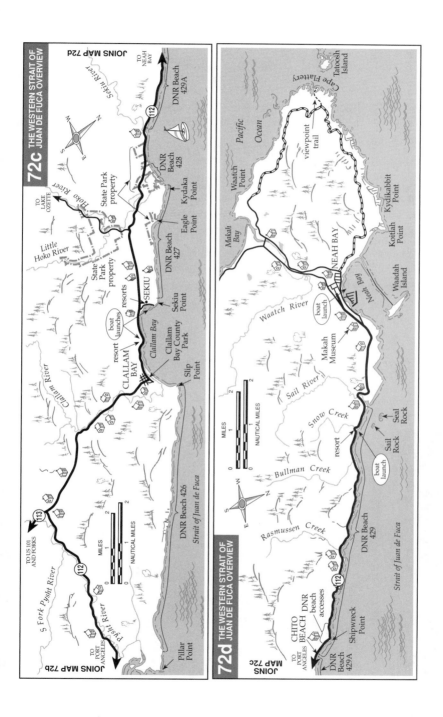

72c THE WESTERN STRAIT OF JUAN DE FUCA OVERVIEW

Sekiu River

TO NEAH BAY

DNR Beach 429A

112

DNR Beach 428

Kydaka Point

Eagle Point

DNR Beach 427

State Park property

TO LAKE OZETTE

Hoko River

Little Hoko River

SEKIU

Sekiu Point

State Park property

resorts

boat launches

Clallam Bay

Clallam Bay County Park

CLALLAM BAY

Slip Point

resort

Clallam River

S Fork Pysht River

113

112

TO US 101 AND FORKS

112

TO PORT ANGELES

Pysht River

Pillar Point

DNR Beach 426

Strait of Juan de Fuca

MILES
0   1   2

NAUTICAL MILES
0   1   2

72d THE WESTERN STRAIT OF JUAN DE FUCA OVERVIEW

Pacific Ocean

Cape Flattery

Tatoosh Island

viewpoint trail

Waatch Point

Makah Bay

NEAH BAY

Kydikabbit Point

Koitlah Point

Waadah Island

Neah Bay

boat launch

Waatch River

Makah Museum

Sail River

Snow Creek

Seal Rock

resort

Sail Rock

Bullman Creek

boat launch

Rasmussen Creek

DNR Beach 429

Strait of Juan de Fuca

MILES
0   1   2

NAUTICAL MILES
0   1   2

TO PORT ANGELES

CHITO BEACH

DNR beach accesses

Shipwreck Point

DNR Beach 429A

112

the state-owned land is below the mean high water level; several locations are paralleled by SR 112, however, giving easy access. At other places, the beaches can be reached via county parks or commercial resorts. At any of the commercial facilities, beach users must obtain permission from the property owner. In some cases, the resorts have rental boats and pay launch ramps; even those with cartop boats can expect to be charged a fee.

STRIPED PEAK
Map 72a

About 12 miles beyond Port Angeles, 1166-foot Striped Peak is a prominent landmark with its thickly wooded slopes rising abruptly from the strait. Striped Peak Scenic Area, Salt Creek County Park, and Tongue Point Marine Life Sanctuary encompass a total of some 1700 acres of land and 4 miles of shoreline, with attractions ranging from dense forest to wave-washed rocks to a sublime saltwater estuary.

Freshwater Bay County Park (Clallam County) Map 72a
Boating • Paddling • Fishing • Picnicking • Beachcombing • Clamming • Scuba diving

Facilities: 1-lane paved launch ramp, restrooms, toilet, picnic shelter, picnic tables
Area: 17.5 acres; 1450 feet of shoreline on the Strait of Juan de Fuca

Freshwater Bay County Park is heavily used by anglers, paddlers, and scuba divers.

🚙 From the junction of US 101 and SR 112, head west on SR 112 for 4³/₄ miles. Turn north on Freshwater Bay Road to reach the park in 2¹/₄ miles.

🛥 Freshwater Bay is on the south shore of the Strait of Juan de Fuca 1¹/₂ miles west of Port Angeles and ³/₄ mile southeast of Observatory Point.

Launch ramps are infrequent along the western end of the strait, and well-appointed ones are even more rare. This 1-lane launch ramp on the east side of Striped Peak is well surfaced and has a spacious parking lot adjoining it. Overflow parking is available just outside the entrance to the park off Striped Peak Road. The only disadvantage to the ramp is that it gradually slopes out onto a long tideflat, making it unusable at low water except for hand-carried craft. The picnic area uphill near the park entrance has a number of tables and a picnic shelter shaded by a magnificent grove of old-growth cedar.

The 4-mile-wide bay, bounded by Angeles Point on the east and Observatory Point on the west, is quite open, but some anchorages can be found in 6 to 10 fathoms. Bachelor Rock, a 20-foot-high sea stack, lies just off Observatory Point.

Boats launched at Freshwater Bay have easy access to three DNR beaches to the east. Beach 417, which is 2800 feet long, and Beach 416, a 1345-foot strip, are 1 to 2 n.m. east, slightly past Colville Creek. Beach 414 lies 4¹/₂ n.m. from the launch ramp on the east side of Angeles Point; the eastern edge of this 5580-foot section of tidelands begins just east of a riprap bulkhead at the Port Angeles city limits. The public land of all three beaches is the area lying below mean high water. At low tide, the gravelly shores might yield some horse and butter clams.

Striped Peak Scenic Area Map 72a

Hiking • Mountain biking

Facilities: Viewpoint, hiking trail, no water
Area: 1500 acres

🚙 See directions to Freshwater Bay County Park, described previously. At the entrance to the park, take Striped Peak Road to the northwest, which soon deteriorates to a 2-lane gravel road. At a junction in 2¹/₄ miles, take the steep uphill spur to the north to arrive at a dirt parking lot.

This large section of DNR property abuts the east boundary of Salt Creek County Park. At the end of Striped Peak Road, reach an expansive viewpoint on a shoulder of the mountain. The view here is north across the Strait of Juan de Fuca. To hike to Salt Creek County Park, follow a road that leaves the east edge of the parking area and quickly deteriorates to a trail. At a trail junction in ¹/₄ mile is the upper end of a steep switchback path from Salt Creek County Park.

Another alternative to reaching the viewpoint is to hike either the road or trail from Salt Creek County Park. To do this, start at the gated road on the east side of the park, just past the entrance information booth. A sign here indicates a 2½-mile-long hiking trail that circles the north side of Striped Peak. In 1 mile, a spur leads to a cove and the lower of two vistas. Continuing, the trail climbs along a wooded flat for another mile, and then starts a murderous series of switchbacks to reach the viewpoint parking area.

Salt Creek County Park (Clallam County) and Tongue Point Marine Life Sanctuary   Map 73

Fishing • Hiking • Camping • Picnicking • Beachcombing • Scuba diving • Swimming • Paddling • Tidepooling • Historical interpretation

Facilities: 90 campsites, picnic tables, fireplaces, group kitchen shelter, restrooms, children's play equipment, softball field, horseshoe pits, RV pumpout station, informational and historical displays, abandoned harbor defense emplacements, hiking trails

Area: 196 acres; 5000 feet of shoreline on the Strait of Juan de Fuca

From the junction of US 101 and SR 112, take SR 112 west for 7¼ miles. Turn north on Camp Hayden Road to reach the park in another 3½ miles. To reach

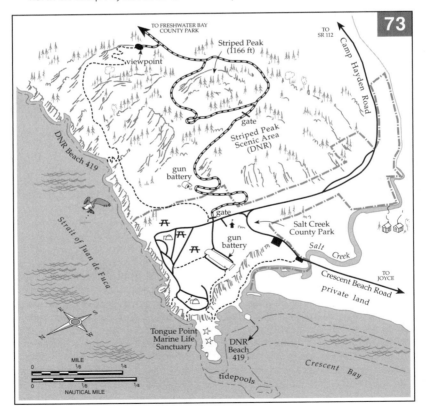

A family treks along the shore at Tongue Point Marine Life Sanctuary.

the day-use area at the mouth of Salt Creek, at the park entrance follow Crescent Beach Road north and in a short distance reach a small parking area. Overflow parking is just uphill to the east.

The recreation area lies 10 n.m. west of Port Angeles. Boats and paddlecraft can be put in at Freshwater Bay to explore along the shore all the way to Crescent Bay, 5 n.m. to the west.

Here is a treasure of a park, with stunningly beautiful scenery, acres of tide-pools to explore, and a sheltered sandy beach for summer lazing. Inside the park entrance, a branch road to the west leads to the World War II 16-inch gun battery built when this area was a military fort. Camping is in two areas: to the east, near the park entrance, RV sites spread around a large open field; to the west, tenting sites lie in light timber on a road that loops around a small peninsula. None of the campsites have utility hookups. Several short trails from the camp areas descend to the beach.

At the entrance to the campground, the gated road that heads up Striped Peak provides an added attraction for hikers: a glimpse of one of the old gun batteries from Fort Hayden. The concrete bunker, which is just off the end of the first sharp switchback, is not maintained and is heavily overgrown.

The concrete gun emplacements of Fort Hayden are quite different from those built at Fort Worden and other World War I forts.

Two 6-inch guns that sat on concrete pads on either side of the battery were covered with thick armor plate. Use care in the area because broken bottles and trash make it hazardous. The road continues eastward across logged areas on the south flank of Striped Peak. It eventually connects through a maze of active logging roads to the last road junction below the Striped Peak viewpoint.

The rocky shoreline east of Tongue Point, along the north edge of the park, drops off abruptly. East of the boundary of the park, the public shoreline, designated as DNR Beach 419, continues nearly all the way to Observatory Point. The rock and gravel shore is difficult for casual walking but, with some effort at low tide, interesting rock formations and marine life can be seen. At high tide, the beach is impassable.

This is a favorite area for scuba divers who explore the submerged rocks and sand channels. Kelp beds, strong currents, and heavy surge conditions are hazards; only expert divers should dive here, and then only on calm days during slack tide.

Tongue Point is a layer of erosion-resistant volcanic basalt that juts out on the east side of Crescent Bay. At low tide, a ¼-mile-long tidal shelf is revealed, filled with a dazzling array of marine plants and animals in a jewel-like mixture of reds, pinks, purples, and greens hidden in the purple-brown seaweed. A single tidepool might contain as many as a hundred different species, including limpets, hermit crabs, sculpin, nudibranchs, and sea urchins. One tiny golf-ball-sized rock the author picked up had five different kinds of life in its hollows: a sponge, lichens, barnacles, a limpet, and a shore crab. A good field guide on seashore life will help identify the many creatures you might see. This is a marine sanctuary—do not remove or destroy any of the life. Put rocks back where you found them; moving them to different locations could cause the creatures they harbor to die.

Tongue Point shelters the sandy estuary of Salt Creek, on the east side of Crescent Bay. The estuary can be reached by trails from the campground, or by a road that goes west from the park entrance for 1/2 mile to a day-use area. Moderate to low tides expose a broad sandy beach punctuated by a remarkable pair of little wooded islands of rock that stand as lonely sentinels on the beach.

WHISKEY CREEK TO TWIN RIVERS
Map 72b

Fishing • Boating • Paddling • Beach walking • Hiking

Facilities: *Whiskey Creek Resort:* Beachfront cabins, campsites, picnic areas, hiking trails, restrooms, 1-lane paved launch ramp. *Harrison Beach Campground:* RV and tent campsites, restrooms, hand-carried boat launch

Whiskey Creek Resort: Follow SR 112 to 1 3/4 miles west of the town of Joyce and turn north on Whiskey Creek Beach Road, which is signed to the Whiskey Creek

A fish-cleaning station sits near the beach at Whiskey Creek Resort.

Recreation Area. Follow signs 1½ miles to the beach. *Harrison Beach Campground:* Follow SR 112 to 4½ miles west of the town of Joyce and turn north on W Lyre River Road. In ½ mile, head west on Harrison Beach Road to reach the resort in another ¼ mile. Do not be confused by a sign on SR 112 ½ mile to the east on East Lyre River Road pointing to a DNR campground. *DNR Beach 422:* 1 mile west of the W Lyre River Road intersection. Turn off SR 112 on an unmarked dirt road at the middle of a onetime clearcut. The narrow, steep road twists down to a branch in ½ mile; bear right. At 1 mile from the highway, the road is barricaded with boulders; a dirt parking area here can accommodate a couple of cars.

🛥 Whiskey Creek is 13 n.m. west of Port Angeles, Lyre River is 2 n.m. farther, and Murdock Creek is 1½ n.m. beyond that.

Whiskey Creek Resort and DNR Beaches 420 and 421 •

Continuing west along the Strait of Juan de Fuca, public shore accesses become more primitive, offering only basic amenities for hardy anglers and boaters who venture out on the waters of the strait. At Whiskey Creek, a commercial resort has a 1-lane launch ramp, usable only at high tides, that is protected by a short rock breakwater. The resort is open from May to October. Resorts such as this have been hard-hit by depleted salmon runs and season closures.

Whiskey Creek Resort provides the only land access to DNR Beaches 420 and 421. Because this is a commercial facility, persons wanting to walk the beaches must be guests of the resort or obtain permission from the property owner and pay a day-use fee. DNR Beach 420, which lies east of Whiskey Creek, is 8750 feet long; Beach 421, west of Whiskey Creek, is 8010 feet long. The public beach, which is below the mean high water level, is gradually sloping gravel and hard clay, with ample room for beach walking at low tide. ❀ Boat landing can be dangerous under severe wave or surge conditions.

Limpets are found in tidepools all along the Strait of Juan de Fuca.

Lyre River and DNR Beach 422 •

The Lyre River was originally called "singing waters" by local Native Americans for the musical lilt of the water rushing over rocks. Early explorers changed the name to Lyre, after the musical instrument that has a similar soothing effect.

West of Whiskey Creek and immediately west of Lyre River, Harrison Beach Campground, a commercial facility offering primitive RV and tent campsites, has a beach access where guests can put in hand-carried boats. The resort is on the eastern edge of DNR Beach 422. Nearby is the Lyre River DNR Campground. While that public forest camp is very pretty, it is on the bank of the river and has no saltwater access.

The Murdock Creek access offers long beach walks.

Murdock Creek Access • At Murdock Creek, the road once went all the way to the beach, but recurring vandalism and off-road vehicle use caused its closure; walk from the barricade to the open timber at the beach. The shale intertidal shelf extends out for about ¼ mile, exposing a fascinating assortment of marine life at low tide. Small pools are filled with a variety of chitons, barnacles, starfish, and "Chinese hat"–shaped limpets. Notice how different the forms of life found here are than those found on the protected shores of Puget Sound. The beach can be walked east for a mile to the Lyre River or west for 4 miles to the point just east of Twin Rivers. ✿ Paddlers should attempt landing only when seas are calm.

TWIN RIVERS TO CLALLAM BAY
Maps 72b and 72c

Fishing • Boating • Paddling • Beach walking • Picnicking • Clamming

Twin Rivers and Silver King Resort   Map 72b

Facilities: *Silver King Resort:* RV camping with hookups, picnic tables, toilet, gas, propane, store with limited groceries and fishing tackle, 2-lane paved launch ramp

🚐 *Twin Rivers:* Twin Rivers lies 22¾ miles west of the intersection of SR 112 and US 101. *Silver King Resort:* About 8¼ miles west of Twin Rivers, a sign on SR 112 points north to the Jim Creek Recreation Area. The gravel road twists downhill for ½ mile to the resort.

🛥 *Twin Rivers:* The closest boat launch is at Silver King Resort, ½ n.m. west.

Twin Rivers • As it journeys west, SR 112 finally touches the shores of the Strait of Juan de Fuca at Twin Rivers. Suddenly, a wealth of sand and shale beaches is revealed, only a jump from the bumper. But don't jump too soon, because the uplands of the first beach encountered are owned by a private camping club. Two obscure side roads lead to the private beach; a third road spur (the last to be reached before the bridge over West Twin River) ends at a narrow public access to DNR Beach 423A, where cartop boats can be put in. This access is heavily used when the weather is good, and parking nearby might be difficult.

Beach 423A, which is a 3415-foot section lying below the mean high water level, extends from East Twin River west to a landfill jetty owned by a quarry. Some clams might be dug in the sandy beach. Beyond the quarry property, where the road pulls away from the shore, Beach 423 begins. This 3-mile section of beach is easily accessed from its west end, where the highway returns to the shore by Deep Creek. Some limited parking is available along the road.

Beach 424, which begins west of the delta of Deep Creek, is 5925 feet in length. It has no upland access—it must be reached by boat. ❀Unfortunately, boat landing at this or any of the other beaches along the Strait can be hazardous. It should be attempted only during calm seas, and even then with great care.

Silver King Resort • Silver King Resort, at Jim Creek, offers the only protected moorage for small boats along this section of the strait. Off-season, if the resort is closed, the road might be gated at the highway.

A dredged basin, with floats in summer, is protected by two curving rock jetties; however, it is not suitable for boats with much draft. The 2-lane surfaced launch ramp inside the jetty is usable during all but minus tides.

Pillar Point County Park (Clallam County)   Map 72b

Fishing • Boating • Paddling • Beach walking • Picnicking • Clamming

Facilities: 1-lane paved launch ramp, picnic tables, fireplaces, picnic shelter, toilets

Area: 4.3 acres; 240 feet of shoreline on the Strait of Juan de Fuca

🚗 At 32½ miles west of the junction of US 101 and SR 112 (6¾ miles east of the junction of SR 112 and SR 113), turn north at a signed intersection to reach the park in ½ mile.

🚤 The park launch ramp is on the south side of the Strait of Juan de Fuca 1¼ n.m. south of Pillar Point.

Pillar Point is rated as one of the fishing "hot spots" along the Strait of Juan de Fuca. In spring and summer, king and silver salmon are caught just offshore, and this is a top area for blackmouth, when winter storms permit. A small county park at Pillar Point is used by anglers for launching boats, although the park's wide tideflat and scenic location make it popular with anyone who loves the shore.

Pillar Point is a distinctive, 700-foot-high knob with a prominent pillar-shaped sea stack lying off its eastern tip. The point encloses an open, shallow bay at the drainage of the Pysht River. ❀Some anchorages can be found in 10 fathoms of water southeast of the point. The surrounding land gives protection from westerly swells; however, there is little shelter from winter storms. Numerous rocks lie offshore east of the county park.

The 1-lane launch ramp empties onto a shallow flat and is usable only for cartop or small, trailered boats. Some anglers use waders to reach boats launched at high tide and anchored out. A picnic shelter and a few picnic tables are in a grassy bluff above the beach.

Two nearby DNR beaches can be reached by boat from Pillar Point. Beach 425, which is 4520 feet long, lies east, midway between the county park and Silver King Resort at Jim Creek. This beach is a continuation of the long tideflat at the mouth of the Pysht River. To the west, Beach 426 stretches for 8 miles from a cove ½ n.m. west of Pillar Point all the way to Slip Point at the east side of Clallam Bay. ✿ This beach lies beneath a 300-foot bluff, and the rocky shores drop off steeply. Landing boats is possible only in a few small coves, and even there the shore should be approached with caution and only during calm seas.

Sometime between March and April, during the brief annual spawning run of smelt, the area from Pillar Point east to Twin Rivers is a prime spot for catching smelt with large long-handled nets. Smelt dippers work from shore on the incoming tide, scooping the little fish from net to bucket to a waiting frying pan.

CLALLAM BAY TO SEKIU
Map 74

Clallam Bay Map 74

Boating • Fishing • Shopping

Facilities: *Town:* Gas stations, grocery stores, restaurants, lodging, shopping. *Clallam Bay County Park:* Restrooms, picnic tables

Area: *Clallam Bay County Park:* 33 acres; 9850 feet of shoreline on the Clallam River and the Strait of Juan de Fuca

🚙 *Town:* On the west side of Port Angeles, turn off US 101 on SR 112 and follow it for 45½ miles to the town. Clallam Bay and points west along SR 112 can also be reached by driving US 101 west from Port Angeles 45¼ miles to Sappho and turning north on SR 113. In 10½ miles, the road joins SR 112 and continues on to Clallam Bay. This route eliminates some of the narrow, twisting sections of SR 112 (or swaps them for the narrow, twisting road around Lake Crescent). *Clallam Bay County Park:* Where SR 112 enters the town of Clallam Bay from the east and takes a left turn, a stub road at the intersection goes straight ahead to the county park's parking lot.

🛶 Paddlecraft can be landed on the beach, but boating destinations are at sister city Sekiu, 1¾ n.m. west.

Clallam Bay is the only protected harbor along the Strait of Juan de Fuca between Port Angeles and Neah Bay. The bay has two small communities along its shore—Clallam Bay and Sekiu. A sandbar at the mouth of the Clallam River fronts the town of Clallam Bay, giving it some shelter from storms sweeping in off the Strait, but it also keeps boats at a distance. The major boating center is at Sekiu, on the west side of the bay, where a rock jetty forms a well-protected basin for the fleet of small recreational fishing boats that arrive via trailer in the summer.

The 2-mile-wide bay has some protected anchorages in 6 to 10 fathoms near the Sekiu jetty. The floats within the jetty are primarily for small boats—some sit on the mudflat at low tide.

Extensive DNR public beaches flank either side of the bay. Beach 426 (see Pillar Point County Park, described previously), runs east from Slip Point, which is marked by a light at the east side of the bay. Beach 427, 17,890 feet in length, goes west from Sekiu Point all the way to Kydaka Point near the Hoko River. Both of these beaches lie beneath high bluffs and are accessible only by boat. At low tide, Beach 427 has some sandy stretches that hold clams and mussels.

Scuba divers sometimes enter the water at the resort at Sekiu and work their way around the point to Beach 427. With permission, divers can cross Coast Guard property by the Slip Point light to reach Beach 426. The underwater area at Beach 427 is rocky, with ledges and caves containing brightly colored rockfish, anemones, and, in dark corners, octopus and wolf eels. Thick beds of kelp, strong currents, and surge are hazards, making this a dive only for the experienced.

Clallam Bay County Park (Clallam County) •
As it reaches the strait, the Clallam River meanders westward, paralleling the shore before emptying into Clallam Bay. A wide sandy bar that had been built up at the mouth of

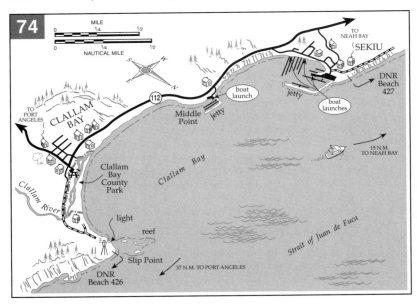

the river is managed by the county as a day-use. In winter 2003, park features were drastically altered by some severe storms, which carved a new river channel through the park and damaged facilities. At present, the only amenities are restrooms and an adjoining lawn with a few picnic tables.

Sekiu Resorts   Map 74

Boating • Fishing • Paddling • Scuba diving

Facilities: Guest moorage, numerous launch ramps (some with boarding floats), gas, outboard mix, restrooms, showers, laundromat, camping, RV sites, cabins, motels, restaurants, groceries, ice, fishing tackle and bait, boat and motor rental, charters

Sekiu is just off SR 112, 2 miles west of the town of Clallam Bay.

Sekiu's extensive dock complex lies behind a rock breakwater on the south side of the Strait of Juan de Fuca and west side of Clallam Bay.

Resorts along the shore at Sekiu cater to the hordes of anglers who arrive during the spring and summer to fish for prized salmon or halibut. Accommodations tend to be plain rather than posh; reservations are usually necessary during good weather. Some limited charters are available through the resorts; however, many anglers trailer their own boats or rent kicker

During fishing season the rows of docks at Sekiu will be filled with boats.

boats. Not all the resorts and motels have full facilities; some primarily offer overnight accommodations, while others have full boating services.

While a number of the resorts close off-season and remove their floats to protect them from storms, a few remain open year-round to take advantage of bottom fishing when an occasional break in winter weather permits.

The Coho Resort is at Middle Point, halfway between Clallam Bay and Sekiu. The resort's own rock breakwater protects a 2-lane launch ramp and two long moorage floats. An RV park, motel, and restaurant are across the highway.

SEKIU TO NEAH BAY
Maps 72c and 72d
Fishing • Beach walking • Tidepools • Boating • Informational displays

🚐 Continue driving west on winding SR 112. The Hoko River is 2½ miles from Sekiu, Chito Beach is 5 miles more, Shipwreck Point is another ½ mile, Snow Creek is 5¾ miles more, and Neah Bay is an additional 3¼ miles. The total distance from Sekiu to Neah Bay is 17 miles.

🛥️ Boats launched at either Sekiu or Neah Bay can access the numerous public beaches along this section of the Strait. ❄Use care approaching the shore as offshore water is riddled with rocks, seen and unseen. Waves and surges are an added hazard.

Approaching Neah Bay, the shoreline becomes even more spectacular, with wave-torn beaches, sea stacks, and imposing offshore rocks. Low tide reveals a boulder-strewn shale shelf with cracks and crevices holding tidepools. Abundant marine life inhabits this shelf—some of it bright and obvious, but much of it blending into the overall purple-brown color scheme. Even flamboyant, bright pastel sea anemones contract into nondescript brown nodules as the tide recedes.

Near Snow Creek and Sail River two massive rocks, nearly 100 feet tall, rise ¼ mile offshore. When seen from the southeast, Sail Rock resembles the mainsail of a giant sloop; Seal Rock is an even larger rectangular-shaped monolith lying to the west. The vast numbers of birds that nest here, including cormorants, gulls, and tufted puffins, have found a spot safe from the encroachment of real estate developers.

DNR Beaches • At several places, SR 112 comes close enough to the shore to permit easy access; a few pulloffs provide limited parking. All the beach between the Sekiu River and Sail River is public DNR beach below the mean high water level, with the exception of a narrow strip at Chito Beach. Beach 429A, which is 12,210 feet in length, is east of Chito Beach; Beach 429, 37,440 feet long, is to the west. Chito Beach, a scattering of homes and summer cabins along the highway, has no public access. A commercial RV and camping park might be open in the summer.

Beach 428, at the mouth of the Hoko River, is 2750 feet long. It is located below a housing development. However, there is no public access through the residential area; the beach must be reached by boat.

Several exquisite sea stacks are next to the highway near the west end of Beach 429. They are not as large or dramatic as those found out on the coast at La Push and Shi-Shi Beach, but they are much more accessible and equally fascinating. The surrounding beaches are prime areas for tidepooling.

Hoyt State Park Property (Undeveloped) ● At ¼ mile east of the Sekiu River, SR 112 skirts a broad sandy beach below a low bank. The beach and uplands for ½ mile to the east are undeveloped properties owned by the state parks commission. Two or three roadside pulloffs permit hand-carried boats to be put in along 1520 feet of saltwater shoreline on the Strait of Juan de Fuca. Boating in the Strait during times of waves, surge, or strong current can be hazardous.

Shipwreck Point ● At Shipwreck Point, 8¾ miles east of Neah Bay, there are three pulloffs along a half-mile section of SR 112. Each has a sign identifying it as a DNR Natural Resources Conservation Area and describing some aspect of the natural environment, ecology, or geology.

Snow Creek ● At Snow Creek, 3½ miles east of Neah Bay, a small resort offers tent and RV camping, a few tiny cabins, a marine rail launch facility, a dock and float, offshore buoys, and a store with ice, bait, firewood, scuba

The docks of Snow Creek Resort are close to prime fishing grounds around Seal Rock, left, and Sail Rock, right.

air, and limited groceries. The resort provides access to DNR Beach 429 and some sensational views of Seal and Sail Rocks, just offshore. Nonguests should ask permission before crossing private property to reach the beach.

NEAH BAY AND CAPE FLATTERY
Map 72d

Neah Bay   Map 75

Fishing • Boating • Museum

Facilities: Guest moorage, launch ramps, gas, outboard mix, camping, RV sites, cabins, motels, restrooms, showers, laundromat, groceries, ice, bait, fishing tackle, restaurants, boat rental and charters, U.S. Customs

Neah Bay can be reached by driving either SR 112 or US 101 west from Port Angeles. If following US 101, turn north at Sappho on SR 113 to join SR 112 about 10 miles south of Clallam Bay. The distance is about 70 miles either route, and much of the way is on narrow, twisting roads.

Neah Bay is 14 n.m. west of Sekiu.

Neah Bay is the only town on the Makah Indian Reservation. Facilities in the town are decidedly utilitarian—a general store offers a range of groceries and supplies, and resorts have fishing tackle and bait. There are no marine repair facilities. Motel and camping accommodations, too, are rather spartan,

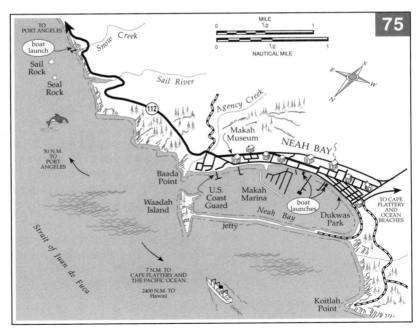

appealing primarily to sport anglers whose main interest is catching a prize salmon. During the last weekend of August, at the annual Makah Day celebration, tribes from throughout the Northwest gather to celebrate their heritage with traditional dances and costumes, a salmon bake, bone games, athletic contests, and canoe races.

The traditional fishing economy has remained one of the mainstays of the Makah tribe, and today the town is the center of large commercial and sport fishing industries. The deep, natural harbor provides moorage for both large and small fishing boats, while ocean-bound yachts often use the bay as a last stop before hitting true open water. Fishing resorts such as this have been hard-hit by decreased salmon runs and cutbacks in fishing seasons. An annual vehicle permit, which can be purchased at almost any business in Neah Bay, is required for recreational use of anything in the Makah reservation such as trailhead parking, hiking, picnicking, and camping.

Waadah Island, a 1/2-mile-long wooded knob, lies on the east side of the bay, off Baada Point. A rock breakwater that stretches for 1 1/2 miles between Waadah Island and the shore shelters the inner bay from all but easterly

The Makah Nation

The Makah people, who are more culturally allied with the Nootka tribe of Vancouver Island than tribes of the inland waters of Puget Sound, at one time occupied all of the coastal land down to Lake Ozette. Archaeological evidence shows their presence here for around 3000 years. The Makahs built large sea-going canoes in which they pursued whales. Using ritualistic preparation and hunting techniques very similar to those of the Eskimos far to the north, they harpooned and killed the whales, towed the carcasses back to their villages, and butchered the whale then smoked and dried the meat. The Natives were also highly skilled at hunting seals and fishing.

Neah Bay was the site of the first attempt by Europeans to settle the area. In the spring of 1792, a group of Spanish colonists landed here with instructions to build a fort and clear land, in an attempt to establish a claim to the coast north of California. The Spaniards evidently found the coastal climate too bitter for them, even in the summer, and the fur trade not to their liking; the settlement was abandoned after four months.

Some fifty years later, Samuel Hancock, a Yankee pioneer, established a trading post here for storing and shipping oil from whales harpooned by the Natives. At the time of the arrival of white men, the Makah Nation was large, but smallpox, brought in 1853 via a trading ship, ravaged the tribe, reducing it to a mere 150 individuals. Today, the tribe numbers about 1400 members. In the Neah Bay Treaty of 1855, initiated by Governor Isaac Stevens, the Makah Indians were assigned 23,000 acres of land at this westernmost tip of the state. The present reservation covers about half the original area.

weather. The low jetty does not give complete protection from severe northerlies, but such storms are rare, especially in summer.

❄A reef and numerous rocks extend from the southwest side of Waadah Island. The entrance channel, marked by buoys, should be followed carefully all the way into the bay, slightly favoring the south side. Anchorages can be found in 20 to 40 feet of water, protected by a second rock breakwater within the bay itself.

A small shoreside park in Neah Bay provides a place to munch a sandwich and observe waterfront activity. Dukwas Park is marked by a totem pole and picnic tables.

Floats for recreational boats are found at marinas and resorts along the south shore of Neah Bay, east of a long pier belonging to a commercial fishing company. The Makah Marina has more than two hundred modern slips with power and water. The complex lies behind an inner rock breakwater in the bay that is tied to a jetty on the east side of the marina. Onshore are restrooms, showers, and a small grocery/deli.

Makah Cultural and Research Center • On the east side of the town, adjacent to SR 112, a splendid museum houses artifacts from the Makah culture. Many of the items are from the Ozette archaeological dig, where part of a coastal village had lain buried in a mudslide for more than 500 years. The items are beautifully presented, with photos, drawings, and text explaining their use in everyday Makah life. The museum is open from 10:00 A.M. to 5:00 P.M. daily during the summer, and is closed on Mondays and Tuesdays from mid-September to the end of May.

Displays cover a wide range of Native life, including whaling, fishing,

This display and diorama at the Makah Museum in Neah Bay shows sealing methods. (MARGE AND TED MUELLER PHOTO, © MAKAH CULTURAL AND RESEARCH CENTER.)

hunting, gathering, food preparation, basketry, weaving, and trading. In the heart of the museum is a replica of a longhouse; when your eyes become accustomed to the dark interior, you recognize dried fish hanging from poles from the ceiling, mats decorating the walls, and benches and baskets surrounding the glowing embers of fires. Voices speaking the native Makah language, and then singing, drift through the longhouse, like ghosts from an ancient time.

A full-size version of a traditional longhouse on the grounds is used for community gatherings, and other group activities. Adjacent to the museum, a loop trail through the woods of the Makah Ethnobotanical Garden has signs identifying native plants, giving their English, Latin, and Makah names, and telling how the Makah used each plant. A pronunciation guide to the Makah language invites visitors to try to say the Native names.

Cape Flattery   Map 76

Hiking • Views • Birdwatching

Facilities: Trail, view platforms, toilets

At the west end of Bayview Avenue, the street that edges the beach at Neah Bay, head southwest on Fort Street for two blocks. Go northwest on 3rd Avenue for two blocks, and then southwest on Cape Flattery Road. In 2¹/₂ miles, pass the Makah Tribal Council Center; the pavement ends in another ³/₄ mile. A gravel road continues northwest for 4¹/₄ miles to a trailhead parking lot with room for two dozen cars.

Cape Flattery marks the northwest tip of the coterminous United States, where the crashing surf of the Pacific Ocean continues to gnaw at the rugged cliffs of this remote point of land. The cape is laced with wave-carved

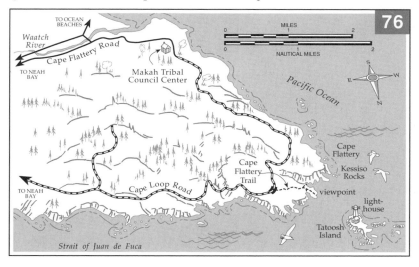

coves separated by high, razor-thin headlands; a myriad of near-shore rocks stubbornly resist the grinding of the powerful surf. These rocks are home or a migratory resting place for a variety of marine birds; seals and sea lions also haul out here for sunny respites from the sea. Shoreside trees provide lofty observatories for eagles scanning the beaches for prey.

A half-mile offshore is Tatoosh Island, the site of the Coast Guard lighthouse that marks the entrance to the Strait of Juan de Fuca. Before the lighthouse was erected here, the island had been used for centuries by the Makahs during summer months for salmon fishing and whaling, and it also served as a Native burial ground. The Native Americans did not take kindly to an invasion of their traditional summer outpost and regularly harassed crews when construction of the lighthouse began in 1855.

Severe weather and waves, coupled with the difficulty of landing on the harsh shore, presented a major challenge to the undertaking. Despite these problems, the lighthouse was completed and commissioned on December 28, 1857. The remoteness, weather, and Indian problems made it difficult to recruit lighthouse keepers, however. History records many wild tales: an attempted suicide by a keeper depressed by the site's loneliness, fierce storms that shook the whole island, a diphtheria epidemic, and haunting by ghosts of Natives buried there. As with other lighthouses, the Tatoosh light has now been automated, and the station is no longer manned.

Cape Flattery Trail • A ³/₄-mile-long trail permits a visit to remote Cape Flattery, with views of Tatoosh Island. At the parking lot, a signed trail heads west into the trees. The route is not overly steep, and boardwalks and stone steps span tree roots and muddy spots, making it a negotiable trail. Near the end of the cape, spur paths and a short stair lead to view platforms.

The view more than rewards the effort of the trip—jagged sea cliffs, 100 to 200 feet high, stretch along the coast as far as the eye can see. Waves crash against the rocky narrow beach below, bursting into plumes of frothing water as they collide with rough beach. Offshore, Kessiso Rocks and a jumble of other rocks have a legion of gulls and other seabirds perched atop. The lighthouse on Tatoosh Island, the westernmost point of the continental United States, flashes a continuous warning to mariners. Notice the frame of a derrick stretching out above sea cliffs on the north end of the island; over time this proved the easiest way to transport personnel and supplies onto the steep, rocky island.

⛴ Hawaii is 2400 n.m. to the southwest. Raise the sails!

Opposite: *Waves swirl around rocks at Cape Flattery.*

Appendices

A. Emergency Phone Numbers and List of Contacts

All Western Washington counties use 911 as the number for fire and police emergencies. For nonemergency situations, contact the local sheriff or police department at their business number.

Other important contacts:

U.S. COAST GUARD

Anacortes: (360) 293-9555
Bellingham: (360) 743-1692
Neah Bay: (360) 645-2236
Port Angeles: (360) 457-4404
Port Townsend: (360) 385-3070
Seattle:

    Emergencies: (800) 321-4400
    Search and Rescue Emergencies: (800) 982-8813
    Other business: (206) 220-7000
    Cellular Telephone Emergency Access: *CG (*24)

RADIO CONTACTS

Marine VHF:

Coast Guard distress or hailing: Channel 16
Coast Guard liaison: Channel 22
Coast Guard Vessel Tracking Center: Channel 14 (1 watt only)
Marine Operator (Tacoma): Channel 28
Marine Operator (Seattle): Channels 25 and 26
NOAA Weather Service: Channel WX1
Citizens Band: Distress: Channel 9

Other Contacts:

Marine Toxins/PSP Hotline: (800) 562-5632. Website: *www.doh.wa.gov /gis/mogifs/biotoxin.htm*
Whale Hotline (to report sightings or strandings): (800) 562-8832. Website:*www.whale-museum.org*

Washington State Parks

General information regarding the state parks is available from Washington State Parks and Recreation Commission, P.O Box 4250, 7150 Cleanwater Lane, Olympia, WA 98504-2669. Phone: (360) 902-8500. Fax: (360) 753-1594. Telephone for the deaf: (360) 664-3133. Information Center: (360) 902-8844. Website: *www.parks.wa.gov*

Campsite reservations for reservation parks can be made by calling (888) 226-7688, or through the Washington Telecommunications Relay Service at

(800) 833-6388 between 7:00 am and 8:00 pm, PST, except Christmas Day and New Year's Day, or anytime on the State Parks website.

Washington State Department of Fish and Wildlife

Natural Resources Building, 1111 Washington Street SE, Olympia, WA 98501. Mailing address: 600 Capitol Way North, Olympia, WA 98501-0191. Phone: (360) 902-2200. Website: *www.wdfw.wa.gov*

Washington Water Trails Association
4649 Sunnyside Avenue N, Suite 305, Seattle, WA 98103-6900. Phone: (206) 545-9161. Fax: (206) 547-0350. Website: *www.wwta.org*

B. Nautical Charts, Maps, and Tide Tables

Charts

Sketch maps in this book are intended for general orientation only. When traveling by boat on any of the Northwest's waters, it is imperative that the appropriate nautical charts be used. The following small-craft folios cover all areas that are included in this book, except for the Strait of Juan de Fuca west of Sequim Bay. These charts, as well as more detailed ones, can be purchased at map stores or many marine supply centers.

NOAA chart folio 18423 SC, *Bellingham to Everett Including San Juan Islands*

NOAA chart folio 18445 SC, *Puget Sound—Possession Sound to Olympia Including Hood Canal* (1:80,000)

Maps

USGS topographical maps are not necessary for any of the hiking described in this book; however, the 7½-minute series maps are both useful and interesting.

City maps or various books of street maps, especially *The Thomas Guides*, are helpful for navigating through metropolitan areas.

Tide Tables (all published annually)

Tide Tables—20___, West Coast of North America and South America. NOAA

Tidal Current Tables—20___, Pacific Coast of North America and Asia. NOAA

20___ Current and Tide Tables for Puget Sound, Deception Pass, the San Juans, Gulf Islands, and the Strait of Juan de Fuca. Island Canoe, Inc., Bainbridge Island. (Extract from the above NOAA tables for local areas.)

INDEX

About the Authors

Marge and Ted Mueller are outdoor enthusiasts and environmentalists who have explored Washington State's waterways, mountains, forests, and deserts for more than forty years. Ted has taught classes on cruising in Northwest waters, and both Marge and Ted have instructed mountain climbing. They are members of The Mountaineers and The Nature Conservancy, and have served on the Board of Directors of Friends of Washington State Parks. They are the authors of twelve regional guidebooks.

The Muellers can be contacted at *margeted@comcast.net.*

THE MOUNTAINEERS, founded in 1906, is a nonprofit outdoor activity and conservation club, whose mission is "to explore, study, preserve, and enjoy the natural beauty of the outdoors.... " Based in Seattle, Washington, the club is now the third-largest such organization in the United States, with seven branches throughout Washington State.

The Mountaineers sponsors both classes and year-round outdoor activities in the Pacific Northwest, which include hiking, mountain climbing, ski-touring, snowshoeing, bicycling, camping, kayaking, nature study, sailing, and adventure travel. The club's conservation division supports environmental causes through educational activities, sponsoring legislation, and presenting informational programs.

All club activities are led by skilled, experienced instructors, who are dedicated to promoting safe and responsible enjoyment and preservation of the outdoors.

If you would like to participate in these organized outdoor activities or the club's programs, consider a membership in The Mountaineers. For information and an application, write or call The Mountaineers, Club Headquarters, 300 Third Avenue West, Seattle, WA 98119; 206-284-6310. You can also visit the club's website at *www.mountaineers.org* or contact The Mountaineers via email at *clubmail@mountaineers.org.*

The Mountaineers Books, an active, nonprofit publishing program of the club, produces guidebooks, instructional texts, historical works, natural history guides, and works on environmental conservation. All books produced by The Mountaineers Books fulfill the club's mission.

Send or call for our catalog of more than 500 outdoor titles:

The Mountaineers Books
1001 SW Klickitat Way, Suite 201
Seattle, WA 98134
800-553-4453
mbooks@mountaineersbooks.org
www.mountaineersbooks.org

The Mountaineers Books is proud to be a corporate sponsor of The Leave No Trace Center for Outdoor Ethics, whose mission is to promote and inspire responsible outdoor recreation through education, research, and partnerships. The Leave No Trace program is focused specifically on human-powered (nonmotorized) recreation.

Leave No Trace strives to educate visitors about the nature of their recreational impacts, as well as offer techniques to prevent and minimize such impacts. Leave No Trace is best understood as an educational and ethical program, not as a set of rules and regulations.

For more information, visit www.LNT.org, or call 800-332-4100.

OTHER TITLES YOU MIGHT ENJOY FROM
THE MOUNTAINEERS BOOKS

Kayaking Puget Sound, The San Juans, and Gulf Islands: 50 Trips on the Northwest's Inland Waters, 2nd Edition
All-inclusive guide to the world's best kayaking area.

A Waterfall Lover's Guide to the Pacific Northwest
The comprehensive field guide to viewing hundreds of spectacular waterfalls in Washington, Oregon, and Idaho.

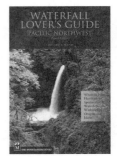

Nature in the City: Seattle
For suburbanites, city slickers, and newcomers, this book reveals the best places for nature lovers to see deer, eagles, and seals, or find flower gardens and other wild gems without leaving the Seattle area.

The Outdoor Knots Book
Guidelines and know-how for selecting the best rope and knots for any activity. Written by Clyde Soles, former senior editor of *Rock & Ice Magazine*.

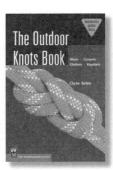

Afoot and Afloat: South Puget Sound and Hood Canal, 3rd Edition
Puget Sound's best places to play both on and near the water—paddle, sail, motor, hike, cycle, drive, GO!

Available at fine bookstores and outdoor stores, by phone at 800-553-4453 or on the Web at *www.mountaineersbooks.org*

THE MOUNTAINEERS BOOKS